White Gloves

THE FREE PRESS

New York   London   Toronto   Sydney   Tokyo   Singapore

WHITE GLOVES

*How We Create Ourselves
Through Memory*

JOHN KOTRE

The Free Press
A Division of Simon & Schuster Inc.
1230 Avenue of the Americas, New York, N.Y. 10020

Printed in the United States of America

printing number

1 2 3 4 5 6 7 8 9 10

LIBRARY OF CONGRESS CATALOGING-IN-PUBLICATION DATA

Kotre, John N.
    White gloves : how we create ourselves through memory /
John Kotre.
        p.   cm.
    Includes index.
    ISBN 0-02-918464-9
    1. Autobiographical memory.   I. Title.
BF378.A87K67   1995
153.1'3—dc20   95-13616
                                CIP

The excerpt on page 50 is taken from the DEAR ABBY column
by Abigail Van Buren. Copyright © 1992 UNIVERSAL PRESS
SYNDICATE. Reprinted with permission. All rights reserved.

To

FRANK KOTRE

and the spirit of his gloves

CONTENTS

ACKNOWLEDGMENTS

I am grateful to the individuals whose memories have become part of this book, many of them people whose stories I recorded over the years. In the early stages of writing, I profited from the guidance of my literary agent, Donald Cutler, and from several long conversations with the late Erwin Glikes, who was then publisher of The Free Press. I will remember Erwin and his story of the brass ruler. Along the way, my colleague Jeff Stern not only checked what I had written about the brain but gave me a new way of seeing it, and my wife Kathy offered the depth of her clinical insight. At the end, The Free Press's Susan Arellano and Edith Lewis stepped in to provide exactly the right finishing touches. My thanks to all of them.

The setting in which I worked was important too. I could not ask for a better atmosphere than that which exists at my home campus, the University of Michigan—Dearborn. Where else can you find a class of twenty-five that includes someone from every decade of life, from the second to the ninth? And where else is one still free to pursue knowledge rather than grants? I thank the students with whom I exchanged ideas, the colleagues with whom I shared them, and the administrators whose policy it has been to support the diverse talents of their faculty.

THE WHITE GLOVES

There's a pair of white gloves that live in my memory. I can see them now, lying on top of some old clarinets in the cramped, dusty attic of my grandmother's house, back in the niche where the roof meets the floor. Nearby is a black clarinet case with a cracked skin. The case itself is open, and you can smell the must in its lining. Everything in the memory is gray, save for the light from a small window at the end of the attic. Although I see the gloves only in memory—I have never done so in actuality—I know they are spotlessly white.

The gloves became part of my memory nearly a decade ago, during a turning point in my life. They originated in the words of my father, words lost among thousands of others that are part of the story of his life, a story I had tape-recorded years before. Ten years ago I was in my midforties, and it was then that I first listened to the tapes I had made. The gloves were only a detail in my father's story, but for some reason they spoke to me, and I felt a great release of emotion when, in my mind, I put them on. They seemed to cleanse me of guilt and confirm a path, seemed to con-

1

nect me to a mythical ancestor who sacrificed himself for me. There was life in them, my grandfather's life.

I never met my grandfather, and for most of my life never even knew his first name, but I do remember that my father once told me I looked like him. I was standing on the back stairs of my house and my father was in the yard, looking up at me. He said my grandfather was tall and thin, like me. My dad was shorter and stockier, physically stronger. I didn't pay much attention to his comment, though I was pleased by it. Later, when I saw the only picture I have of my grandfather, I was pleased again. He was a handsome man in his twenties and the woman standing behind him was beautiful—my grandmother in her physical prime. The wide-eyed infant in the white gown was my dad; he had a look in his face that he could have today, at seventy-nine, his mind diminished and nearly gone. In the picture, my grandfather holds him firmly in his lap with his right hand.

My grandfather died before I was born. From my father's story, I learned that it was of a lung problem. Years of breathing dust from the coal he shoveled into a furnace at the public gas company were compounded by a traffic accident that broke his ribs. He lingered for a few years after the accident but died before he was fifty. In my memory, the whiteness of the gloves stands against a background of the black coal dust that killed him.

That wasn't the way my grandfather's life was supposed to end. It had begun in Hungary, in a region where the spoken language was German. As a youth, my grandfather played the clarinet in what was probably a military band. "I think his whole soul was music," my father said; never before did I hear him talk about someone's "whole soul." Before he was twenty, my grandfather was playing, writing arrangements, and touring Europe. When he came to the United States in 1912 and then sent for his wife, he tried at first to make a living with what he loved. But musicians were "a dime a dozen," and after about a year, he gave up and got a job making bricks. What I remember from my father's story is the absolute decisiveness with which my grandfather took that step. The clarinets were put away, not very carefully it seems, and with them the white gloves that were part of his uniform. It was his wife, my grandmother, who wanted to keep them. I doubt my grandfather ever picked them up again. As a child poking around in my grandmother's attic, I had come across the clarinets, but not the gloves. At the time I had no idea who the instruments belonged to or what they meant. I didn't know a thing about my grandfather.

What did it cost him to lay down his music and turn to bricks and then to coal in order to support his family? What part of him died at that moment? My dad told me his father would play at home only once a year, on Christmas Day, and it would not be the clarinet, but the accordion. There were times he would listen to his children practicing on the piano or to music playing on the radio. Every now and then he would bolt up in his chair and cry out "*Falsch!*" Someone must have missed a note. But it seems as though the only way he could let go of something he loved was to make a complete break. If he could not make music, he would not, except in rare instances, even listen to it.

The break he made lasted for several generations. Neither my father nor I can carry a tune, and though I enjoy and am moved by music, I do not know it. (My sons, fortunately, are different.) And my father's temperament is far from artistic. He was a practical, hard-working man, a laborer with strong hands and short, thick fingers. He took over my grandfather's role in the family after he died. He went to work for the same company and was with them all his life. He was a family man, involved with his children and invested in them. He held them firmly in his hands, doing what his own father did after his music was silenced.

I grew up in my father's family and in a Jesuit high school was taught the riches and the discipline of classical literature. More important, I was exposed to the stuff of the spirit, though I would never have said it that way as a teenager. Eventually I became a psychologist, always interested in *seeing,* always trying to put into words what I saw. Not a "scientific" psychologist, not a "clinical" psychologist, but one who wanted to make portraits of individual lives. An artist, if you will, if only in temperament. In my midforties, my life changed dramatically. My children grew up, my marriage died, I received a large grant that turned my work life upside down, and I met a new woman. In many ways I was alone, and at that moment, I listened to the story of my father's life.

I am still amazed at my reaction to the white gloves, still in awe of the power the image has today. I've tried replaying the tape to find the source of that power. Here are my father's words, edited only slightly: "The gloves were made out of suede. My mother couldn't get her hands into them because the fingers were long and slender. The thing that was bad was that after he worked at the brickyard doing manual labor, he couldn't fit into them any more. And he was a very proud man." From a technical standpoint, the recording of my father's voice isn't that good. Nor do the gloves play much of a role in his life story. He had no idea at the time and, given the present state of his mind, he never will have any idea of what they have meant to me. So their power isn't to be found on the tape.

Where is it to be found? In me—in the use I made of the memory at a critical moment in my life, in the use I still make of it. Back then the gloves confirmed a decision to go through with a divorce, to choose life over a deadening sense of responsibility. They connected me with a kindred spirit, a resource I never knew existed in my family. In my grandfather I found roots for something in me that seemed to have sprung out of nothing. I think I understood what it meant for him to sacrifice his "whole soul." I saw that my father sacrificed too, living his life in a way that enabled me to have mine. Ultimately, I put the gloves on because they fit. No one else in the family has fingers like mine. No one else has the same temperament.

Back then, all these thoughts came in an instant. But more were to follow over the years. Often the gloves have returned with their whiteness to ease the guilt over choices I have made and help me cope with the small deaths that permit life. I have to separate from people, people I work with, people I live with and love, to pursue my soul. The gloves make my hands clean and tell me what to do: start fresh, stick to the soul, get going. It's been eighty years since my grandfather put the white gloves aside. If only he knew how much they have mattered today!

This book is about autobiographical memory, and it's dedicated to the man who reached out from the past to touch me. Autobiographical memory is memory for the people, places, objects, events, and feelings that go into the story of your life. For many years, clinical psychologists, psychiatrists, and social workers have dealt with this kind of memory. So have lawyers, police, politicians, interviewers in the media, teachers, clergymen, and lovers. I have worked with autobiographical memory, too, but in a different context. I have recorded the stories of people's lives and put them, or parts of them, into books, audio programs, and on one occasion a public television series called *Seasons of Life*. And I've wondered again and again about the mystery of memory, about mental pictures from long ago that warm the face of one storyteller, moisten the eyes of another, and bring the "shakes" to a third. Are these memories photographic, or even remotely accurate? And, accurate or not, what do they mean? What do the memories speak of and how do they speak?

What, for example, lies in the past of a woman in her late thirties who finds it difficult to breathe whenever she gets into a situation that is even mildly threatening? Her ears start to ring, sounds become distant echoes, her eyes dim, and she feels very much alone. Then part of her starts to float away, going off to the side where it can watch her. What events occurred in her past, why do they seem to be stored in her body, and why does the feeling of dissociation come back unbidden? We hear so much these days about "repression" on the one hand—and, on the other, about "false memories" that are "implanted" by therapists. What is the status of these concepts? We are told how beneficial it is to "recover the child within." Is such a thing even possible?

What about the little things that endure? Once, on a summer night, a girl of eleven or twelve held her baby toe and asked her mother why it was "squished in." It was bedtime, and her mother had just come into her room to tuck her in for the night. Her mother took a finger and pushed on the side of the toe just the way a shoe would. She explained that the girl's shoes had done it, and she added that the same things had happened to her own toes. It's a gentle, reassuring memory, says the girl at thirty-eight. But why, when she has forgotten so many incidents from childhood, does this one stay in her mind?

How powerful is the fear of losing a memory, or never having one? A man in his late twenties peers out of a window on a rainy day, thinking of a younger brother who was killed in a car accident just six weeks before. The man notices how the water disappears into cracks in the ground. Suddenly he is filled with panic. He cannot remember a thing about his brother, cannot even picture him. He rushes to his parents' home and digs out the family photo album. He is reassured that memories of his brother will not disappear. Another man the same age remembers times as a boy when his great-grandfather, once a minor-league baseball player, saw him play ball—and play well. He remembers his great-grandmother's lemon meringue pies, the best he's ever had. These are cherished memories, but there's a hitch. The young man was adopted into his family only after his great-grandfather had died, and only after his great-grandmother had stopped baking because she was in a nursing home. The man's family tells him that he has turned their stories about his ancestors into memories, but he insists they are genuine recollections.

Finally, what beliefs about memory were going through the minds of United States senators in the fall of 1991 as they questioned a law professor who had come forward with charges of sexual harassment against a man being considered for the position of Supreme Court Justice? The professor remembered being disgusted and humiliated by the explicit nature of what the man had said eight to ten years before. Though it was difficult for her to say the words in public, she did so, and in graphic detail. She talked about "sex with animals," "pubic hair," and "Long Dong Silver." "He made a comment I vividly remember," she added. "He said that if I ever told anyone of his behavior, it would ruin his career." For his part, the man denied he ever said any of those things. He recalled nothing of what she alleged, and no other witnesses to the conversations existed. Did the senators really believe that, even if there were no lying, autobiographical memory could preserve the details of what was said in conversation a decade before?

In the 1970s, a new breed of memory researchers ventured forth from their laboratories to shed light on phenomena such as these. Abandoning research on nonsense syllables and word lists—on memories of a few minutes' duration—these scientists began to investigate such real-world phenomena as legal testimony, diaries, and recollections of historical events. Proceeding independently, researchers on the brain were finding that the principal organ of memory is not what we thought, that it revises itself over and over in the course of a lifetime. In still another branch of psychology, scholars interested in narrative were reminding us of the storied nature of human thought and insisting that we pay attention to the human drive to make meaning. Taken together, this work calls for a dramatic shift in our basic beliefs about autobiographical memory, a shift that will have profound implications for everyone from lawyers to lovers, for everyone who needs to know what memory can and cannot do.

Not everyone believes in the "old" view of memory, but research shows that a solid majority of people do. They believe that every experience of their life is stored somewhere in their brain; even if they cannot remember a particular incident, they assume that some special technique can call it forth—in its true, original form. But the new breed of researchers is saying this isn't so.

My goal in this book is to present the science of autobiographical memory without losing touch with its spirit. In Washington, D.C., there's a memorial to great Americans, a simple wall of polished black marble etched with the names of those who died in the Vietnam War. Depressed in the ground, the memorial is lost among the other great monuments in the area. But anyone who comes upon it feels there is life in that stone. A man who lost someone in the war once described what it was like to find his loved one's name among all the others. You see the name carved on the wall, he said, but you also see your own reflection in the marble. When you lift your hand to touch the name, you also see a hand from the past reaching out to touch you. There is no better symbol of a meeting in memory, no better statement of what the journey in this book is about.

Chapter One

THE WHEREABOUTS OF MEMORY

To begin thinking about the prevailing view of memory, I'd like to ask a strange question. Where is it? That's right—*where* is memory? The quick answer is to point to your head. But if you pursue the question thoughtfully and thoroughly, you will see that the quick answer is too insular. Leave the island of your mind, follow a memory wherever it leads, and you'll find yourself on quite an adventure. At its end, you will realize that the context of autobiographical memory at the end of the twentieth century is vastly different from what it was at the beginning, and light years away from what it was for almost all of human existence. You will also get an idea of where the present view of memory comes from.

Here's how to follow a memory. Think of an object from the past that figures in the story of your life—a baseball glove, perhaps, or maybe a paper doll, a violin, a brass ruler, a cigarette lighter, a flag. Or you can take some episode in your life that's not known to many people. Now what would it take to erase all vestiges of that object or episode from the face of the earth? To remove any and all reminders? You'll find it fascinating to trace the lineage of a memory, and you will get an idea of where, and in what form, human memory now exists.

It took me days to discover all the places and forms in which my grandfather's white gloves still exist. The search began with the gloves themselves. Where were they now? I didn't know, of course, but I was startled to realize when they might have left my grandmother's house. It was when she could no longer take care of herself, and my father had to put her in a state-run "mental institution." We kids had to help clean out her little bungalow. I was fifteen at the time, and I remember going through her drawers and finding all sorts of things. There was some money, and there was a long letter written in a strange language. I can still see the elegant handwriting in purple ink. I can't believe I threw out the letter, but I did. (The money was another story.) What startled me was the possibility that this was the time we got rid of my grandfather's gloves. Could I have touched them, even been the one to throw them out? However and whenever it actually happened, the gloves were probably buried by the city of Chicago along with tons of other things that people considered garbage. The leather they were made of would have decayed by now. No trace of them would remain.

That leaves their memory. For many years it was carried inside my father's head, and probably his alone. When he told me the story of the gloves, it went into my mind and the minds of whoever of my family was sitting around the kitchen table. It also went by way of a microphone onto a thin ribbon of cassette tape. It sounds like an impersonal place for so human a story, but the memory fared far better there than it did in any of our very personal minds. I promptly forgot all about the gloves, and I'm sure everyone else did too. Eventually their memory decayed in my father's mind much as the gloves themselves disintegrated in the earth. Today he has no recollection of them; he has, in fact, only the dimmest sense of who I am. And yet . . . perhaps the memory

is still there, in his mind, but cut off from the surface by the neuronal plaques and tangles in a brain beset by Alzheimer's disease.
If that's the case, maybe the memory never left my mind either,
even during the years I forgot about it. Perhaps something other
than plaques and tangles kept it from the light of day.

Had I lived half a century ago, the memory of the gloves might
have come to an end in the years following that reminiscing at the
kitchen table. But I had a portable tape recorder at my disposal,
and that enabled me to hear the story again. A tape recorder is a
wonderful invention: it converts sound waves in the air into an
electric current, which in turn magnetizes little rust-like particles
of iron oxide that coat a plastic tape. The process creates a permanent record. To retrieve it, I have only to put the tape back into
a recorder and push the "Play" button. The magnetized particles
re-create sound, and I hear my father's voice—just the way I
heard it the first time.

The machine that preserved my father's voice has had a profound effect on my life. Sound recording in general goes back to
1877, when Thomas Edison recited "Mary Had a Little Lamb"
onto a tinfoil cylinder, the world's first phonograph record. Tape
recording is more recent, introduced by the Germans in 1935 on
a "magnetophone." When tape recorders became commercially
available after World War II, they enabled Columbia University to
institute an oral history program, America's first. They've enabled
me to do life histories since the late 1970s. Without them my
work would have taken a different path, and I would not be writing about autobiographical memory today.

Now once I played back the tape recording of my father's story,
the white gloves reentered my mind. Or maybe they activated a
memory of them that was always there, but buried. After listening
to the tape, I told two other people about my reaction to the
gloves. That's two more places where the memory existed for a
time. Whether it's still there, I don't know. I do know, however,

that it still exists at its next major stop. In the course of an on-camera interview for *Seasons of Life,* I told the story of the gloves. I hadn't intended to, but my memory was jogged by a question of the producer. The story was dropped in the editing room, but the producing station, WQED in Pittsburgh, sent me a videocassette of the original interview. Now another machine, a videocassette recorder, was figuring in the lineage of my memory. It had converted light from my face as well as sound from my voice into more magnetized particles on plastic tape. The process was far more complicated than that in audio recording, and the plastic tape was larger, but the idea was the same. A machine had made a lasting record that I could access with just the right equipment.

Now I had to hit the library. I learned that the first videocassette recorder (VCR) was introduced in America in 1956. It wasn't the first device to record pictures, of course. In the 1820s the Frenchman Joseph Niepce used a primitive camera to preserve still images on pewter, and in 1839 his partner, Louis Daguerre, went public with "daguerreotypes," images on silver-plated copper. Photography had come into existence. Pictures that moved came along about fifty years later, developed principally in France and the United States. In 1895 Auguste and Louis Lumière projected the first movie on film to a paying audience.

When the story of my grandfather's gloves went on videotape, it occupied only a few minutes out of an interview of several hours. The tape went to a transcriber who used yet another machine to get it into still another medium: the printed word. Now the memory was getting into a form with a real history. Still pictures go back a century and a half; audio records, just over a century. But Gutenberg's Bible goes back to the middle of the fifteenth century, and the movable type that made his press so important was probably in use in China in the eleventh. Nine centuries before that, the Chinese had carved religious texts in stone, put ink on the raised surfaces, and taken multiple impressions. It was the first form of printing that we know of.

At this point in the journey of the white gloves, they existed in four types of places. There was an audio record, a video record, a print record, and a record in people's minds. Nothing new happened to the memory for several years—until I began to think about this book and got out a yellow pad. I put the memory into writing, a form more ancient than printing. It's difficult to pinpoint when writing began, or even what kind of scratchings, drawings, or painting you want to consider writing. There are cave drawings in southern France and northeastern Spain that date from the last Ice Age. They are more than 10,000 years old, and perhaps as much as 30,000. An early type of writing represented objects in just this way, by drawing miniature pictures of them. Later, writing was based on the sounds of words, and alphabetic scripts like the kind you're reading came into being. The first was developed at least 3,500 years ago. Much early writing was probably done on leaves, bark, or wood; the first record of paper comes from China and is attributed to Ts'ai Lun nearly 1,900 years ago. His paper was probably as perishable as the stuff on which I first etched my memory of the gloves. I don't have that paper any longer; it's probably in a landfill in Ann Arbor, Michigan. Whatever its present condition, the paper brings to five the number of forms in which my memory of my grandfather's gloves exists.

Make it six. After writing the story of the gloves I went to my computer and entered what I had written. My Macintosh took electric signals from its keyboard and converted them, once again, into miniature magnets coated on plastic. This time the magnets were laid out not on a reel of tape, but in concentric circles on a shiny black disk three-and-a-half inches in diameter. The transfer from the keyboard to the disk was made possible because of a machine that was developed in the 1940s and offered to the public in the 1950s. Today, computers have become smaller and more "personal." Once mere aids to calculation, they have become, among other things, repositories of memory. Everything that is entered in them stays there; all it takes is a special technique, in this case a set of keyboard commands, to call it forth. And the "memories" come out in their true, original form.

The final destination for the memory of my grandfather's gloves involved no new media, but it represented an exponential leap in propagation. A typesetter took a copy of my computer disk and used more machines to convert the magnetic recordings there into a pristine printed copy. Other typesetters did the same thing with translations of the story that had been made into languages other than English. Printers photographed those copies and made tens of thousands of others, including the one in your hands. Through that copy, the story of the gloves is now entering your mind.

Where is memory? Not where it was a thousand, a hundred, or even fifty years ago. If you look back on human history, you start with *Homo sapiens* relying only on the memory inside his head, just one of the six places where the white gloves exist today. That was several hundred thousand years ago. Somewhere along the line humans invented external devices to aid their memory: notched sticks to carry messages from one tribe to another, knotted cords to record important legal transactions. Native North Americans made wampum belts of colored shells to ratify treaties, confirm alliances, and conclude contracts. Early Australians put geometrical markings on sacred tablets to help them remember the story of their tribe. In recent years the progression of memory aids has been extraordinary. Writing with an alphabet appeared about 3,500 years ago; paper and printing, less than 2,000. Photography has been in existence just over 150 years; sound recording and motion pictures, about 100; audiotape, videotape, and computers, about 50. The new electronic machines of memory continue to become smaller, more efficient, more personal, and (with the exception of sound recording) more visual. At the end of the twentieth century, the setting of human memory is radically different from what it was at the beginning.

A new generation of children is growing up with the newest of the memory machines. A four-year-old named Clare has been videotaped by her father since her first year. Today, her favorite television program is "The Clare Show." She asks to see it almost every day, and she'll tell you what her favorite parts are. One of them is when one-year-old Clare has no idea what her father is talking about when he says, "Show me your nose." Four-year-old Clare can point to her nose, so she thinks the Clare on her television screen is pretty silly. I was born well before camcorders came into being, so my equivalent of "The Clare Show" was a "baby book" of mementos that my mother carefully put together. Thankfully, the "baby book" became a "scrapbook" in my adolescence, but it continued to hold the fascination for me that "The Clare Show" has for Clare. Still, there's a huge difference between these two repositories of personal history. Mine was static, voiceless; hers, fluid, with sound, and generally more lifelike. I can't imagine how Clare, and all the children of her generation who grow up with VCRs, will think of themselves in relation to what they see. What kind of self-image will they form? How will they relate their own memories to those in the machines? How will they end up picturing their memories?

There is a paradox that runs through the entire history of human memory. As each new external aid came along, it became a picture for that portion of memory that remained inside our heads. Once writing was in place, we could conceive of "verbatim" memory—and later, with printing, of "scripts" from childhood that have been "imprinted" in our minds. After the invention of the camera there came "photographic" memory; after the tape recorder, "human" tape recorders (remember John Dean during the Watergate hearings?); after the computer, "information processing" in the brain. And think of what's coming: helmeted body suits that produce "virtual reality." All these devices create powerful metaphors for the memory that remains in us. They embody the current view of human memory. But every one of them, from first to last, is inanimate.

The Memory in Us

As I look back on my life, I see other places where memories reside. They're not the recording devices that figure in the story of my grandfather's gloves, but rather the sites where significant events in my life took place. If you could tell the story of your life by taking someone to half a dozen places, where would you go? To the yard of the home you grew up in? To the farm where you hid while making an escape during wartime? To a pair of sycamore trees where you and your lover used to meet? To the street corner where a child of yours was killed in an accident? The brick building where you worked for thirty years? The temple where your family worshiped? These are "autobiographical places" where the walls and trees can almost talk. They have always been part of the human experience, but the memories they contain do not survive our death the way the sounds and the pictures in our machines of memory do. That's because the memories in yards and streets and trees and buildings are really memories in us.

So let's turn inward in our pursuit of memory. That which exists in us—where exactly is it?

Once again, the quick answer is to point to your head, meaning that memory is situated in the brain. But think of where else in the body we experience autobiographical memories. The thought of my grandfather's gloves has brought tears to my eyes and a tightness to my throat. A ringing in his ears is the only direct memory a World War II veteran has of riding in a tank and hitting a land mine. Smell is powerfully evocative. Candles, horseradish, cigars, baby powder, sliced apples with honey, sticks of cinnamon, roses: when my wife and I brought these to a group of retirees, they were taken in an instant back to their childhood. In *Remembrance of Things Past,* Marcel Proust wrote of a now-famous incident involving a tea-soaked morsel of cake: "No sooner had the warm liquid, and the crumbs with it, touched my palate than a shudder ran through my whole body, and I stopped, intent upon the extraordinary changes that were taking place." Proust later traced the experience to a boyhood treat connected with visits to his aunt: when he went in to say good morning, she gave him bites of madeleine dipped in tea. Other memories bring with them difficulty in breathing, sweaty palms, a sinking feeling in the pit of the stomach, pain in the lower back, a stirring in the loins, a sense of the body floating away. Gentle memories, as William Wordsworth wrote in *Tintern Abbey,* exist as "sensations sweet, felt in the blood and felt along the heart."

Many therapists who work with victims of childhood abuse describe terror as being stored in the body and say it must be treated as it is experienced—as a bodily memory. Phenomenologists who study memory speak of the body as a "memorial container." You must touch old objects, they say, smell old aromas, hear old sounds, stoop down to the level of a little person to recapture the experience of childhood. And you will experience your memories more deeply if they are embodied in gesture and movement. "After my husband died," said a woman, "I would go into his closet and hug his suits, because they smelled of his own body odor, slight cigarette smell, and aftershave. I'd stand there, hugging his clothes, making believe, close my eyes, and cry."

And yet, when we get away from the lived experience of memory and explore it the way a scientist would, we discover that there is something essentially correct about the impulse to point to our head when asked about the seat of memory. Nothing makes this clearer than the "phantom limb" experience: people who have lost an arm or leg often continue to experience the missing limb as an integral part of their body. So real is the feeling, reports psychologist Ronald Melzack, that patients may attempt to step off their beds onto a phantom foot or to lift up a cup with a phantom hand. One man who felt that his missing arm was bent behind him could not sleep on his back—his phantom hand got in his way. Another who felt that an arm he had lost extended straight out to the side had to turn at an angle to get through doorways.

Amputees experience phantom limbs, but so do people who were born without a limb (which shows that the phantom experience is not a memory experience). Sadly, a deep and burning pain often accompanies the experience of a phantom limb. It's a pain from which physicians are not yet able to provide permanent relief.

After years of studying phantom limbs, Melzack has come to the conclusion that the experience originates not in the body—where the limb has been severed, for example, or in the spinal cord—but in the brain. Even in the absence of input from a missing arm or leg, the brain's own activity creates the sense of an intact body. If a phantom foot dangles in the air a few inches beneath its related stump, as it may on occasion, it is still felt to be a part of the body and to move with the body. Making it so, says Melzack, is primarily the work of the brain.

Phantom limbs suggest by analogy that the memories we experience in the body are actually stored in the brain. So we're back to where we started—that organ in our heads. What's it really like?

Some scientists have described the human brain as the most complex structure in the known universe. Take all the stars in the Milky Way and squeeze them into into a three- or four-pound galaxy the size of a (Chicago-style) softball: that's close to the scale we are operating on. The stars in the brain, perhaps a hundred billion of them, are nerve cells, or "neurons." Neurons conduct electricity, but not the way wires in our machines of memory do. Electricity in a neuron comes from a momentary penetration of ions through its outer membrane; the penetration creates an impulse that moves down the neuron's length the way a spark moves down a long firecracker fuse. The spark in a neuron is at least a million times slower than an electric signal in a copper wire, but it's still capable of speeds of up to 200 miles per hour. Once the spark reaches the end of the neuron, it causes the release of chemicals across a narrow gap known as a synapse. These chemicals are able to ignite another neuron, thus relaying the signal. Put a thousand wires on each and every star in the

Milky Way, start running the wires throughout the galaxy, and you will begin to grasp how many connections the brain can make.

I wonder what stars in the galaxy of my brain have seen my grandfather's gloves. At the moment my father told me about them, I *saw* and I *heard*. That means myriads of nerve impulses went down a pathway from each of my eyes, passed through a crossing station and then a relay station, and arrived in my cortex, the convoluted outer layer of my brain. More precisely, the impulses reached two areas of the cortex in the rear of my head, one on either side of the fissure that divides my brain into two hemispheres. There they encountered neurons firing rhythmically in clusters of a hundred or even fewer. Each cluster worked as a unit, like a flock of starlings in flight, flowing this way on one collective whim, darting that way on another. When the nerve impulses from my eyes hit the neurons in my cortex, they were suddenly energized. Some of them responded to the color (and only the color) of my father's face, others to the shape of his head, still others to its movement. The neurons met in a place where color, shape, and movement were assembled into an image of his face. In monkeys, researchers have identified nerve cells that respond to faces but not to the separate visual stimuli that make up a face. "Face cells" are higher up in the hierarchy that processes sight.

The words I heard from my father took a different route, setting out from each ear and crossing the brain to a place in the cortex just above the opposite ear (at least most of them did). There are hierarchies of processing here as well. Investigators have found neurons in the male zebra finch that react to a song but not to the pure tones that make it up. Amazingly, these neurons react to the song of the bird's father, not to that of any other finch. My father's song was in the form of language, so neural impulses also traveled to a number of places in the left hemisphere of my brain. (Because I'm right-handed, I can be 99 percent sure that language is processed in my left hemisphere. If you're left-handed, you can be only 65 to 70 percent sure.) At various points in the journey of these impulses, a large set of neuronal structures categorized all the meanings of "gloves," from the concrete and literal to the abstract and metaphorical. Working separately and nearly simultaneously, a smaller set of structures limited to the left hemisphere dealt with the sounds, the words, and the sentences of language, including the rules for making a story. A third set of structures, spread throughout the left hemisphere, mediated between the first two, so that my father's words were able to evoke all the corresponding concepts in me.

At least that's what happened the second time around, when the tape recording of my father's voice struck deep and hard. The first time is a mystery. Was a memory even created at that point, only to be forgotten? I can't tell you. But when I heard the story a second time, neural excitations must have reached a crescent-shaped system deep within my brain, the so-called "limbic" system. (Put a finger a little above each ear and imagine pushing it an inch and a half into your brain. The tip of each finger will be tickling that side's limbic system.) The limbic system is involved in emotion, and we know from brain-injured patients who experience amnesia that a part of the system called the hippocampus is critical to long-term autobiographical memory. Amnesics with hippocampal damage can learn how to solve a puzzle, can demonstrate that learning, and then insist after five straight days of practice that they have never seen the puzzle before. "Why should I even try to do it?" they ask, and then proceed to do it beautifully. What they have learned is stored somewhere in their brain as "implicit" memory. But it has not become "explicit," a part of autobiographical memory.

The hippocampus isn't the final resting place for long-term autobiographical memories; it's more like a processing station that holds them for a while—several weeks at least—before transferring them back to the cortex. Damage to the hippocampus prevents new long-term memories from being formed but doesn't eradicate old ones that have been processed. Patients with particular kinds of hippocampal damage have no memories beyond the time of their injury. Asked how old they are, they give their age in the year their hippocampus was damaged, and then are shocked when handed a mirror. One patient with a very old injury had lived in a time capsule since 1945. He insisted the president of the United States was Harry Truman and could make no sense of a picture of the earth taken from outer space. In his mind, it had to be the moon.

Patients with hippocampal damage make us realize how distinctive autobiographical memory is. So do people with certain other disabilities. In those who suffer from multiple personality disorder, implicit memories transfer from one personality to the next, but explicit autobiographical memories do not. My father, who suffers from Alzheimer's disease, has forgotten the story of the gloves and does not recognize me, but he still remembers what to do when lining up a shot at a pool table. Implicit memory survives, at least for now. Explicit autobiographical memory is gone.

But back to our mental galaxy. When it became my turn to tell the story of the gloves, other areas of my brain became involved. Once again, networks of nerve cells in the left hemisphere introduced the medium of language. They helped me choose the right words, nouns from one part of the cortex, verbs from another. Research has gotten very precise about the location of these lexical items. Proper nouns, for example, are represented further forward in the left hemisphere, just as specific concepts are positioned to the front of general ones. Verbs are harder to find; preliminary evidence points to sites higher and more frontal. Neuroscientists have been able to be so precise because techniques such as MRI (magnetic resonance imaging) can pinpoint the damage in brain-injured individuals. Some of these individuals can retrieve verbs but not nouns, nouns of one type but not of another. And men and women may allocate the tasks differently.

One researcher reports that speech disorders occur most often in women when an injury damages a region in the front of the brain and in men when it damages a region in the back.

In any event, a number of neural networks in my left hemisphere recreated a story from my ideas and shipped it to areas on either side of my "motor" cortex, which runs in an arch from ear to ear. Now all I had to do was write the story off the top of my head—that's where the nerve cells that guide the movement of my hands and fingers are located. Or I could tell it from the side—the center of control for mouth and tongue.

My grandfather's gloves had seen a lot of my brain, all right, but had they ever lodged in a place called Memory? Almost fifty years ago neuropsychologist Karl Lashley tried to answer that question. He trained rats to run a maze, systematically removed parts of their cortex, and then tested their knowledge of the maze. He was hoping to discover where a record of the maze was stored. But no matter where Lashley cut, parts of the memory survived, and after years of looking for a single site, he gave up.

Other researchers pursued the idea that Memory wasn't a place but an activity, a particular pattern of electrical impulses. An experiment by Robert Ransmeier ruled out that possibility. Ransmeier trained hamsters to run through a maze of doors to get food. Once they learned the route, he lowered their body temperature until all the electrical activity in their brains ceased. When the hamsters were revived and their brains became active again, they showed no loss of learning. Their brains had been turned off, but their memories remained intact. So long-term memory must involve more than a change in neural activity. A record must be made in the neurons themselves.

But where in the brain is the record? Most probably in millions of places. Neuroscientist Patricia Goldman-Rakic and her colleagues recently trained a monkey to fix its gaze on a small spot in the center of a television screen. An object would appear, then disappear, somewhere near the edge of the screen. After a few seconds, the central spot would also disappear, which was the monkey's cue to move its eyes to where the object on the edge *had been*. Once the monkey was executing this procedure, Goldman-Rakic used fine electrodes inserted into its brain to find where the vanishing object was "remembered." She discovered that when the object first appeared near the edge of the screen, there was an increase in electrical activity in a tiny pocket of neurons in the monkey's prefrontal cortex, that part of the brain's outer layer that lies beneath its forehead. When the object vanished and the monkey had to remember where it was, there was a peak of activity in a pocket close to the first. And when the monkey actually moved its eyes to where the object had been, an electrical burst appeared in a third place. Nerve cells in the first position were connected with seeing, those in the third with doing. The ones in the intermediate position had to be "memory" neurons. Their only assignment was to keep alive an image of where an object had disappeared from view.

This kind of memory is hardly autobiographical (it lasted between three and six seconds), but it gives researchers a fresh perspective on a very complex problem. All that goes into an autobiographical memory—the sights, the sounds, the smells, the emotions, the meanings—is probably represented by the brain in separate pockets close to where the original seeing, hearing, smelling, feeling, and making of meaning were done. The pockets involved must be tiny—no more than a thousand neurons in each, according to one estimate. And the neurons in the pockets must be highly specialized: in monkeys, certain nerve cells increase their rate of firing when the monkey is remembering a red circle but not a green square.

When a memory is made, at least three things happen. First, a bond between neurons is strengthened. What strengthening means and how it occurs is still uncertain. We know that electrical impulses bridge the gap between one neuron and another by means of chemical messengers. But how is the leap across a synapse made easier the second and third time around, so it becomes a fledgling memory? One possibility is that the second neuron in a sequence sends its own chemical messenger back to the first. The messenger says "do it again" by freeing more of the original messengers.

The chemical strengthening of connections explains short-term memories, but lifelong ones require something more. That something appears to be major anatomical change—the growth of new branches on nerve cells. When laboratory rats are moved from an ordinary environment to a stimulating one, their brains show such growth; close examination reveals that it occurs at the very places where particular experiences are processed. The same effect has been found in monkeys: when they use their three middle fingers to rotate a disk for an hour a day, the areas in the cortex that represent those fingers expand; adjacent areas representing the unused thumb and little finger do not. The effect is not limited to young animals, nor does it seem to exclude us.

It's likely that many long-term memories are stored in the same sites as short-term memories, but that they reflect the complex wiring that comes from stimulation. The neurons involved may also live longer—a third kind of change. The reason is that genes turned on by repeated firing seem to manufacture proteins that promote survival. For nerve cells, electrical activity may be something like lifting weights or jogging. The exercise may build them up to the point where they become capable of maintaining memories for a lifetime.

Though I'm not about to let neuroscientists wire me up to prove the matter conclusively, I think it's safe to say that a number of nerve cells in my brain have changed in response to my grandfather's gloves. With some kind of help from the hippocampus, they have made a thicket of their branches. Even now, as I think of the gloves, those nerve cells are firing faster, helped along by chemical messengers that know how to get where they're going. My odd question, "Where is memory?" led me far and wide, but I ended up where I began, pointing to my head. The only difference was that, at the end of my journey, I was using all of my fingers.

Which means I had no way of pointing to an historic landmark, an organ shaped like a pine cone and the size of a pea that sits in the middle of the brain. It's the pineal gland, and though scientists aren't sure of all that it does, they think it may be the remnant of an ancestral sense organ. But 350 years ago René Descartes thought it was the center of consciousness, the place where matter meets spirit. Descartes was wrong about the function of the pineal gland but not about the question he posed. How indeed are excitations in neural networks turned in on themselves to become the subjective experience of memory—the sound of a father's voice, the vision of a grandfather's hands, the meaning of both of their lives? Where is the great Cartesian Theater, the place where the chemical messengers of memory become actors before our mind's eye? Everywhere, somewhere, or nowhere?

No one knows, of course, and it may be a century (if ever) before anyone can hazard a guess. In the meantime, let us understand our metaphors. Is memory like a machine? At the present moment, we know this: the human brain is sluggish in comparison with a computer, though it more than makes up for that with the complexity and organization of its connections. The brain wasn't designed for a specific purpose, as was the computer, but rather took millions of years to evolve. It has countless more things to do than preserve memories, things like controlling our breathing, walking, and talking. And as long as it's alive, the brain is "on." Its plug is never pulled, even when we go to sleep. In fact, researchers have known since the early 1950s that sleep brings brainstorms of electrical activity—dreams—about every ninety minutes. Finally, though there is stability in the brain's wiring, a hard precision laid out in its genetic program for growth, it's far softer than any machine. It's malleable, revisable, its gray matter a clay that hardens very slowly over the course of a lifetime.

Does this mean that the memory in our minds is less accurate than that in our machines? Yes, but accuracy does not ensure truth. Let us never forget that we're the ones who create and control the machines. We process the memories in them with the memories in us. We now have the capacity to sit in front of a computer, take apart a photograph bit by bit, and reassemble it any way we wish. We call it digital alteration. And we can edit. We can fashion "docudramas" that are "based on" or "recreate" actual events and movies that unabashedly mix fact and fiction. The power of the visual image is so strong that many in our audience accept what they see as history. As memory machines improve in the twenty-first century, as they make knowledge more and more visual, as they bring on "virtual reality," as they begin to do things we cannot even conceive of today, our capacity to preserve accurate records will increase. But so will our capacity to make bad memory look good.

There's a whole new world of memory out there, a world my grandfather could hardly have imagined. But the stuff of memory in him is no different from the stuff in me. I know much more about it than he ever could, thanks to some remarkable research on the brain. But my grandchildren will know more than I, and they will live in a world of memory devices and "Clare Shows" that would boggle my mind if I ever saw them. I hope my grandchildren realize, in that dazzling world, that the memory in them is different from the memory in their machines, that they control it, and not vice versa. May none of their generation forget what eludes some of us, even the scientists: the memory in humans is alive.

⚭

Chapter Two

IS EVERYTHING "IN THERE"?

Just as the audio tape recorder was coming into being, a Montreal neurosurgeon was listening to the human brain as no one had before. In the late 1930s, Wilder Penfield began treating patients with severe epileptic seizures by removing damaged tissue from their brains. To pinpoint where he should cut and check for possible side effects, Penfield would see what parts of the body moved when he applied gentle electrical stimulation to various regions of the cortex. Since the brain has no pain receptors, his patients were able to remain awake during the procedure. As Penfield explored the area of the cortex just above the ear, patients would occasionally report flashbacks, like the sound of old folks singing a hymn or a mother calling a little boy, or the vision of big wagons at a carnival. These flashbacks were so lifelike that Penfield believed he was activating long-forgotten memories. When he published a summary of his work in 1969, he said of the *living* brain he had touched with his very fingers that it was rather like "a tape recorder." Later, he used a different metaphor. "The mind seems to act independently of the brain," he wrote, "in the same sense that a programmer acts independently of his computer."

These were no idle metaphors. Penfield believed that "electric recall" summoned up exact reproductions of past experiences. "It may have been a time of listening to music, a time of looking in at the door of a dance hall, a time of imagining the action of robbers from a comic strip, a time of waking from a vivid dream, a time of laughing conversation with friends, a time of listening to a little son to make sure he was safe, a time of watching illuminated signs, a time of lying in the delivery room at childbirth, a time of being frightened by a menacing man, a time of watching people enter the room with snow on their clothes." Only forty of over 1,100 patients experienced these flashbacks, but Penfield was so astonished by "the stream of a former consciousness flowing again" that he left a detailed record of every case. Included in the records were diagrams of the brain with numbers corresponding to where the patient had been stimulated. The sample below, from a man, begins with a point marked "28":

> 28. *"Oh gosh! There they are, my brother is there. He is aiming an air rifle at me." His eyes moved slowly to the left. . . . When asked where he was, he said at his house, in the yard. His other little brother was there, that was all. When asked if he felt scared when he saw his brother, he said, "Yes."*

Penfield moved his electrode:

> 30. *"I heard someone speaking, my mother telling one of my aunts to come up tonight."*

Again:

> 31. *"The same thing as before. My mother was telling my aunt over the telephone to come up and visit us tonight." When asked how he knew she was talking over the telephone, he said he did not*

see her, but from the way his aunt's voice sounded when she answered he knew it was over the telephone.

And again:

32. *"My mother is telling my brother he has got his coat on backwards. I can just hear them. . . ." When asked if he thought these things were like dreams, he said, "No."*

Standing over his patients, Penfield believed that every experience of their lives lay beneath his electrode. Neural activity, he said, left a permanent trail of connections "that can be followed again by an electric current many years later with no loss of detail." Though Penfield never came across certain kinds of events—memories of tasting food, having sex, making decisions, and suffering were among them—he persevered in the belief that all of life's experiences are stored somewhere in memory. Newly developed memory machines had created irresistible metaphors for his mind.

Earlier in the century Sigmund Freud had come by a different route to essentially the same conclusion. Although he had taken a variety of positions over the years, Freud ended up by saying that all our autobiographical records are "in there," hidden or not. "In mental life nothing which has once been formed can perish," he wrote in 1930, adding "that everything is somehow preserved and that in suitable circumstances (when, for instance, regression goes back far enough) it can once more be brought to light." Penfield used an electrode to bring memories back, while Freud used the techniques of psychoanalysis, free association and the analysis of dreams among them. The techniques were needed to get through the pain, the fear, the shame, and the guilt that keeps memories repressed. Although a surgeon's table is far from a psychoanalyst's couch, it's interesting to realize that both Penfield and Freud came to their conclusions by having patients lie on their backs and talk.

The two were not the only ones to explore the memories of people who had been rendered passive. In the 1940s hypnotists were encountering fascinating experiences when they took people on "age regressions." Under hypnosis subjects were told that they were three or four years old; they started to talk like children and produce vivid memories of events they had long since forgotten. In 1949 Robert True published in *Science* magazine a study in which he took hypnotized volunteers back to Christmases and birthday parties at ages four, seven, and ten. He then asked them what day of the week it was. The results were astonishing: 82 percent of the answers were correct. Had subjects simply been guessing, only one in seven answers would have been right.

Therapists saw in hypnosis a way of uncovering trauma in a client's past; criminal investigators, a way to induce "hypermnesia" (or supermemory). They could turn a spotlight on memory traces that were beyond the conscious recall of victims and witnesses. Hypnotically retrieved memories provided leads in the cases of the Boston Strangler, the San Francisco cable-car nymphomaniac, and Sam Sheppard, the Cleveland physician who was charged with killing his pregnant wife. In 1968 a Maryland court declared such memories to be admissible as evidence and placed no restrictions on their use. In 1975 a spokesman for the Los Angeles Police Department said in *TV Guide* that hypnosis had proved useful in 65 percent of the cases in which it was tried. "Through hypnosis," he stated, "we make the conscious mind passive and communicate with the subconscious to release what's buried there." Hypnosis was certainly critical in the case of Ed Ray, a school bus driver who in 1977 was kidnapped and imprisoned, along with twenty-six of his charges, in an abandoned trailer truck buried six feet underground. After the group was rescued, Ray was able to see under hypnosis all but one of the digits of his captors' license plate, enough to enable police to hunt down them down. In a variety of settings, hypnosis appeared to be doing the same thing as Penfield's electrodes and Freud's psychoanalysis—

finding the light switch in the darkest regions of the storehouse of memory. Everything lay in the storehouse, waiting to be found.

Today, most lay people see memory the way Freud and Penfield did. Some 70 to 85 percent of those who are asked believe that everything that ever happened to them is stored somewhere in their brain. The things they can't remember are "lost" or "buried," but they can be "found," "dug up," or "tapped into" if you just know the trick. The trick is a certain technique: electrical stimulation of the brain, psychoanalysis, hypnosis in the cases mentioned above; the right kind of interrogation, drugs, meditative imagery tours, prayer, body massage in others. In this view of memory, everything gets in and nothing gets out. Amnesia means that memories of an event are blocked from recall, not that they have been removed from the storehouse, or never put there in the first place. I once thought this view of memory was confined to young people, but my sampling of older audiences (I usually ask for a show of hands) has proven otherwise. People of all ages seem to believe in the permanence of memories. Everything is "in there" and potentially accessible.

And why not believe this? In addition to the influence of thinkers like Penfield and Freud and the periodic claims of some hypnotists, we have personal experiences of more being "in there" than we know, experiences of words getting to the tip of our tongue but not crossing over into consciousness, experiences of knowing we're supposed to do something but forgetting what it is. On the other hand, a scene from childhood pops into mind, unasked for, after decades of absence. And there's the eerie sense of *déjà vu,* which has been experienced at least once by some 60 percent of adult Americans. You walk into a room and have the feeling that you've been in this very place before. But you know you haven't. What is it, deep down, that tells you this is not a new experience? Sometimes a call from the deep leaves wonder and dread in its wake. Therapists have told me how the face of a client will go white with terror, how muscles will slacken, how eyes will widen and stare as something appears in the corner of memory. The client doesn't know what it is, doesn't *want* to know, but cannot escape the feeling that something is lurking.

These experiences of knowing that *some* things are hidden in memory slip easily into the belief that *all* things are hidden in memory. Along with this belief come some corollaries: the original records still exist, and once you find an original, you'll be able to recognize it as such. The corollaries make sense if you think of memory as a machine. When I'm working at my personal computer, I'm aware that much more is "in there" than appears on my screen. In fact, I know that everything that went in, now matter how deeply, is ready and willing to come back out. I know the technique, in this case a set of keyboard commands, that will summon it forth. And I have perfect confidence that when it does come forth, I will see an exact replica of what was originally processed. It's no different when I put a tape in my VCR, listen to someone on audiotape, go through old family pictures, or, for that matter, take a book off my shelf and open it to a particular page. I can get back to the original records and know they are authentic.

In the prevailing view of memory, you judge authenticity by the vividness of an image and its wealth of detail. A clear picture is thought to be an original picture, a photograph that hasn't faded with time. During World War I, Frederick Bartlett, a psychologist at Cambridge University, gave a small group of subjects a simple task: to remember the sequence in which five picture postcards were shown to them. Some of Bartlett's subjects relied on visual cues in remembering the cards; others, on the words they had used to describe them. Two weeks after seeing the cards for the first time, the visualizers were more confident of their memories than the verbalizers, even though they were no more accurate in their recall.

To Arthur Mann, a biographer of Fiorello LaGuardia, the former mayor of New York City, exactness in particulars was the test of authenticity. Mann accepted the credibility of one witness "when he remembered the exact day that the Germans broke through at Caporetto, the middle names of his commanding officers, and the day and the time of day that LaGuardia's first wife was buried in 1921 as well as the street address and the name of her undertaker." In a recent episode of the television series *Murder, She Wrote,* a man was cleared of a killing when a hypnotist helped him recover a hidden memory showing he acted in self-defense. Everyone accepted the memory as an original record. But in the same episode, a woman's entire story was discounted because the timing of a detail was off. She remembered a refrigerator being in the basement of a house years before it was actually there. Because no one accepted as normal the transposing of detail from present to past, the woman was considered a liar. And so she would be if the prevailing view of memory were correct.

The New View: Reconstruction

It is the prevailing view of memory that I called in the prologue to this book the "old" view. How old it is in the history of humanity is hard to say, because the records that would tell us already represent the externalization of memory. But I suspect the "old" view has truly prevailed only in the last century or two, when the machines of memory created their powerful metaphors. In the last few decades, a new line of research, and a new breed of researchers, have called this view into question.

In a way Frederick Bartlett, who showed during World War I that vividness is unrelated to accuracy, was a forerunner of the new breed. He thought that memories were "reconstructed" rather than "recovered," a view not incompatible with occasional comments of Freud. Half a century after Bartlett and Freud, psychologist Elizabeth Loftus began to accumulate evidence supporting the reconstructionist viewpoint. As part of her research, she and her husband, Geoffrey Loftus, examined the flashbacks of Wilder Penfield's patients more closely. They found enough inconsistencies and impossibilities to question his belief in the permanence of memory. In one instance, a woman had changed the location of a memory from "the neighborhood" to "the lumberyard" when a particular spot in her brain was stimulated a second time. She added that she had never been near a lumberyard in her life. In another, number "31" above, the patient overheard his mother talking to his aunt on the telephone. Though he was not on the phone himself, he heard both sides of the conversation—an impossibility in real life. Penfield's conclusions were also called into question when a different group of researchers described the case of a patient whose "memories" consisted of thoughts that happened to be present just prior to the stimulation of her brain. They appeared to be recordings from the past but were not.

Similar doubts about the stability of memory traces were created as the claims of hypnotists began to be checked out. When researchers were unable to replicate Robert True's age-regression results, it was discovered that he had not asked subjects, "What day is this?" but rather, "Is it Sunday?" "Is it Monday?" and so on, and that he himself had known the correct answer when asking the question. That tiny detail made all the difference: it takes only the merest vocal inflection, even unintended, to communicate the right answer to a subject. What True had demonstrated was not the power of memory but the power of suggestion.

The power of suggestion was demonstrated more directly in a number of subsequent experiments on hypnosis. In one, participants were asked to choose a night from the previous week, a night for which they had no specific memories of dreaming or waking up. Told under hypnosis to relive that night, they were asked a specific question: had they heard any loud noises that awakened them? That question was the experimental implant. In the study, seventeen of twenty-seven subjects said yes, they now remembered such a noise. Thirteen of them maintained the memory even after hypnosis was lifted and they were told that the loud noise was only a suggestion of the hypnotist. Of the thirteen, six were sure they had a direct recollection of the nighttime sounds. "I'm pretty damned certain," said one. "I'm positive I heard these noises." The other seven had no direct recollection of the sound, but concluded there must have been one. "I'm pretty sure it happened because I can remember being startled," was a typical comment. In general, research has shown that people under hypnosis recall more fact but also more fiction, and they become less able to distinguish one from the other. At the same time they become more confident of their memories and turn into compelling witnesses. As a result of this research, fewer courts (including those in the state of Maryland) are now accepting testimony based on hypnotically refreshed memories.

In the early 1970s Loftus demonstrated the power of suggestion in the memories of subjects who were not hypnotized. College students in her experiment watched a brief film in which a few seconds were devoted to a traffic accident. Afterward, some of the subjects were asked to estimate how fast the cars in the film were going when they "hit" each other. Others were asked to estimate the speed when the cars "smashed" into each other. Both groups saw the same film, but the "smashed" group gave higher estimates of speed than the "hit" group. A week later both groups were asked if they had seen any broken glass. More members of the "smashed" group, and more of those who had given high estimates of speed, said yes. Actually, there had been no broken glass in the film. Subsequent research has convinced Loftus that leading questions can change the mental picture of rememberers; they now *see* a moustache, or curly hair, or broken glass, or a white vehicle, or a stop sign, or a barn, or whatever has been suggested. Loftus believes that two kinds of information go into a memory. The first is the original perception of the event; the second is information supplied after the event. With time the two become blended into a single memory that replaces what was originally present.

Researchers are now able to do more than replace memories in nonhypnotized subjects; they can implant totally new ones. In one case, they replicated the results of the loud-noises-at-night experiment simply by asking subjects to imagine and describe such noises. Even without hypnosis, some of the descriptions turned into memories. There's a well-known story about the Swiss psychologist Jean Piaget, who grew up with a vivid memory of nearly being kidnapped at the age of two. In the memory he saw a man assaulting him, his nurse trying bravely to defend him, and her face being scratched in the ensuing scuffle. The memory lasted throughout his childhood and into his adolescence. But when he was fifteen, the nurse wrote to his parents, confessing that she had made up the whole story. The clarity with which Piaget had seen the event in his memory, and the personal conviction he had about its truth, was no proof that it ever happened.

Former President Ronald Reagan used to tell the story of the commander of a bomber who was posthumously awarded the Congressional Medal of Honor during World War II. His plane had been hit and a young gunner who couldn't get out was panic-stricken. "Never mind, son," said the commander, "we'll ride it down together." The commander stayed with the plane, accompanying the young man to his death. Reagan told the story during his campaigns of 1976 and 1980, and again in 1983. But then a journalist did some checking and found that no such Medal of Honor had ever been issued. He also discovered a World War II movie called *A Wing and a Prayer* in which a pilot goes down with a wounded radioman, saying, "We'll take this ride together." A *Reader's Digest* story contained the same words: "We'll take this ride together." What Reagan remembered as fact had probably come from fiction. A false memory like Piaget's, it illustrates a phenomenon known as cryptomnesia.

The term itself is esoteric (the Greek root means "hidden memory"), but the situation it denotes is commonplace: you remember *what* someone told you but you forget *that* you were told. I've seen a lot of it in groups that work together on a creative product. After a while, an individual starts to remember what he heard in a hallway conversation or a group meeting, but he forgets where he heard it, and even that he heard it. An old idea becomes his original creation. (In a way, this is the opposite of *déjà vu,* in which something new seems old.) Because of cryptomnesia it's possible to believe that a picture actually planted in your memory by a photograph, a film, or someone else's words originated in a direct experience of your own. Nor can you tell if a memory has been cryptically implanted by the way it looks or feels. Unreal memories look and feel like real ones.

Alterations and fabrications in memory add up to what Bartlett in 1932 and psychologists today call reconstruction. The idea is that memories don't sit inertly in our minds they way they do on an audiotape or the shelves of a library. They are constantly refashioned. Reconstruction is well illustrated in research on John Dean's testimony at the Watergate hearings. In June 1973, Dean testified before the Senate committee investigating the Watergate coverup regarding a meeting he had had with then-President Nixon nine months before, on September 15, 1972. Dean prefaced his testimony by saying that he believed he had an excellent memory. After hearing him testify, the press began to call him "a human tape recorder." When it was later revealed that an actual tape recorder had been playing during the meeting about which Dean testified, an experiment of nature was created. Psychologist Ulric Neisser compared the transcript of Dean's testimony with the transcript of the actual tape-recorded meeting. He found rampant reconstruction. In a literal sense—who sat where, who said what—Dean's testimony wasn't even close to being accurate. Neisser's comparison showed that Dean inserted into his memory something he yearned for at the meeting but never received— an opening compliment from the President. In memory, Dean gave himself the benefit of hindsight, reversing a prediction that had proved to be wrong. And in his recollections he saw himself as more central to ongoing events than he really was. "What his testimony really describes," said Neisser in conclusion, "is not the

September 15 meeting itself but his fantasy of it: the meeting as it should have been, so to speak. . . . By June, this fantasy had become the way Dean 'remembered' the meeting."

Surprisingly, Neisser did not conclude that Dean was lying. In the larger scheme of things, what he said was all true. Nixon had the knowledge Dean attributed to him; there *was* a coverup. In Dean's mind, a single event—his meeting with the President—symbolized a pattern of repeated events. The symbol was so compelling that Dean "remembered" specifics that never took place on the occasion in question.

Any time autobiographical memories are checked against external records, they come up short, at least if you expect them to do what our machines of memory do. And yet those expectations persist. In the Senate Judiciary Committee hearings that investigated Anita Hill's charges of sexual harassment against Clarence Thomas, there was no hidden tape recorder, as there was in the Watergate case. The only belief on which the hearings could even proceed was that everything was "in there," that original records of words spoken long ago were still stored in the heads of two individuals. Intense interrogation, it was thought, could produce those original records. When the testimonies of Hill and Thomas clashed, senators, television commentators, and people in the street tried to establish criteria for truth. If a memory was vivid and full of detail, it was accurate. If witnesses had nothing to gain from talking about a memory, if they did so despite pain, if they spoke with emotion, if they were consistent and confident, if they calmly looked questioners in the eye, they were truthful. Scientific research, however, has found that none of these criteria has any bearing on the accuracy of recall. And conversation is just about the most difficult thing to remember accurately, especially when you're being interrogated.

The scientific evidence on memory is quite clear: qualities like vividness and exactness cannot prove a memory to be true, nor can the lack of them rule out a memory as false. For a Senate panel, a judge, or a jury—for any of us—to be sure of a memory, we need to have corroboration from other people's memories or from some kind of external record. We also need to remember that false details and even false episodes can be implanted in memory, and that memories can be essentially true even though significant details are wrong.

The Ins and Outs of It

To get an idea of how material gets into memory and then back out again, let's take something quite commonplace, something you've seen almost every day of your life. A penny. How much can you remember about a penny? A lot, you say? Well, try drawing one—now.

It ought to be easy, but it isn't. When you get stuck, compare what you've drawn with an actual penny. On the "heads" side, did you have Lincoln facing toward the right, where the year 19— appears? Did you have "In God We Trust" written across the top and "Liberty" on the left? For "tails," did you start with a building in the center? (It's the Lincoln Memorial, and if you look closely you can make out the statue of Lincoln between a pair of pillars in the middle.) Did you add "United States of America" across the top, "E Pluribus Unum" just below that, and "One Cent" across the bottom? In a study of memory for a penny, only 20 percent of the participants recalled even half of these eight features correctly. But one of them got everything right. He happened to be an avid coin collector; he could picture pennies in minute detail because they had a special place in his life.

When I've tried the penny exercise with groups, people perform as poorly as the experimental subjects. But they still retain their belief in the permanence of memory. Although they can't draw a penny, the majority nevertheless insist that all a penny's features are stored somewhere in their heads.

I tell these people what we know from research: that a penny would register on their eye and their brain in amazing detail, but in a few tenths of a second much of the image would be gone. What would be left—all they needed to identify and use a penny—would first enter short-term, then long-term, memory. What this means is that many aspects of our experience never get "in there" in the first place. If you doubt that, go to a local store and ask to watch a week's worth of videotape from a surveillance camera. Make it a store that's open twenty-four hours a day. Very little of that 168 hours would stay with you because very little of it would be worth remembering. But you'd get a good idea of what is potentially available to memory, and how boring most of it is.

Not everything gets into autobiographical memory, not even the details of a penny, and once something manages to enter, it may never return. Sometimes memories "decay" during storage, usually from a lack of use. Like white gloves buried in the earth, they literally go out of existence. Neuroscientists have yet to find direct anatomical evidence of such decay in humans, but they are coming close. Some time ago they learned that if one of a kitten's eyes is sewn shut at a particular stage in its development, nerve cells running from that eye to the brain's cortex will lose branches. Lack of use leads to their atrophy. At the same time, nerve cells running from the open eye to the cortex will grow thicker branches and actually take over some of the space in the cortex that normally belongs to the closed eye. The same thing happens with young monkeys, and in both animals it leads to impaired vision in the adult, long after the sutured eye has been reopened. It is not far-fetched to say that there is competition among neurons and that the strong survive at the expense of the weak.

How do we recover memories? Usually "retrieval cues" point the way. Go over an old high-school yearbook and you'll see such cues at work. The names and faces will bring back a flood of remembrance. So will the farewell notes your classmates may have written in the book. Go back to the school itself, walk through the halls and classrooms, and you'll discover even more cues. Autobiographical places that hold memories illustrate that memory is dependent on context. When scuba divers in one experiment listened to a list of words ten feet underwater they recalled the list better when they were again underwater, as compared with sitting on the beach. A second group of divers who heard the list while sitting on the beach remembered it better on the beach than when they were underwater. Take young children to a park and ask them the next day what they did on the trip; they'll remember more if you ask your questions in the park than if you do so in their nursery school.

To recover even more memories of high school, use other cues—"autobiographical objects" like an old sweater or textbook. Should you go to a reunion, you will see how one person's memories stimulate another's. (You will also see how different those memories are.) As stories ricochet through the gathering, as the mood gets more nostalgic, you will realize something else—that memory is dependent on emotional state. If people are in a happy mood, they come up with happy memories. In a sad mood they think of what's depressing. There's an old Charlie Chaplin movie, *City Lights,* in which Charlie plays a tramp who saves a drunk from leaping to his death. The drunk turns out to be a millionaire who treats Charlie to a night of drinking and carousing. The next day, after the two have sobered up, the millionaire has no idea of who Charlie is. Then he gets drunk again, sees Charlie, and remembers. After another round of drinking and sobriety, the millionaire finds Charlie in his house. He believes him to be an intruder and has the butler kick him out. Charlie doesn't get it.

Psychologist Gordon Bower would explain to Charlie that different emotional states are like different libraries. "A given memory record can be retrieved only by returning to that library, or physiological state, in which the event was first stored." One of the reasons episodes of childhood abuse are so hard to remember is that they often enter memory under extreme emotional conditions. Only when something in the present evokes those conditions (and only when an ever-present fear is lifted) will a memory of the event actually return. A person may genuinely forget committing a crime of passion because extreme rage has given way to overwhelming remorse. The dramatic shift in emotional states creates a kind of amnesia.

When psychologists test for memories, they usually do it the way your high-school teachers did. They use either "recall" or "recognition." When I asked you to draw a penny, I was testing your recall. It's like asking you to answer an essay question on an examination; there are no answers for you to choose from. Sometimes recall fails, and we do better recognizing the correct answer from a range of possibilities, as on a multiple-choice test. When researchers in the penny experiment asked subjects to select the correct drawing of a penny from a sample of fifteen look-alikes, 42 percent were able to do so. That was far better than their recall performance. In another study, people who had difficulty recalling many of their high-school classmates from twenty-five years before were still able to recognize 90 percent of their names and pictures. Often something "in there" enables us to recognize what we cannot consciously recall.

But recognition has its problems, mainly that suggested alternatives contaminate memory. In one study of criminal identification, subjects were told that the perpetrator of a staged act of vandalism was in a lineup of five people. In reality he was not, but 78 percent of the subjects "recognized" him. When another group of subjects were told that the vandal *might be* in the lineup (once again, he wasn't), there was less misidentification, but 33 percent still selected an innocent person. One of the problems with police lineups is that they are based on relative judgments. Witnesses gain confidence from eliminating possibilities, which makes them less likely to question the absolute value of their final choice. And once they express that choice, thus accusing someone of a crime, it becomes very difficult for them to change their mind.

Recall, on the other hand, is capable of producing trustworthy memories if it is allowed to proceed without interruption. There is less pressure on witnesses to fill in their accounts with details they're not sure of. One study found that recall was 50 percent more accurate if police investigators held off on any questions until after witnesses had visualized a scene and described every detail they could remember. Interrupting recall with questions implants suggestions that falsify recollection. Other studies have found that if witnesses are not forced to choose between alternatives, if they are told that "I don't remember" is an acceptable response—and if they're not out to prove a point—their recall will be virtually error-free. They simply do not volunteer information they are unsure of.

The variety of cues that bring memories back tells us how rich the brain's associative networks are. When we recollect, the brain literally *re-collects* all the neural events that took place on a prior occasion. When you consider how many individual neurons fired the first time around (the number is beyond imagination), it's easy to see why many of them will be missed in the second collection. Then, when you think about how many associations may have been added to a neural network over time, it's easy to see how nonoriginal elements work their way into a memory. Finally, when you realize that all the neurons involved, both originals and nonoriginals, grow and decay over time, it's not at all surprising that psychologists who check memories against external records find evidence of reconstruction. Actually, it would be stunning if they didn't. Today, neuroscientists appreciate what Wilder Penfield did not, that what is stored in the brain changes because the brain itself changes.

Repressed Memories

In 1990 George Franklin, Sr., was brought to trial in Redwood City, California, for the brutal murder of an eight-year-old child that had occurred in 1969. The chief witness against Franklin was his own adult daughter, Eileen, who had been a close friend of the victim, Susie Nason. Eileen had forgotten the incident for some twenty years. Then one day when she was playing with her own five-year-old daughter she had a flashback. She saw Susie's look of betrayal just before the murder. This flashback was followed in due time by others, until Eileen had pieced together an entire episode. It began with her father sexually assaulting Susie in the back of a Volkswagen van. Eileen remembered the exact words of the victim as she begged, "No, don't!" and "Stop!" and the precise tone of her father's voice as he responded, "Now, Susie." She remembered that her father took Susie outside the van after the assault and that she herself screamed as he raised a rock over his head. The next scene was of her friend lying on the ground, covered with blood. Eileen recalled another detail from that scene, a crushed silver ring on Susie's finger. Some features of her story changed as Eileen recounted it first to relatives, then to police, and finally in court. One of the changes concerned who else was in the van when Susie was picked up and what time of day it was. Another involved the circumstances in which Eileen first had her flashback. In the beginning she had said it was under hypnosis; only later did she maintain it was while playing with her daughter. Still, the images Eileen spoke of were so vivid and compelling that it took the jury only a day to find Franklin guilty of first-degree murder—a verdict that was subsequently upheld by the California Court of Appeal. This was the first time in history that the return of a repressed memory was the primary factor in convicting an American citizen of a crime.

A year after the Franklin conviction, comedienne Roseanne Barr Arnold appeared on the cover of *People* magazine to reveal memories of her mother abusing her from the time she was an infant. The memories had recently come to light during therapy. Other stories of repressed childhood trauma, including that of a former Miss America, had come out in *People,* the *Washington Post, Seventeen, Glamour, Newsweek,* and *Time,* and attorneys had begun to file civil suits on behalf of clients whose memories of abuse were breaking through repressions. The clients were seeking financial compensation for emotional and physical distress, counseling and medical expenses, and lost earnings. State legislatures had to reconsider statutes of limitations. The state of Washington was among the first to do so, deciding in 1989 to recognize lawsuits filed within three years of the time a person *remembered* being abused, with no reference to when the abuse actually occurred. Repression wasn't a new idea, but the public (and the law) was suddenly coming to terms with it. But was it a valid concept? Was there any merit to the notion that experiences can be so painful that they are pushed out of awareness, remaining "in there," but inaccessible? And what shape are repressed memories in when they finally return to consciousness?

If you believe the television movie *Fatal Memories,* which aired on NBC two years after the conviction of George Franklin, repressed memories are in very good shape. Based on the Franklin case, the script was true to much of what we know about the sexual abuse of children, and it showed sophistication in its understanding of autobiographical memory. But it's interesting to note what the film did *visually.* Visually, Eileen's flashbacks came as grainy black-and-white sequences in a color film. They looked exactly like original records, and the movie's Eileen Franklin never doubted that they were. The picture of autobiographical memory in *Fatal Memories* was in the tradition of Penfield and Freud, old film inside of new, and all of it produced by a machine.

At the heart of anyone's beliefs about autobiographical memory are the concepts addressed by Eileen Franklin and *Fatal Memories,* the concepts of repression and the unconscious. Freud is usually given credit for introducing these ideas, but they go back much farther. In the seventeenth century, Descartes spoke of the difference between conscious and unconscious processes; at the beginning of the eighteenth, Leibniz wrote of "an infinity of perceptions, unaccompanied by awareness or reflection." With the advent of Freud and the spread of psychoanalysis came the idea that the unconscious was a place that held repressed memories. Therapists believed that some experiences bring such pain, fear, shame, or guilt that the only way one can cope with them is to lock them out of awareness, to forget they ever happened. What is locked in the unconscious doesn't go away, however; it returns in symptoms that eventually make life unlivable. In the case of childhood sexual abuse, a person may feel something in her body—a huge lump in the throat, a feeling of wanting to throw up, an impulse to hold muscles tight during lovemaking. The victim may have repressed the specific episodes that brought on these symptoms because the perpetrator of abuse threatened to harm her if she ever told anyone about it. But when the perpetrator ceases to be a threat, pictures of the episodes may start to come back and the repression begin to lift.

There are phenomena akin to repression, the so-called "psychogenic" amnesias that conceal memories of trauma, and that disappear as mysteriously as they come on. Some traumatized individuals may leave their home, travel to a distant place, and forget who they are for months and even years. Though they retain their knowledge of how to talk, to work, or to drive—examples of implicit memory—they lose their autobiographical memory. From a clinical standpoint, there is ample evidence for the existence of an unconscious that holds repressed memories.

But the descriptions of clinicians haven't been enough for experimental psychologists looking for scientific proof. So for over a century they have been pursuing evidence of the unconscious in their laboratories. In the June 1992, issue of *American Psychologist,* they came to a collective conclusion: the existence of unconscious mental processes was "solidly established in empirical research." It was "no longer questionable."

One experiment that enabled laboratory psychologists to detect the unconscious, if only as a faint and distant signal, involved subliminal perception. Octagons of irregular shapes were flashed on a screen so quickly (each for one one-thousandth of a second) that subjects were unable to see them. All they were aware of was a brief burst of light. Then each of the octagons was presented again, this time in combination with a new one. The exposure lasted a full second, which is plenty of time for a good look. Asked to guess which of the two had been presented the first time around, subjects were right only 50 percent of the time, no better than chance. But asked which of the two they *liked* better, they picked the old one 60 percent of the time. That was better than chance. Some unconscious recognition predisposed them to prefer the familiar octagon, even though they had no recollection, indeed no experience, of ever seeing it.

Analogous results have been obtained when surgical patients under general anaesthesia are read a list of names. Once the anaesthesia wears off, patients judge the names that were read to be more "famous" than names that were not, even though they can't tell you why they feel that way. More remarkable still is the phenomenon of blindsight. Patients with a particular form of injury to their visual cortex are able to "see" without knowing they see. Blind for all practical purposes, they can nevertheless point out the location of an object and even track it with their eyes. Their ability is limited to certain aspects of vision, and they make a number of mistakes, but they perform better than chance and are as surprised as their doctors when informed of what they've done. One woman with an injury that deleted only certain features of her vision was presented with two drawings of the same house, one of which showed the house on fire. Asked which she would prefer to live in, she said the question was silly—both houses were the same. But when told to pick one anyway, she regularly chose the house that wasn't burning. Something in her knew about the fire, but she couldn't say what it was. Normal subjects given suggestions for hypnotic blindness react in much the same way as blindsight patients. So do individuals with tempo-rary blindness that is purely psychological in origin. So, in a sense, do any of us who drive a car and respond to traffic lights with little awareness of seeing them.

Unknown pathways of neurons must be operative in blindsight, but brain researchers do not yet know where they are. It's also possible that the neural activity involved is so weak that it does not produce conscious awareness, even though it gets to the motor system that controls actions. Neuroscientists really don't ask what makes something *unconscious*; they're more likely to turn the question on its head and ask what makes it conscious. What is added when awareness comes in? The answer may be more electrical activity, activity in certain places, even activity in certain rhythms. But the neural manifestations and the location of consciousness are even more mysterious than those involving memory.

The scientific debate over what is conscious and what is not has made it clear that there is no sharp distinction between the two. What about that itch in your foot that you had forgotten about while reading this paragraph? It wasn't exactly *un*conscious, so how about *pre*conscious or *sub*conscious? *Un*conscious can refer to mental *content,* as in the case of repressed memories, but also to mental *process,* as in experiments on seeing and hearing without awareness. Much of our learning and creative inspiration result from unconscious processes. So, as we shall see, does much of the shaping of the story of our lives.

Today, the argument in psychology is not over the existence of the unconscious, however defined, but rather over its level of sophistication. Is it smart or dumb? (Those are the very words that researchers use.) The unconscious found in the laboratory is actually pretty dumb. It may have helped forerunners of *Homo sapiens* to get a split-second feel for an object before they saw it, to sense it before they heard it, but what can we do with that ability today? Anticipate a fast ball maybe, but not much more. And a proclivity for retaining names "heard" under anesthesia won't help you pass an exam any more than listening to audio tapes while asleep. Of course, it's not terribly bright of researchers to expect the unconscious to look smart in an experimental setting. Going into a laboratory to hear the unconscious is something like going into a closet to hear an orchestra.

To hear all that the unconscious has to say, you have to come out of the closet. Regarding repressed memories, you either have to listen to therapists who say, "I believe what my clients tell me," or you have to accept studies like those of John Briere and Jon Conte, who asked adult survivors of childhood sexual abuse if there had ever been a time when they could not remember the abuse. Fifty-nine percent of their sample said yes. Briere and Conte found that those who reported amnesia were more likely than other survivors to have been abused violently, to have been abused early in life and for a long time, and to have been threatened with death if they ever revealed what happened, all in keeping with Freud's theory of repression. While it is hard to determine how common repression actually is (because, paradoxically, you are asking people to remember periods of forgetting), there is no doubt that the phenomenon does exist. More than once, an adult has recovered a memory of abuse and subsequently verified it, sometimes with an admission from the perpetrator.

But something else exists, too, the possibility that phantom memories of abuse can be implanted in our minds and look like repressed memories coming back. Listen to what the authors of a widely read book tell women who suspect sexual abuse in their past: "If you are unable to remember any specific instances . . . but still have a feeling that something abusive happened to you, it probably did. . . . Assume your feelings are valid." The assumption has never proven wrong, they state. "If you think you were abused and your life shows the symptoms, then you were." And again: ". . . even if your memories are incomplete, even if your family insists nothing ever happened, you must still believe yourself." A pamphlet on the same subject advises those with no specific memories of actual abuse: "The best thing is to proceed as if you had been abused." These instructions may indeed help to bring repressed memories to the surface, but they can also lead a reader to fabricate an event that provides a simple explanation for some very complex problems. Therapists on the lookout for abuse in their clients' past can make similar suggestions: "Your symptoms sound like you've been abused when you were a child. What can you tell me about that?" One woman seeking help for depression and anxiety spent two years trying unsuccessfully to remember the abuse her therapist seemed certain was there. "I have no direct memories of this abuse," she wrote Elizabeth Loftus. "I've tried self-hypnosis and light trance work with my therapist. And I even travelled to childhood homes . . . in an attempt to trigger memories." Another client "recovered" a memory that stunned and bewildered her parents. Her father wrote a famous newspaper columnist:

> *Dear Abby,*
>
> *My wife and I have been married for 36 years. Our only child, "Ellie," is 34.*
>
> *She was having emotional problems, so she started seeing a therapist, and is now convinced that I—her father—raped her when she was an infant!*
>
> *She said she had repressed the memory of this rape, and her therapist helped her to remember it.*
>
> *Abby, there can be no such memory, as I would never do such a terrible thing! This is the greatest tragedy of my life, and I can't convince Ellie this "memory" of hers never happened.*
>
> *Thank God my wife believes me; in fact, this crisis has brought us closer together. We have cried bitter tears over this. Can you please help us?*

Can a memory of rape be implanted by a therapist? For ethical reasons, the relevant experiments cannot be done, but in a pilot study Loftus and her colleagues have been able to induce memories of a less traumatic nature. One of the subjects in the study was a fourteen-year-old boy named Chris. Chris was told by his older brother that he had gotten lost in a shopping mall when he was only five, and that he had eventually been found in the company of an old man in a flannel shirt. The story was a complete fabrication, but two days after hearing it Chris started to "remember" his feelings on the occasion in question. "I was so scared that I would never see my family again," he said. "I knew that I was in trouble." The day after that, he recalled his mother telling him "never to do that again." On subsequent days, he remembered the old man's flannel shirt, some stores in the mall, and even a conversation with the old man. In a matter of weeks there was more:

> *I was with you guys for a second and I think I went over to look at the toy store, the Kay-bee toy and, uh, we got lost and I was looking around and I thought, "Uh-oh. I'm in trouble now." You know. And then I . . . I thought I was never going to see my family again. I was really scared you know. And then this old man, I think he was wearing a blue flannel, came up to me . . . he was kind of old. He was kind of bald on top . . . he had like a ring of gray hair . . . and he had glasses.*

Did Chris believe this memory was authentic? When he had first been told the false story about being lost, he had also been told some true ones. Several weeks later he was let in on the experiment and informed that one of the stories was a fake. Could he guess which one? Chris chose one of the true ones. Like all four of the other pilot subjects, Chris thought that the false memory was genuine.

A more dramatic case, one with severe consequences, involved Paul Ingram, a prominent public figure in Olympia, Washington, who was arrested in 1988 for alleged child abuse. The charges were brought by his two daughters, aged twenty-two and eighteen, whose apparently repressed memories were triggered by an emotional talk on sexual molestation at a religious retreat. The speaker, who felt the Lord prompting her, told one of the girls directly, "You have been abused as a child!" and indicated that the abuser was her father. When confronted with the charges, Ingram said he had no knowledge of any abuse on his part; he could remember nothing. Several hours later he made an official statement on a tape recorder. "I really believe that the allegations did occur and that I did violate them and abuse them and probably for a long period of time. I've repressed it."

Over the ensuing months Ingram's daughters remembered much more. They had been abused for many years by Ingram, his friends and co-workers, and even his wife. They had been subjected to Satanic rituals in which babies, perhaps twenty-five of them, were stabbed to death and buried. They themselves had been stabbed, forced to have intercourse with animals, and defecated on. Whenever a new charge came forward, Ingram would have trouble remembering the event in question. The investigators tried to help; if only he confessed, they said, the memories would start to flow. Ingram would pray feverishly, go into a trance, and begin to see what they were talking about. Or he would imagine going into a warm white fog and wait for the pictures to come. He felt confident that the pictures were real because his pastor had assured him that God would show him the truth. The pictures seemed different from ordinary memories, but he thought that was because they had been repressed.

At one point the prosecution brought in a specialist in cults, Richard Ofshe, to help Ingram recover more of his memories. But Ofshe decided to test the process. He made up a completely false incident, telling Ingram that his daughter had reported that he had forced her and her brother to have sex in his presence. Ingram couldn't recall the episode, but Ofshe assured him that it did happen and told him to return to his cell to pray about it. Ingram did and eventually wrote a three-page statement describing the incident in vivid detail and admitting his guilt. No bones of murdered babies were ever discovered by police. No signs of abuse were ever found on the girls' bodies, even though they said they were covered with scars. There was no physical evidence substantiating any of the charges, and Ofshe tried to convince Ingram that neither his nor his daughter's memories were true. But Ingram pleaded guilty to six counts of third-degree rape and was sentenced to twenty years in prison, with the possibility of parole after twelve years. In prison, he now realizes that his visualizations were fantasies, not memories. According to Ofshe, this was not an isolated case. Other people have been made to "remember" a repressed crime they never committed.

It seems there is no clear answer to the dilemma posed by the unconscious, but in actuality there is. When confronting any particular case we must keep two possibilities in mind: (1) memories can be repressed, and (2) suggestion can implant phantom memories that look like they're repressed. How common is the first possibility? How common the second? Is repression more powerful than suggestion, suggestion than repression? The answers to these questions will never be determined with any degree of accuracy. And even if they were, they would be statistically normative answers, answers *in general;* they would be of little help in an individual case. In an individual case, all we can do is remember the possibilities and look for verification of either.

Can I Trust My Memory?

As a life-historical researcher and writer, the role in which I encounter autobiographical memories is different from that of a therapist or juror. Most of the work I do involves the fertility or sterility that people experience in their lives, so the memories I elicit are imbued with these themes. When I edit the memories into stories, the accent gets stronger still. Years ago I may have believed I was getting pure memories, but now I know better. Now I know that the memories are the product of two people, myself and my subject, and that they serve a social purpose. Not only do they offer a view of one person's past, they also keep a relationship going in the present.

The therapist's office, the courtroom, and the back porch on which I often find myself all offer differing perspectives on memory. Yet they all make us wonder: can we really trust it? Can we know the truth about our past? The problem is compounded by what George Orwell pointed out in *Nineteen Eighty-Four*: "If it is necessary to rearrange one's memories or to tamper with written records, then it is necessary to forget that one has done so." When memory changes the record in our heads, it doesn't tell us about it.

Trust is not a simple notion, nor is truth, but neither are they hopelessly complicated. Take some of the cases cited in this chapter. Even though we can't recall all that's on a penny, we still know the truth about it—what it is, what it's worth, how to use it, and so on. We can trust what we know. The subjects in Elizabeth Loftus's experiment who incorrectly remembered broken glass still knew what they had seen on film: it was a car accident. They could trust that knowledge. And for all that John Dean got wrong about his conversation with President Nixon, he got the big picture right: what he said was going on in the White House actually was going on. When it comes to memory, we have to ask more than "Can I trust it?" We have to ask, "Where can I trust it? In what setting? To what end?"

The autobiographical memory of humans evolved in a multitude of settings over a vast number of years. It has wound up in some pretty strange places. One of them is on a witness stand in an adversarial legal system in the late twentieth century. In such a system, one person's story is pitted against another's—prosecution versus defense, Thomas versus Hill. Everything in that setting, from initial interrogations and depositions to final courtroom presentations, is designed to elicit memories that are *convincing.* It is difficult in such circumstances to be open-minded or tentative about memories, to take them on their own terms. When forced to make public statements about what is uncertain, people become very certain, persuading themselves in the course of persuading others. Gradually, the qualities that generate confidence start to look like those that signify truth. But they are not.

Were I a juror, I would find it impossible to convict someone solely on the basis of a repressed memory returning to consciousness. The problem is getting beyond a reasonable doubt: it is simply reasonable to doubt when dealing with these kind of memories. Even in a civil suit, where the legal standard of evidence is less stringent, I would need external corroboration. Were I a therapist, however, the situation would be different. I wouldn't be concerned with a single event, much less with particular details, but with the pattern the event represented. I would have no qualms about reaching a conclusion that someone's father was abusive, and though I couldn't be certain that he performed a particular act on a particular occasion, I could well conclude that such an act would have been consistent with his character. As a counselor, I would have time to get to know my client, time to study the context of his or her memories, and time to consider other explanations. In short, I would be in a position to take a repressed memory on its own terms and, as a result, to trust what I encountered.

But a therapist's office, different though it is from a courtroom, makes its own impression on memory. A therapist will color her clients' recollections with the suggestions of her particular brand of therapy. If she's a psychoanalyst, her patients will have psychoanalytic memories. If she takes a cognitive approach, they will remember their irrational thinking. If she's interested in birth order, they will recall what it was like being the oldest or the youngest in their family. If she runs an inner-child workshop, they will find their infant self. Some schools of therapy more than others will engender the belief that our memories are bottomless reservoirs, that ever more is "in there." So counseling sessions may never come to an end.

The solution is not to take memory out of these settings, but to know how it behaves in them, and to adjust our expectations and alter our practices accordingly. Donald Spence, for example, no longer believes that he can dig up memory's original records when doing psychoanalysis. He cannot recover "historical" truth. All he can get is "narrative" truth, coherence that takes on "aesthetic finality" and fits the present character of the client. But narrative truth is sufficient for the client to get better. In response to research on the suggestibility of witnesses, it is now becoming standard legal practice to allow them to tell their story in free narrative form before asking specific questions. There are new recommendations for obtaining identifications in police lineups: start with one that does not contain the suspect before moving to one that does (witnesses who make no identification on the first prove to be more accurate on the second); present lineup members sequentially, not simultaneously (it eliminates the problems associated with relative judgments); provide no feedback after an identification (telling witnesses that someone else made the same identification artificially increases their certainty). In these and other ways, the findings of scientific research can be brought to bear on the question of trusting one's memory.

But science raises a question of its own. How far can we trust *it*? For all that systematic research has told us about memories, it cannot address our most important ones—the spontaneous recollections that come and go on their own. These are the sudden flashbacks, the conversations we find ourselves mulling over, the thoughts that play on our mind when we're not even trying to remember anything in particular. Some psychologists have come close to capturing spontaneous memories, but they always run into a basic dilemma: as soon as you sneak up on one, much less haul it off to the laboratory, you destroy its spontaneity. Even "free" recall and "free" association cannot get around the problem. Can you simply watch memories fly in and out of your mind and do nothing to them? No, says one psychologist who has tried, for as soon as you become vigilant you inevitably change what you are watching.

We are left, then, with what mysteriously moves our spirit—the sound of a mother calling on a summer evening, a hymn from long ago that plays gently in our mind, the sight of brightly colored carnival wagons, and yes, the horror that pounds on our door when we thought we were safe. We do not ask for these memories, we do not control them, and yet there they are, the stuff of life. Sometimes they bring tears. Sometimes they bring a smile that crosses our face without our even knowing it. Conscious and unconscious, but very smart, they flow like a river through our souls.

Chapter Three

LIKE A RIVER

I think my wife has a better autobiographical memory than I do. There are just too many times when we're reminiscing that I find myself saying, "Did I really do that?" or, after a reminder, "Oh yeah, now I remember." Only rarely am I able to spring a memory on her that she doesn't already know about. But though she's the one with most of the records, I'm the one who wants to play them. I want to retell the story of our life together, particularly of the events in the beginning. I know that if I don't put our memories into words, I'll lose touch with them, and something will die in me. Maybe the urgency I feel to go over our past is really a foreboding. If what happened to my father happens to me, Kathy is destined to become my memory.

Something tells me she'll be good at the job. During late elementary and early high school Kathy had what's known as eidetic or photographic memory. She didn't call it that or even think she was unusual; she just knew she did very well on tests. She remembers how she studied: on the day of an exam she would get up early in the morning and read the assigned material in a state of concentration. It would remain in her mind for her to see. One of her teachers thought she was cheating, and more than one advised her against depending on that kind of learning. But there was an eighth-grade teacher, a Mr. Byrd, who told her she had an extraordinary gift. He regularly excused her from homework for getting up in front of the class and reciting five or ten pages from the textbook. Kathy didn't realize she was different until other students were given the same opportunity and failed to make the grade. Her photographic memory was fun while it lasted, but by the twelfth grade, for whatever reason, it was gone.

Psychologist Ulric Neisser believes that transient abilities like Kathy's may be more widespread than we think. One woman told him that in her school years she needed only one reading of an entire blackboard of information to have it memorized. She could recall a painting in a museum as if she were standing in the museum looking at it again. In her twenties, she worked for several years mounting insects in a zoological laboratory. At the start of each day, her director would give her 100 to 200 specimens along with instructions for how each was to be positioned. Writing nothing down, she carried out those instructions flawlessly, a fact Neisser was able to confirm with the director. This woman's ability vanished like Kathy's, but not until the age of twenty-nine, when she developed a temporary psychotic reaction to some medication for an intestinal disorder. Neisser suspects that cases like Kathy's, in which extraordinary abilities disappear by the end of adolescence, are far more common.

There has been documentation of other machine-like memories. It's reported that a Dr. Leyden in the late nineteenth century could repeat correctly a long act of the British Parliament, or some similar document, after having read it just once. More remarkable are the feats of some Jewish scholars who were discovered in Poland around the turn of the century. These scholars had memorized the entire contents of the Talmud, twelve volumes and thousands of pages. In demonstrations of their ability, the scholars would ask a volunteer to pick any volume of the Talmud and open it to any page. Then the volunteer would take a pin and touch it to one of the words on the page, any word at all. The scholar would then ask people in the room to call out other pages. Without looking, he would tell them what words were in the same position as the pin on those other pages. To see if he was right, someone would push the pin through to the other pages and check. Cases were documented in which the scholar never failed.

Then there's the case of a Russian newspaper reporter named Shereshevskii, whose editor was disturbed by the fact that he never wrote down assignments. When he brought the matter up, Shereshevskii was puzzled. *He* remembered everything people told him, word for word. Didn't everybody? Amazed, the editor referred him to a young psychologist named Alexander Luria, who began to test his memory. Over the years Luria found "there was no limit either to the *capacity* of S.'s memory or to the *durability of the traces he retained.*" If words were read to him slowly, he could memorize a list of seventy in four minutes. Fifteen years later he could recall the list perfectly, forwards or backwards. In demonstrations of his ability, a questioner would ask about a series of words Shereshevskii had learned long ago. Shereshevskii would close his eyes, pause, and then say something like, "Yes, yes . . . this was a series you gave me once when we were in your apartment. . . . You were sitting at the table and I in the rocking chair. . . . You were wearing a gray suit and you looked at me like this. . . . Now I can see you saying . . ." and then he would reel off the words in the precise order he was given them years before.

Shereshevskii was a powerful visualizer. "If I want something to happen," he said, "I simply picture it in my mind. I don't have to exert any effort to accomplish it." His normal pulse rate was between seventy and seventy-two beats per minute, but he could decrease it to the midsixties by seeing himself drop off to sleep, or he could raise it to 100 by seeing himself running after a train that had just begun to pull away. He could raise the temperature in his right hand by imagining it on a hot stove while lowering that in his left by imagining he was holding a piece of ice. But Shereshevskii wasn't just a mental seer. Visual images in his mind were often accompanied by sound, taste, touch, and feel—a rich sensory mix known as synesthesia. Of one occasion he said, "I heard the bell ringing. A small round object rolled right before me eyes . . . my fingers sensed something rough like a rope. . . . Then I experienced a taste of salt water . . . and something white." The list of words that Luria read to him created images in his mind, and the images were so clear they never went away.

Other superstars of memory include "calendar calculators" who can tell you what day of the week any date in the past fell on. Some claim to know the weather on that day, and even events that occurred, but there's no way of checking the latter details. There was a way to check out another memorist, however, Hideaki Tomoyori of Japan. Recently, Tomoyori correctly recited the first 40,000 digits of pi, a feat that took over seventeen hours. Conductor Arturo Toscanini qualifies as another legend when it comes to memory. It's estimated that Toscanini knew by heart every note of every instrument of about 250 symphonic works and the words and music of about 100 operas. One of the many stories told about him involves a second bassoonist who discovered just before a concert that the key for the lowest note on his instrument was broken. Toscanini covered his eyes for a minute, reviewing the score in his mind. "It is all right," he said, "that note does not occur in tonight's concert."

From the standpoint of scientific verification, however, the top photographic memory may belong to a woman who has been tested by stereograms consisting of pairs of random-dot patterns, with 10,000 dots in each pattern. Anyone looking at the pair through a stereoscope sees a figure emerging in depth. (A stereoscope presents one of the patterns to the right eye and the other to the left. No figure appears without it.) The woman in question could combine a pattern presented to her left eye with the memory of a pattern presented to her right eye *the day before*. This is a remarkable feat that no one has since duplicated. The woman, by the way, is an artist who can project an exact image of a scene onto a blank canvas. Once the image is there, she can move her eyes around to inspect the details.

None of these remarkable performers has a perfect memory, however. The only one I know of belongs to Arnold Schwarzenegger's character in the futuristic movie *Total Recall*. In the movie Schwarzenegger receives an electronic memory implant of a vacation to Mars. Getting the implant is cheaper than actually making the trip, and because the implant is perfect, the experience is just as good. Once the implant is in Schwarzenegger's brain, he heads for Mars. Or does he? The memory is so real he doesn't know whether he's living in the past or the present. Neither does the viewer, and no one finds out at the end.

Would you want a perfect memory, one with everything "in there" and in mint condition? What Schwarzenegger discovers about the state of total recall is that it's extremely dangerous. If you were in such a state, you couldn't tell the difference between the words you are reading right now and words you have read in the past. You wouldn't know if a car cutting in front of you was actually there or not. In one scene Schwarzenegger has to make a split-second decision whether to shoot someone. Is he for real or only a memory implant? (When in doubt, Schwarzenegger shoots.) Indeed, one could argue that an imperfect memory is adaptive in an evolutionary sense. If *Homo sapiens* could not distinguish memories from reality, as would be the case with a picture-perfect memory, he would have been too vulnerable to survive.

If you had a picture-perfect memory, you could probably survive, but you might find yourself in the position of Dr. Leyden. Though he could recite a long act of Parliament after just one reading, there was a catch. If he wanted to recall a particular point in something he had read, he could do so only by recalling the entire document *from the beginning*. His "gift" was more of a curse than a blessing. Nor would you want the life of many calendar calculators; in spite of possessing one extraordinary (and rather useless) talent, they are often severely retarded. The ability to visualize the entire contents of the Talmud also came with a hitch. None of the scholars who had this remarkable ability was ever known for his understanding or wisdom. It's as if they had traded away a knowledge of what mattered for a photographic memory. The tragic flaw in Shereshevskii's case was that it was nearly impossible for him to throw something out of memory. He couldn't convert specifics into generalities, form abstractions, or organize all the detail in his mind. Over the years, concrete images kept piling up until they finally overwhelmed him. The slightest cue evoked so many memories that he couldn't go about his daily business. He couldn't hold a job, read, or even follow a simple conversation. By the end of his life, all he could do was travel from town to town demonstrating his peculiar talent for memorizing lists of words.

Many people with extraordinary memories have none of the problems Shereshevskii ran into, none of the overpowering synesthesia, none of the difficulty in generalizing. But his story illustrates a universal—and paradoxical—truth: you have to forget in order to remember. Forget some things, that is, in order to remember others. Suppose you remembered every place you ever parked your car. Would you ever find it again? What if you were a short-order cook who couldn't forget an order once you were through with it? Thousands and thousands of past orders would all be a jumble in your mind; which one were you supposed to cook now? Whereas we work on techniques to improve our remembering, Shereshevskii sought those that would improve his forgetting. He didn't *want* to see so many details. He tried covering them with a "thick canvas" in his mind. It didn't work. He tried crumpling numbers from previous memory tests into an imaginary ball so they wouldn't interfere with the task at hand. That didn't work much better. He even tried writing the numbers down and actually burning the paper on which they were written, but even then they appeared in his mind hovering over the charred embers. Eventually, and quite mysteriously, he found some relief by focusing on essential details in a scene or by concentrating in certain situations on the *absence* of images. His case is one more reason that some psychologists today treat forgetting not as a problem but as a useful mental skill. If you remembered all the trees in your life, you'd never see the forest.

The brain, our organ of memory, works not only by turning nerve cells on but also by turning them off. Most of the messages sent across synapses, in fact, result in the inhibition of the receiving neuron, not its excitation. Neurons must be inhibited because the brain is always "on." If you are to move or speak or think in a coordinated way, certain regions must be quieted even as others are amplified. To flex your arm, for example, you have to tense the muscles on the inside of your arm, but you also have to relax the ones on the outside. So it is with memory. If some of the things we learn are not to interfere with others, we have to clean out our files every now and then. Some neural connections in our brain have to decay so that others may grow.

From the cognitive point of view, the problem with a picture-perfect memory is that it cannot be cleaned out. The same may be true from an emotional standpoint. How often might we have wished to write down some feelings from the past and magically burn them away, only to find them still hovering within us! How often might we have tried to get rid of reminders that cause pain and regret! I can remember sitting in the dark by a frozen pond and wishing my memory could be like that, anesthetized into silence by the cold. It couldn't, of course, and now I'm grateful for the thaw, but the experience makes me wonder why anyone would want an autobiographical memory that's as "good" as the ones in the machines. With a perfect memory we would feel the sting of rejection as intensely now as we did long ago. We wouldn't be able to see the loss, the fear, the guilt, and the waste in a new light.

We'd be frozen in the past, unable to repair it, unable to breathe, change, or grow.

Repairing Memories

Let us now consider the setting in which autobiographical memory is at home—not in the courtroom or in front of an audience, but in the living of our lives. In this context, memory's reconstructive nature appears salvific, for without it we could neither recover from the past nor make use of it.

In the summer when my stepdaughter Adrienne was fifteen, she would occasionally sneak out of the house in the middle of the night. So would her friends from other houses around town, and these teenagers would usually end up at a local restaurant, just hanging out at three or four in the morning. Not that their parents knew where they were, or even know today how many times their children's escapes went undetected. We slowed Adrienne down in her fifteenth summer by screwing a board across the outside of her bedroom window and having my wife, Kathy, sleep on the couch to guard the front door. But occasionally we relaxed our watch. That set the stage for the creation of a memory.

One August night Kathy made a bed check at one in the morning and found that Adrienne was gone. This time Kathy had a hunch that we should search a wooded area near our house. So we got a flashlight and the dog and started down a path, Kathy frantically shouting, "Adrienne!" It was dark in those woods, and while there were two of us and the dog, I was frightened, frightened for myself and frightened for Adrienne. After about fifteen minutes of checking out twisted little trails, sometimes with the flashlight off, we decided to turn back. At that point we heard a male voice far away, calling, "Adrienne." I kept the flashlight off and ran toward it, Kathy and the dog right behind me. When we got close, I shone the light directly in the faces of two young men I had never seen before.

They must have been blinded because they asked if I was Adrienne. "No," I said, lying a little, "I'm Adrienne's dad." Silence. They turned out to be college kids from Minnesota who were spending their last night in town. They had met Adrienne at an outdoor swimming pool and had arranged to take her to a party that night. They had planned to pick her up at the edge of the woods at one-thirty, take her to the party, and get her home before we woke up. I explained that Adrienne was only fifteen and that she was legally a minor. Whether it was the implications of that speech or the fact that these were pretty decent fellows, they joined in the search. As it turned out, their help wasn't necessary. Adrienne had seen us enter the woods and had decided to head for home.

At the moment we walked in the door and saw her in the living room, Kathy was flooded with relief and I was contemplating murder. It didn't take Kathy long to see the merit in my point of view. We were both very angry, and though I can't remember exactly what Adrienne's punishment was, I'm sure it was, shall we say, "firm." Fear and anger permeated our original memory of that evening's activities.

Three days later I watched the memory change before my eyes. Kathy and I were taking a birthday cake to my daughter My-Linh, who was spending the summer as a counselor at a nearby camp. We had our prisoner in tow. There were other young people at the party and soon they were listening to Adrienne's story. All of a sudden, it was hilarious. It was The Great Escape. It was *Ferris Buehler's Day Off.* In fifteen minutes Adrienne went from criminal to heroine. Her offense became an "excellent adventure." No, no, I said to myself, wanting to stay mad, but the momentum was irreversible. Since that evening I have been unable to recapture my original feelings of fear and anger. Dominating them is something that tickles my funny bone.

This is a memory transformed, not only in Adrienne but also in me. But what exactly was different after the transformation? Not anyone's knowledge of what actually happened. Adrienne did leave the house during that August night, Kathy and I did go after her in the woods, we did encounter some young men, and we did go home and find her in the living room. All that was true both before and after the memory changed. Some of the details might have been off from the beginning. Was it at one o'clock precisely that Kathy found Adrienne's bed empty? Were we in the woods for fifteen minutes? Did I actually say to the young men what I think I said? Were there even two of them? My confidence in peripheral details is far lower than that in the central facts. I trust the latter completely.

The central facts didn't change in the telling of the story, but the meaning of the facts did. So did the emotions associated with them. I suspect that I am fated to remember the event the way it was told, as The Great Escape, with the danger a little greater than it actually was, the deliverance more breathtaking, the contemplated filicide closer to execution. I'm afraid I will actually *enjoy* the memory, and believe me, there was no joy the night it happened.

Memories can change like this because they have open spaces. They don't look like they do, but they do. There's an interesting optical illusion that serves as a symbol for the way we unknowingly fill in the spaces in our memories. You can create it for yourself: draw a horizontal bar about four inches long and a quarter-inch thick, leaving a half-inch gap in it somewhere on the left side. Darken the interior of the bar. Now place an "X" immediately above the bar on the far right side. Cover your right eye and focus with your left on the "X." Hold the bar at arm's length and slowly move it in toward your nose. You'll find there's a point where the illusion appears. The gap in the bar suddenly fills in, making the line look continuous.

At that point the bar is an apt symbol for a memory. What creates the illusion is that the break in the bar hits a spot in the back of your eye where there are no sensory receptors. The so-called "blind spot," it's where the optic nerve exits the eye for the brain.

But the brain fills in the missing information and constructs a picture of a solid line, just the way it fills in missing information about an amputated limb with the experience of a phantom. When you look at a memory, you too are filling in gaps with constructions from your brain. The constructions are often the kind of generalizations Shereshevskii had such difficulty making. They represent what events *mean*. They also represent what we feel about them. Memories are transformed when one set of meanings and emotions is exchanged for another. The new set makes you remember from a different perspective, recall this detail and not that, amplify one episode and tone down another.

A young housewife with small children had her memories transformed when she discovered one day that her husband was having an affair. Then she learned through a private investigator that there was more to it than a simple affair, that her husband was actually involved with three women—herself, the mistress with whom he was having the affair, and someone else with whom he was having children. As each new revelation came along she found it more astonishing than the one before. She found herself asking, "Why didn't I see all this?" Now she knew why money was tight, why he was so aloof, why he wasn't around that much. Meanings in her memory changed. Trivial gestures became monumental; off-handed remarks, prophetic. Emotions changed too: words that once stood for commitment now symbolized betrayal. Even new details came to mind—things, it seems, that were always "in there" but never noticed. An experience like this leaves little doubt about the reconstructive nature of memory, about the way events in the present can turn our recollection of the past upside down.

Memories change for the better as well. They can be repaired or, to use a metaphor of life, healed. Consider the story of a middle-aged woman I'll call Sandra, who was having difficulty at work. In tense situations, her breathing would become labored, her ears would start to ring, and she would begin to feel herself floating away. Sandra's history was that of a physically abused child. Her alcoholic father would regularly beat her mother, and if Sandra was present, she too would be beaten. Sandra remembered instructions that she had received from her mother as a small child: when her father became violent, she was to take her little sister and hide. One episode in particular stood out in her mind. When she was four and her sister two, her father went into a rage and began hitting her mother with a telephone. Sandra and her sister climbed out of the apartment window onto the fire escape, went up a flight of stairs, and crawled into the apartment of the neighbor upstairs, where they found refuge.

This particular episode was so clear in her mind that Sandra decided to see how accurate it was. She had already relived it in the presence of a therapist, but now she wanted to go back to the very place where it happened. Her husband accompanied her, physically and emotionally. The apartment was where she thought it would be, and it looked like she thought it would. The fire escape was still there. Her mother lived nearby, although she had divorced her husband long before, so Sandra decided to visit her as well. She learned that her flight up the fire escape at the age of four was not an isolated incident. In fact, the mother had made arrangements with the upstairs neighbor to take the girls in whenever her husband became violent. In that visit with her mother, Sandra learned pieces of family history that she never knew existed. She still knew what had happened to her as a child—in fact, she knew more than before—but much in her memory had changed.

Meanings had changed. Although Sandra knew that her mother had been unable to protect her children adequately, she now saw that her mother was herself a victim. She had borne the brunt of a pattern of abuse that had been passed from one generation to the next. Sandra saw herself differently, too. Although she had suffered abuse, and would carry the scars for life, she had not passed it on to her children. She had been the buffer, the person who said, "The damage stops here." As more memories came to the surface, she made additional connections. She always had to sleep curled up and facing a wall, with a pillow at her back. Now she knew why: it was a position to protect her against a nightime beating. She connected the feeling of dissociation at work with the feeling in her memory, and she understood why the feeling would come back.

Emotions had changed as well. Sandra felt safer now, not as helpless and certainly not as anxious. Her memories didn't seem to control her the way they once did. She still had trouble breathing in difficult situations, but she experienced more freedom and relief, and she found it easier to sleep at night. Another way of saying this is that she was better able to separate *then* and *now*, to take what seemed an ongoing lived experience and turn it into a memory.

All these changes came about as her memories were shared. They now belonged to more people—to an insightful therapist and a supportive husband as well as to her mother and herself. This, I think, is an overlooked ingredient in memory repair: how healing involves a shift in the ownership of our remembrance—or, if you will, its whereabouts. To whom did a traumatic memory belong before a change? Where was it? To whom does it belong after a change? Where is it? The answers to these questions may show that the memory was pruned from one collective meaning system and grafted onto another. I'll have more to say about this blend of individual and collective later in the book.

Sandra's memories were repaired indirectly, in the context of therapy and with the help of other people in her life. But other approaches are more frontal. In the Christian healing of memories, for example, the figure of Jesus is inserted directly into the remembered image. Matthew Linn and his colleagues tell the story of "Sue," who at the age of eighteen was labeled a paranoid schizophrenic and sent to a mental hospital. Thirty years later, she remembered being three years old, sitting in a hospital corridor while doctors frantically worked on her father in his room. "Soon her mother stormed out of the room and dragged Sue down the corridor," writes Linn. "Sue said, 'I want to say good-bye to my daddy.' Her mother hit her and screamed, 'You will never see your daddy again. He's dead. If I ever see you crying or hear you talk about him again, I'll beat you.'"

This memory came to Sue shortly after she began to work with a Christian therapist named Judith. Here's what ensued, first from Judith:

> *"Sue, can you see yourself again sitting on that chair in the hall?" "Yes." "Do you feel like you are three years old?" "Yes." "Now see if you can see Jesus come down the hall." After a minute, Sue said, 'Yes, he is coming down the hall." Then her face lit up and Judith just let her silently be with Jesus for several minutes.*
>
> *Afterwards, Sue told Judith what had happened. Jesus came down the hospital corridor and said, "Hi. How are you?" Sue answered, "Oh, not so good. They won't let me go in there." Jesus said, "Well, they're not going to stop me." So Jesus took Sue by the hand, led her into the room, woke up her father, and placed Sue in his arms. Sue wept her held-back tears and told her father all the things she had never told him, and reveled in his hugs and kisses. . . . Then Jesus said, "Why don't you hug your daddy and say good-bye to him now?" Sue hugged her daddy and said, "Goodby. I'll see you later." Then Jesus carried her out of the room.*

The woman still knew what had happened in her past, but in her mind Jesus was now part of the memory. It belonged to him as well as to others, so it was attached more securely to the Christian meaning system. According to Linn, the ensuing transformation was so striking that the woman was able to leave the hospital.

In the next chapter I will discuss individual memories that are symbolic of enduring themes in a person's life. Called self-defining, these memories are connected to many levels of meaning in the autobiographical memory system. Sue's original memory is an excellent example. It was not a precise account of what happened one day at the age of three but a precise metaphor for what happened over the first eighteen years of her life. It was not about her father's death as much as it was her mother's lack of love. Sue's metaphor had connections so rich that it became the vehicle of a great many changes in her. When one of her self-defining memories was repaired, in other words, so was much of her life story.

Just as direct and frontal as the Christian healing of memories is the approach of psychotherapist David Grove, who works with adult victims of early childhood abuse. At a certain point in his therapy, Grove "softens up" his client's memories—say, those of a female client—by having her play the memories in her mind, as if they were a movie. Then he has her play the movie in reverse, not once, but several times. If the movie freezes at a particular point and won't go on, Grove suggests she turn the movie into a still picture. Then she's to try putting a frame around it and taking different perspectives on it, seeing it from above or below, or turning the picture around and seeing it from behind. After the memory has been made more fluid, Grove asks the client if there's anything that would help her change it. Is there any knowledge she has, any person she knows, any spiritual resources she is in touch with? The client creates a new memory in her mind and stands it next to the old one. Which predominates? If the new memory has the strength to dissolve the old one, the process is complete.

Grove insists that this is not an exercise in fantasy. If it were, the change would not last. What is newly inserted into a memory must be based on reality, on actual knowledge and people. Clients who have been helped by his approach do not lose touch with what really happened in the past; they just experience it differently.

There is no single way in which therapists and others work directly on memories. Sometimes they soften the blow of a past event, but not always. A therapist working with a woman who was frozen with grief over the loss of her daughter two-and-a-half years before constantly drove home the point that she was gone. Only when the woman accepted that fundamental reality did a tearing pain disappear; only then was she able to look at a picture of her daughter and listen to a recording of her favorite song. John Bradshaw, who has written and spoken extensively on reclaiming one's "inner child," advocates combining memory "anchors" from the past and the present. You dwell, for example, on an adult experience of being loved while pressing together the thumb and a finger of one hand. Then you take an infant experience of being unwanted and unloved and enter into it while touching the thumb and a finger of your other hand. To repair the memory from infancy, you activate both anchors by pressing both thumbs simultaneously. "As you hold them, let yourself feel yourself welcomed to the world. Let yourself feel warm hugging. When you are filled with warmth and strength, let go of both anchors and open your eyes." The memories will fuse, says Bradshaw, and you will actually change your remembrance of infancy.

At what point does a frontal attack on memory become manipulative, even coercive? It clearly did in the thought reform, or "brainwashing," employed by the Chinese Communists in the 1950s. When practiced on captured Westerners—doctors, missionaries, and the like—it involved the constant confession of past deeds. Prisoners had to reveal the entire history of their life in China, including any and all details from their personal lives. The details became the target of change. A French physician, for example, admitted that "at the time of the 'liberation,' when I saw the horsedrawn artillery of the Communist army, I told this to an American friend. . . . The judge shouted that this American was a spy who was collecting espionage material for his spy organization, and that I was guilty of supplying him with military intelligence. . . . At first I did not accept this, but soon I had to add it to my confession." Other innocent conversations—mentioning to an American what the price of shoes was or saying he couldn't buy gasoline for his car—were also redefined as acts of spying. As the man's past was raked over, events were stripped of their old meaning and given new ones. Decades of life history were transformed, event by event, not just for the interrogators, but for the prisoners themselves. All this took place in endless hours of group discussion. The Communists were trying to change a person's identity, and they knew full well that they couldn't do that without changing a person's memory. They were willing to take their prisoners to physical and emotional extremes in order to achieve their goal.

When it's part of brainwashing, we want nothing to do with the direct manipulation of memory. Even in normal circumstances, we'd rather have our memories change on their own, without letting us in on what's happening. And yet, why do people go to a friend or counselor with troubling memories if they do not intend to change them, if they have no hope of seeing and feeling the past in a different way? When you realize that the memories you enter a counseling experience with are already reconstructions, replacing them with new ones doesn't seem so artificial.

There are, of course, limits to memory repair, as a woman victimized by rape said so well: "I always think I am finished with the rape experience . . . and I am always wrong. The unimaginable fear, the requirement that I surrender against my will, the power of someone else over me are unforgettable, stamped onto my soul." Another woman discovered the limits of repair when she tape-recorded the story of her father's life. At first he seemed changed, and so did her memories of him. "I felt that I had reached a place where I could accept my past, my parents, and myself. A place where, although I can't forget, I can let go and move on. I felt that I was a separate person who is not consumed by the alcoholism, neglect, and abuse that go back for generations." But her feeling of liberation was only temporary. Several weeks after the taping was over, she listened to what she had recorded:

The old familiar feelings of hurt and abandonment emerged. I detected a change in my father's voice when he reached the point in his history that involved his family. He seemed to become guarded and aloof. I realized that my struggle with my own existence is rooted there. We were so insignificant in his story. Maybe it is because I am female that he doesn't value me. Maybe it is because he doesn't value himself and I am only an extension of him in his eyes.

I realize now that the memories are the same but the function they serve has changed. They no longer control me but rather protect me. They serve as a reminder that the poison in the family is still there even if I don't deal with it on a day-to-day basis. The memories remind me that I must keep my distance because it is not safe. The family pathologies are ongoing, and I must be aware.

Repair in memory might mean many things—that pain is less frequent though never completely absent, that obsessive rumination gives way to meaningful remembrance, even that a kind of repression settles over what cannot be fixed. When autobiographical memory is in a state of repair, it isn't frozen in a machine but flowing like a river. A century ago, William James adopted this most ancient of similes to describe the "stream of consciousness" in our minds. Wilder Penfield adopted it too, but applied it only to the stream of ongoing consciousness, not to the trail of remembrance it left. That he took to be permanent. We now have anatomical and behavioral evidence that Penfield was wrong, that there's a stream of memory in our minds as well as a stream of consciousness. So let a river be our primary metaphor for autobiographical memory. Let the stream flow with all its distortions and all its moods and all its potential for life.

A River's Life

When I call my father up these days, my mother puts him on the phone and the conversations go something like this.

"Hi, dad, this is your son, John." I have to state my name and relationship to give him some idea of what's going on.

"Oh."

"You know, the good looking one." I've used the line dozens of times, and he never ceases to find it fresh and funny. As the loss of memory whittles him down to his essence, there remain two things: religious faith and a sense of humor.

It helps that there are family pictures on the wall by my parents' phone. By now my mother is pointing me out.

I'll ask him how he is, and he'll say, "Well, I'm still around."

"But you're not remembering much, I guess."

"No, that's for sure." He laughs, but there's uncertainty in his voice, a meekness. He may be wondering whether he'll make it through the conversation without embarrassing himself.

I'll ask about the weather and then talk about something of his that I have, the '78 Olds that just passed 100,000 miles ("It's still going good." "No kidding, old Betsy."), or the fishing reel that I just put on one of my rods. "I tried out a reel of yours and it worked pretty good. Got lots of bluegills one night and one small bass." One of my favorite memories is being in a boat with my dad, fishing with fly rods and poppers for bass and bluegills. I remember the smell of the 6-12 that we smeared on our hands and faces, and I can feel the mosquitoes buzzing around my head. We have handkerchiefs hanging out from under our baseball caps to keep the bugs off the back of our necks. That was our "Foreign Legion" getup. A small sucking sound out there in the growing darkness, and you set the hook. Either there's a fish on the other end of the line, or a popper is whizzing by your ear.

"Remember when we used to fish for bass and bluegills?"

"Yeah." He no longer has the pictures in his mind that I do. He doesn't smell the insect repellent or hear the buzzing of the mosquitoes. But there's affection and nostalgia in his tone when he says, "Yeah, those were the days."

I put Kathy on the phone for a change of pace. He doesn't remember her, but she says that she remembers him, "you handsome, sexy guy."

"Well, I used to do that, but I don't do it too much anymore." His remark cracks her up. I guess there are some things you never forget.

As my father's memories of me fade, my memories of him come streaming into consciousness. I don't ask for them, they just remember themselves. Silver Lake, Wisconsin, the late 1940s. I have just caught my first fish, a bullhead. It's on the bottom of the boat and I'm backing up on the rear seat as far as I can go without falling in the lake. My dad is warning me about something on the fish that I shouldn't touch, the whiskers or the spines. He needn't worry—I've never seen anything so slimy. A little while later he is talking to another fisherman on the lake and asking for a live minnow "for the kid." We must have been using dead ones or worms we had dug. With the live minnow I subsequently catch a real fish, a crappie. It replaces the bullhead as my "first."

Balsam Lake, Wisconsin, the early 1950s, opening of the bass season. I've been excused from school for three days to go on a fishing trip with my dad and my uncle. It's my first "man's" trip—I can tell because the two of them don't clean up their language on my behalf. I haven't been taught to use a fly rod yet, but on two successive afternoons schools of crappies pass by our pier and we take our limit on bamboo poles, minnows, and bobbers. That was the best fishing we ever had. A black-and-white photo shows the crappies, all of them good-sized, lying on newspapers, my dad and I crouched behind the display. It was the last year of my boyhood and the prime of his manhood, a moment that will always be.

My father was also a softball player, and I often think of the Sunday morning games he took me to. My dad roamed center field in a blue-and-gold uniform that said "Acorns." Once in a while when his team was up he'd play catch with me or have one of his teammates toss me a ball. There's a picture in my mind of riding with him in the back seat of a jeep after an All-Star game, past a fence where I see his name posted. Years later, after he had quit playing regularly, there was a company picnic where he was working a concession stand. He took time out to play a few innings in a game his division was losing 8–0. (Why do I remember that as the score?) The first time up he hit a smash past the second baseman. It was hit so hard it kept on rolling down a slope in the outfield, and he ended up with a home run, his team's first score. The next time up he went to the opposite field again, but this time it was a long drive and a legitimate home run. Two times up, two home runs, and then back to work at the concession stand. That was the father of my boyhood years. I am amazed at how many memories I have of him from that period—half a dozen years, perhaps, but in the time warp of memory they seem to last decades. And when I'm truly immersed in them, they are forever.

I was present when he made his final attempt to play organized ball. I know I was older because I was shagging fly balls in the pregame warmups, and I was able to hang on to the sixteen-inch "indoor" they use in Chicago. As game time approached my dad called me behind the bench and asked me to throw him some ground balls for practice. This I didn't understand. A center fielder asking for ground balls? He opened that evening at second base, where a team tries to hide its liabilities. He must have muffed a couple of chances because after a few innings he was out of the game altogether. I think we stayed to the end, but I'm not sure. I don't remember talking on the way home.

My father worked all his life for the same public utility that my grandfather did. In fact, the company gave him the job when my grandfather died. In his fifties, my dad's focus became a cabin he had bought in northern Wisconsin for $8,000. (Maybe that's why the softball score is 8–0.) Having a summer cottage was a lifelong dream, but longer vacations, retirement, and the realization of his dream did not bring him peace. I remember all the rocks he used to dig up. There was an area in front, lakeside, that he wanted to be flat so he could establish a lawn that would be easy to mow. He was also adding to a wall behind the house that helped divert rainwater away from the foundation. So throughout the summer he would dig up the stones that broke the surface of the grass and haul them away to his wall. And every spring they would be back, rocks the size of softballs and rocks the size of boulders. Once he started on a rock he couldn't stop. Out it would come, no matter how big, out they would all come, and the next year, others would rise with the thaw to take their place.

He liked the tough physical labor, though he always complained about it, but to me that earth could have been his soul. I don't know much about my father's inner life, but I think it involved a lot of digging—digging up worries in the hopes of getting rid of them, digging up disappointment and bitterness, and, even more so, digging up guilt, softball-size sins and boulder sins, or at least what an essentially good man believed were sins. He had no doubt confessed them many times to a priest, but they always came back. He may have thought he deserved the physical pain of hauling the stones away, that the punishment he inflicted on his body was good for him, that (in the Catholic theology of the day) he was knocking off the "temporal punishment" due to sin and shortening his days in purgatory. Maybe he hoped that if he clawed deep enough and long enough, all the rocks would eventually disappear and he would enjoy peace. But the more he dug, the more the rocks kept coming to the surface.

I have no proof of what was transpiring in my father other than the temperament I have inherited. I know what his obsession is like, and I know the freshness of white gloves. Somewhere along the line I began to see his face coming out in mine. It began in my thirties, I think. A look in the mirror, a remark from someone else. Once I plastered down my hair to see if it were true. It was, and the idea frightened me. The face my father is ending his life with has a deep, harsh scowl. Whether it comes from the genes in his cells or the rocks in his soul I don't know, but it's a look that would frighten a child who didn't know him. And yet that same face smiles back readily when smiled at.

In retirement, my dad became more difficult for my mother to live with. His presence every hour of the day sent her blood pressure soaring, and he became so concerned about it that he began to take it every day. Nothing—nothing!—could raise your blood pressure more than having my father approach you with the cuff. His treatment of her at that point in their lives would warrant today's label "emotionally abusive." I can picture him on the front lawn of our house, probably when he thought no one was looking, pointing his finger in my mother's face, that terrible scowl on his. He was shouting, "Look at me when I talk to you!" The anger was overpowering.

Though she never talked about it, I'm sure there were times after he retired when she thought of getting away from him. But she couldn't imagine her life, in a financial sense, in a family sense, in a religious sense, apart from his. She didn't even know how to drive a car. And though she suffered from living close to him, she would always say that he meant well, that he was basically a good person. And he was.

For years my father was tormented by the idea that he would lose his mind, just as his mother had lost hers. So he denied all the signs and overcompensated by writing himself notes. Endless notes. The '78 Olds I inherited from him when he was no longer able to drive was full of his written reminders. Under the hood, reminders about what fluids go where. On the dashboard, reminders about what switches do what. In the glove compartment, notes about how to use and care for the tire gauge. In the trunk, a complete survival kit. My mother would tell his doctor about his mental slips in the hope that someone else would know, that she could walk away with an official declaration of senility. On visits, I would take him places he had never been and he would say that he remembered being there. Finally, he admitted to what he was losing and began to joke about it. He seemed relieved. What do you do when you forget what you're worried about? When you don't know what disappointed you, why you were so angry? When you can't remember what to confess? There was no longer anything to dig for. My father became simpler, more docile, and found a kind of peace. Now his most important question became, "Where's Bess?"

Bess, his wife of fifty years, was somewhere, and somebody, he couldn't have imagined. Nor could I. For most of my adult life, my mother wrote empty letters and had little to say on the phone. I thought it was her medication, or maybe her personality, but then I discovered that my father censored everything she wrote and said. Suddenly, in her seventies, the oppression was lifted. She began to address him as "Kotre," not "John." She became talkative, capable, independent. I saw a practical intelligence emerge in her, and I wondered where it had been, where it had gone, all these years.

In my fifties, I'm not really curious about the details in my memories of my father. There's a truth in them, and I trust it, and there's a residue they leave in me. Every now and then I dream at night of finding treasure, some resource in me that I never knew existed. The dreams take several forms, but often the treasure is a fish that I see beneath the surface of a lake or a pond. Or it's a fish that I don't yet see but am connected to. I reel it in, but it runs deeper, and I wonder what it'll turn out to be when I get it near the surface. This is the legacy of vacations on northern Wisconsin lakes and the best fishing of all.

Several summers ago I got back to "real" fishing. Not from a boat, because problems with my back meant I couldn't sit for long, but from shore or wading in the shallows of a lake. Then I found stretches of a river near my home. (Like any fisherman, I'm not going to get too specific.) My father had never taken me wading in a river, so this was a new experience. The first summer I caught smallmouth bass, rock bass, and other panfish, even a few small bullheads when I put my fly rod aside. Nothing of any size, but what really mattered was to come home with the smell of fish on my hands. That, and a little 6-12 from a bottle I still have.

I knew nothing about rivers and I loved getting to know this one. Not just the fish that swim in it, but everything about it. When a ribbon of cassette tape passes by you, its pace never changes. Nor do its contents. But water in a river is in constant transformation. In the middle it may surge ahead while near the bank it circles in an eddy, a silent boil at the hub. Close your eyes and you may hear a deep rumble upstream, a softer spill nearby, and a quiet lapping at your feet, all distinct sounds. There are many moods in a river, and they change with time and place. Step into it and you will feel how powerful the current is, how deceptive the bottom. Things can get lost there, so much that the Greeks imagined a river in the underworld whose waters brought total oblivion. They called it Lethe, and souls drank from it when passing from one life to the next.

There is life in a river that you wouldn't imagine. Plants grow, reproduce, and die beneath the surface, and so do all sorts of other creatures—crayfish, snails, leeches, hellgrammites, nymphs with names I still don't know. But for unseen and unsuspected life you have to be in the middle of a mayfly hatch. It happened to me for the first time one summer evening as dusk was turning to dark. I was still in the water in my waders and vest. All of a sudden they were around me, hovering quietly. The moon was rising, and I saw a cloud down the whole length of the river, the mosquitoes of my boyhood transformed. The mayflies were large, white, silent, warm, gentle. I could feel them against my face and I basked in it. I don't know how they came out of the river, but they did, opaque spirits floating like snowflakes, but rising, always rising.

I'll return each summer to be in the middle of that hatch. I might even fish while I'm at it. And I hope that over the years my memory brings me what that river did, in its own way and in its own time. I hope that neither the river nor my memory proves my undoing. But for now I'll trust them both.

I've told my father about the river but not about the mayflies. It would be too much to explain, and he's always in such a hurry to get off the phone. "How's everybody there?" he asks at the end of a typical conversation. It's lasted only a few minutes.

"Fine. We're doing good. Maybe you can't remember us, but we remember you."

"Okay, buddy, take care."

"Yep, you too."

Chapter Four

THE AUTOBIOGRAPHICAL
MEMORY SYSTEM

As the river of memory flows through our lives, something happens within, something foreign to magnetized particles of iron oxide riding a ribbon of cassette tape. The contents of the river organize themselves, forming a kind of hierarchical system. In its precision and stability, the system pales in comparison with those we find on computer disks. But it's a system nevertheless, and there's a self atop it—a product of the hierarchy, a creator of the meaning that infuses it.

You can see how memories organize themselves by following their journey downstream, comparing their condition when you toss them in the river with when you fish them out. In 1972 psychologist Marigold Linton set herself precisely that task. Every day she wrote down on cards brief descriptions of at least two events from her day, one event per card. After a while she began giving herself monthly tests. Could she remember an event well enough to date it? At the end of six years Linton had recorded over 5,500 events and was spending six to twelve hours on her monthly tests.

After twelve years she had learned a great deal about autobiographical memory.

In one way, Linton's memory functioned very much like a library, storing recent events on shelves marked "New Books"—as things that happened last week or last month. Linton was able to retrieve these memories with a simple chronological search. But after a year or so events were moved to the the main stacks of her memory, organized now in terms of their content—as things done with friends, for example, or things done in connection with work. Except for major landmarks, *when* faded as a retrieval cue; in comparison, *what* grew stronger. You yourself can probably remember what you did this past summer; but you would have a hard time recalling the events of three or four summers ago, unless you thought of them, say, as vacations or projects or episodes in a faltering relationship. Few of us are calendar calculators when it comes to the long-term organization of our memories.

If you ever record and write up the story of someone's life (and I heartily recommend the experience), you'll see how little interest memory has in the calendar. You, the writer, will have to reconstruct the missing *when,* making side notes like, "Born 1912, brother born 1915, family moved 1917, started school 1918, bout with measles 1919," and so on. Events from the same year may be spoken of on different occasions and in totally different contexts. But there'll be surprises, like opening up a unit of *what* and finding a string of dates encapsulated within. Such was the case with a World War II veteran who remembered his year of combat in perfect chronological sequence. But most of the time subjects will say, "Well, let's see, that must have been . . .," and then they'll search for a reference point for which they know the date, or for which there is some external record. In some cases they may even remember the hour of the day or the day of the week in which a particular event took place better than they will the month or the year.

Reference points are key. A character in Agatha Christie's *By the*

Pricking of My Thumbs remarked of the people in her vicarage, "They don't say, 'That happened in 1930' or 'That happened in 1925' or things like that. They say, 'That happened the year after the old mill burned down,' or 'That happened after the lightning struck the big oak and killed Farmer James' or 'That was the year we had the polio epidemic.'" An old Armenian man I interviewed wasn't even sure of the date of his birth. "My mother said the time was when we were doing noodles. Noodles, that was September. I said, 'What year?' She said, 'I don't know.' Heh, heh. I think maybe I could say 1905 or 6." His youthful years were divided into two categories: "before massacre" and "after massacre." He had since learned the year of the massacre, 1915, but he had to infer the month, saying it must have been May because the wheat was green. Today, someone may infer the date of an event by relating it to a divorce, a job change, or some other major transition. "That was before we split up," they might say, or "That came after I retired." It shouldn't be surprising that significant events are used to monitor memory time because calendars themselves are built around such markers. Although it's off by about six years, the Christian calendar divides time into the years before Christ's birth and the years after. In Islam, the calendar separates the periods before and after Mohammed's flight from Mecca to Yathrib.

The yielding of *when* to *what* in autobiographical memory is important because it leads to memory's real interest: the creation of meaning about the self. Before we can give an experience a lasting place in memory, we have to decide what it means. Interestingly, once the decision has been made, we no longer need to remember similar episodes. In her self-study, Linton was surprised to discover how much she had forgotten because events had lost their distinctiveness. She remembered a new class she taught but not all the times she had taught an old one, a match with a new racquet partner but not all her matches with a former one. What remained in her memory were unique events, the "first times" but not all the subsequent times. Most libraries are interested in duplicates, but most memories are not. Duplicates contribute nothing to meaning.

Starting with the fourth year of her testing Linton began to notice something else. A few of the cards that were supposed to jog her memory not only failed to do so but made absolutely no sense. She simply could not understand what she had once written. "I could hear my voice describe fragments from my own life that were somehow completely meaningless." The problem wasn't in the original writing. The events, rather, connected with no pattern that had developed in her life. They hadn't led anywhere, didn't fit any theme. They were orphans in an autobiographical memory system fashioning generic memories of *what* events mean.

Psychologists have all sorts of names for generic memories of *what:* scripts, schemas, MOPs (memory organization packets), and TOPs (thematic organization points), to list just a few. No matter what generic memories are called, the idea is that we create them from the specifics of everyday life and arrange them in a kind of hierarchy. At the lowest level of the hierarchy are actual episodes, single events that we still remember as events. These are relatively few, however, because most of what we remember is absorbed higher up in the hierarchy. We don't remember every time we played a neighborhood game as kids, but we do remember that we "used to" play hide-and-seek or statues or stickball. The phrase "used to" is a sign of a generic memory. I don't remember every softball game my father took me to, but I do remember that he "would" take me—another generic memory. We all have general impressions of our high-school days, but we cannot render a day-by-day, blow-by-blow account. So much was so routine that we've forgotten the specifics.

You can tell you're ascending the memory hierarchy when generic recollections become more thematic. They start to cover longer periods of time, periods that psychologists call "extendures." They pull more activities together, become more interpretive, and begin to reflect a self-image. Now it's not "we used to play stickball," but "I was always the last one chosen." Not "My father would take me to his games," but "I did everything with my father." Of the high-school years we might say, "I was a lousy student" or "my best friends are the ones I made at that time." Generic memories near the top of the hierarchy may span a lifetime. Meaning will be present in them, but the specific events that yield the meaning will be absent.

Generic memories introduce an efficiency to the autobiographical memory system. Read through the following string of numbers and then see if you can remember them: 1, 4, 9, 2, 1, 7, 7, 6, 1, 8, 1, 2, 1, 9, 4, 5. Now try it again, grouping the digits into packages of four. When the numbers are combined into meaningful units—in this case, dates that every American schoolchild is taught—there's less to remember. Using this technique of "chunking," a college student was able to remember eighty digits read to him just once. He saw the numbers in sets, some as running times for track events, others as ages or dates. The sets themselves he organized at a higher level of his memory hieriarchy: first came a cluster of five running times, then so many ages, and so forth. Meaningful organization enables superstars of memory to retain strings of numbers that get into the tens of thousands, if they are given an unlimited amount of time to learn them. It also enables expert chess players to remember the position of pieces on the board. Research has shown that the memory of experts is far superior to that of novices when the pieces are arranged in meaningful patterns, but not when they are positioned randomly. Patterns reduce the burden on memory.

The next time you find a word stuck on the tip of you tongue, write down all the words that come up as you try to think of the one you're after. When (or if) you discover the target word, you'll see that it has something in common with the decoys that came first, perhaps the same first letter or the same number of syllables or the same accent. If the target word you couldn't think of was "Cornish," you may have come up with "Congress" and "Corinth" and "Concord." If it was "sampan," as it was in one experiment, you might have come up with "Saipan," "Siam," "Cheyenne," "sarong," "sanching," and "sympoon," not all of them actual words. The common elements in the decoys and the targets suggest the existence of a generic word that memory retains, even when knowledge of a specific word is lost.

Generic memories may also explain the experience of *déjà vu*. You walk into a restaurant and have the strange feeling you've been there before. But you know that's impossible. You've probably activated a generic memory, a "script" for going to restaurants. The script tells you what you normally do in a restaurant: enter, give your name to the hostess, follow the hostess to a table, sit down, greet the waiter, order your meal, eat, have dessert, ask for the check, pay, leave a tip, and exit. Studies have shown that generic memories can alter the recollection of specific details. A professor delivering a lecture may never point to information on the blackboard, for example, but many students will "remember" that she did. Pointing to the blackboard is part of the standard script for lectures. On a trip to northern Michigan, my wife once had a problem with the oil pressure in our old station wagon. Her brother lived in the area, so she took the car to him. He removed the oil filter, tore it apart, found that it was bad, and replaced it. That did the trick. A few years later, Kathy "remembered" how relieved I was when he had finished. *But I hadn't been there* on that occasion, even though Kathy saw me in her memory. She saw me because of the influence of a generic script: normally the two of us go up north together.

Psychologist Craig Barclay has shown that people will accept altered memories as genuine if they are consistent with scripts they already have. In one study, Barclay had graduate students record fifteen events a week for a period of four months—a total of about 250 events. He then tested their memory five times over the next several years. The tests were simple. Students were shown memories they had originally recorded as well as alterations that Barclay had added. They had to look at each item in a test and ask themselves, "Did I write this or did Barclay? Is it my memory or not?" They proved to be quite good at recognizing originals, spotting roughly 90 percent of them. But they also bought many of the alterations, upwards of 50 percent. They did so because the alterations were things they could have done or would have done, something they "normally" or "typically" do. In the absence of other information, they were relying on scripts to judge the authenticity of their memories.

When people tell the story of their life, they leap with the grace of a cat from one level of their memory hierarchy to another, from the general to the specific and back again to the general. They do it so quickly that you fail to notice until you study a transcript of their recollections. "School was bad all the time," began a man in his early fifties in response to a question of mine. He had opened with a generic memory from the middle of his hierarchy. Then he slipped a level, talking about various academic subjects. History and geography were fine; so were the shop classes. English was a major problem, as was mathematics once he got into algebra. Then he wanted to explain, so he leapt upward: "I kept hearing my mother make excuses for me. You hear that as a kid, and it's easy to believe it yourself, you know?" In the next instant he was on the ground, speaking of a specifc event. "I finished the tenth grade, and I saw I was going nowhere. I had nothing but problems. So I told my mother, 'I just can't cut it and I'm gonna quit.'"

Our conversation turned to work and World War II, which had begun when he was twelve years old. That brought back a memory from junior high school. In a shop class "we would make all types of little wooden airplanes, and they would be painted black so guys would learn how to identify planes by silhouette"——a low-level generic memory. Next: "I won two or three prizes for having the best model planes," a remembrance that gets down to the level of concrete events. And then: "I excelled in that type of thing, anything with my hands." This was a statement close to the peak of his autobiographical memory system, reflecting a truth that extended far beyond junior high. The fluidity of this man's movement in memory is no less marvelous for being so common-place: in one breath, an image of some prizes from forty years ago; in the next, a statement about who I have always been.

Everyone's autobiographical memory is different, of course, with its own blend of *when* and *what,* its own mix of the specific and the general. Some of us preserve chronology better than others. Some of our hierarchies are top-heavy and others bottom-heavy, some vaguely abstract and others excruciatingly concrete. Most people's earliest memory of life is of something specific, but I once interviewed a man whose first memory was of "a kind of doubleness." Abstractions like that permeated his entire system. Early in a series of interviews I found myself asking for concrete descriptions of events, but they were few and far between. More came as the interviews went on, when trust between us had grown and when his early years were no longer the focus. Still, his autobiographical memory system had a great deal of what psycho-analysts call intellectualization, a defense mechanism that puts distance between oneself and the felt experiences of life. Recent work on people suffering from depression suggests that they have access to positive memories at the generic level, but not at the level of specifics. In this domain, they cannot get to the bottom of their memory hierarchy. Theirs is a problem that is the exact opposite of Shereshevskii's, a man whose memory was burdened by concreteness and the inability to form abstractions.

It's easy to assume what many superstars of memory initially do, that everyone's autobiographical memory has the same personality as our own. But it's exhilarating to see the assumption break down, to discover the variety in the structure of our memories, to realize how unique our own system might be. The template in this chapter describes the ways in which all our memories are alike. May it not obscure the ways in which all of them are different.

Why Are Some Episodes So Vivid?

Let us turn now to the ground floor of the autobiographical memory system, where recollections of specific events are found. Later we can climb to the top, where the self resides. At the base, we wonder about all that has happened in our lives. It shouldn't be surprising that so much has been lost as memory flows on. What should astonish us is the reverse—why so much has survived. Why are some episodes so vivid? Why as clear as the freshest of water?

Marigold Linton's diary study provides one answer to that question: we remember events that are novel, at least at the time we experience them. When something is surprising or shocking, or simply has never happened to us before, a flashbulb seems to go off in our mind, and the event is imprinted in memory. Neurologically, the equivalent of the flashbulb may be a massive increase of activity in the cortex, fueled perhaps by a sudden release of hormones. The hormones increase the availability of glucose, which serves as the fuel. A neurological flash doesn't ensure that the resulting "photograph" won't change over time (research shows that it will) but that the changing impression will last a long time. When researchers asked a sample of people between twenty and eighty-seven years of age to write down six of their most vivid memories, 73 percent of all the memories collected were of unique events. Another 20 percent were of first times, i.e., of unique events that were followed by others of their kind. In contrast, only 4 percent of the vivid memories were of generic events, and only 3 percent were of last times.

Sometimes what's unique about an event is the twist it gives to what's routine. Long after I had formed a script for going to restaurants, and long after trips to individual restaurants were being absorbed into that script (and so forgotten), I had a memorable dining experience. It was at a family restaurant in a small Indiana town, and it began with a heavy-set waitress dumping a bowl of soup in my lap. She brought towels and apologies and cleaned me up as best she could. Then she returned with the main course. As she was setting my plate before me, she slipped on some soup that was still on the floor. Down she went with a thud. I'll never forget the sound when she landed or the embarrassment that all of us felt for her. Not one mishap that evening, but two.

Another memorable twist on my generic restaurant script came when my wife and I were going to take advantage of a promotion by a local home builder. Visit one of our model homes, the ad said, and we'll give you a certificate for a free dinner. So we visited the model, got the certificate, and called some friends. When we arrived at the restaurant, I insisted we tell no one that we were "certificate" customers. I wanted to be treated like everyone else. And we were—royally. Drinks, appetizers, the most expensive entrées, desserts we didn't have room for. We were like kids let loose in a candy store, and whenever we said, "This is too good to be true," I checked my pocket for that certificate. It was always there. Then came the real moment of truth. The waiter brought the check and I placed the certificate on his tray. He hesitated and said, "I'll have to talk to the manager." In an instant I knew it was over. When the waiter returned, I learned that the builder was no longer honoring his certificates. We left muttering an eternal truth: there's no such thing as a free lunch.

Unusual outcomes that break a script are known as tags; they make otherwise ordinary episodes stand out. But episodes stand out in memory for another reason: they prove to be consequential. Now it's not a flashbulb that goes off at the time of the event, but a spotlight that casts a retrospective glow. When Linton was giving herself one of her monthly memory tests, she came across a diary card that described meeting a shy scholar. There was nothing exceptional about the event, nothing particularly emotional. But when she realized five years later that the person on the card had become her husband, the spotlight of consequences came on. She felt more emotion in connection with event; it became more vivid in her memory, "a beacon in a previously unmarked terrain." If you can imagine leafing through an old appointment book or diary and discovering an insignificant meeting that brought you the love of your life, or finding a mountain that turned out to be a molehill, you will appreciate the effects of consequentiality. Sometimes autobiographical memory waits to see what becomes of things before it decides if they are worth remembering.

Now imagine how vivid a memory might be if it's both novel *and* consequential, if it initially entered memory with a flash and continues to stand in the spotlight. On rare occasions we even know *as we experience* a new event that it's a major turning point, that it will change our life forever. Sudden tragedies fit into this category, but so do moments of unexpected bliss. Upon first hearing the sound of a man's voice, a woman said, quite in contrast to Linton, "I knew I loved him from that instant." And a man, just before he first made love to a woman, said, "This is my night to remember." Both persons eventually married the ones they loved. Both felt the seed of consequences at the very beginning of their relationships.

If an event in your life is both unique and consequential, chances are you've worked it into a good story. You've "rehearsed" it, to yourself if to no one else, and that rehearsal has kept it clear in your mind. When a young Tennessee man known as J. T. was called by the Army for a physical examination in 1944, he had no idea what to expect. He only knew that this would be an unusual day, and a fateful one. He thought the Army wouldn't want him because of a knee ailment that had laid him up as a child. He was in for a surprise:

> *Hundreds and hundreds of naked men were going through a line down there in Clarksville. I remember so damn well when I got to the desk. This guy was settin' there lookin' at my record. "Any childhood diseases?" he said. "Things like that?"*
>
> *"Yeah," I said, "here are the papers that the doctor sent down with me. I have a leg problem."*

He looked at the papers and said, "Well, how do you feel now?"
"Well, there's no problem now."
"One-A! You'll do!" And he stamped the record. Then he asked me, "Do you want to go in the Navy?"
"Hell no," I said, "I can walk a hell of a lot farther than I can swim."

Three words—"One-A, you'll do"—changed J. T.'s life irrevocably. After fighting in World War II, he reenlisted and made a career of the Army. By the time I got to know him, an event that was both novel and consequential had become a classic Army story. How much had it changed in the telling and retelling? Did the punch line, the one about walking farther than he could swim, actually go back to Clarksville, 1944, or was it added at a later date? I surely don't know, and at this point I don't think J. T. does either. But it doesn't make much difference. The function of the line is to make the story tellable, to keep a turning point in his life memorable.

Military stories often involve major historical events, happenings that have consequences not only for oneself but also for one's country, and even for the planet. When you are a participant in those events, the memory never fades. Another veteran of World War II, this one a Navy man, told me about being on "Operation Crossroads" just after the war ended:

I had no idea what it was. They took almost all the planes off the "Saratoga" and brought aboard a couple tanks and a bunch of army trucks and jeeps, and anchored them on the flight deck. We were cut down to just a bare crew, 600 men from 4000. We got out to sea and somebody said, "We're going to Bikini." I didn't know what Bikini was. Everybody started looking on maps, and it was a little dot out in the middle of the ocean.

That dot in the ocean would be the site of atomic bomb tests. There were two of them, and they were unforgettable:

The first test, they had a bomber come in and drop a bomb by parachute—a little, tiny bomb, only five megatons. It was a cloudy day and we could hear the pilot and bombardier talking back and forth. They made a run and they couldn't see the target, so the bombardier told the pilot to bring it around again. On the second run, he still couldn't see the target. Finally, on the third run, he dropped the bomb. We had our backs turned and they said, "Okay, you can turn around." Well, there was no explosion. I didn't hear nothing. I looked over on the horizon and I could see little puffs of smoke here and there. And I said, "Well, this is a big deal. Here we come all this way, been out here sweating our rear ends off, and for this?"

And then all of a sudden, somebody said, "Look up there," and above the clouds was this massive cloud of orange fire. It looked like whipcream rolling up, just this big mushroom coming up. You can see all the pictures you want, but you cannot really visualize what this thing is like. The heat was so intense. The "Saratoga" was fifteen miles away from where the bomb went off, and it set it on fire.

After that test was over we went to the underwater test. Now we were real close. We were outside the atoll, but we were close enough that you could read numbers on the sides of ships. The "Saratoga" was right next to the target ship. When that blast went off, I've never ever seen anything like that in my whole life. It was so fabulous that words can't describe it. The water came up like you took a big steam hose and shot it up in the air and the steam hit a ceiling. In a split second the water shot up and covered the whole atoll, and I mean it just sunk ships all over the place. It lifted the "Saratoga" completely out of the water, and it did a 360 in the air and split open on the backside. And that was only five megatons, sixty feet underwater.

Research is showing that you don't even have to be a witness to historically significant events for them to stay fresh in your memory. Just before the turn of the century, F. W. Colegrove found that a sample of middle-aged and elderly people had vivid memories of nothing more than *hearing the news* that Abraham Lincoln had been shot. They remembered where they were when they heard, what they were doing, the time of day it was, and who told them. Over thirty years later the memories were quite specific. Here's what one respondent said:

> *My father and I were on the road to A_____ in the state of Maine to purchase the "fixings" needed for my graduation. When we were driving down a steep hill into the city we felt that something was wrong. Everybody looked so sad, and there was such terrible excitement that my father stopped his horse, and leaning from the carriage called: "What is it, my friends? What has happened?" "Haven't you heard?" was the reply. "Lincoln has been assassinated." The lines fell from my father's limp hands, and with tears streaming from his eyes he sat as one bereft of motion. We were far from home, and much must be done, so he rallied after a time, and we finished our work as well as our heavy hearts would allow.*

Older Americans who read this book can probably remember the occasion on which they first heard the news of the bombing of Pearl Harbor. Younger readers weren't alive then, but they no doubt have equally vivid memories of the assassination of John F. Kennedy, of the time a human being first set foot on the moon, or of the time, almost twenty years later, when the space shuttle *Challenger* blew up. Studies have shown that a surprising number of us remember where we were and what we were doing when we received news of these events. We also recall who brought us the news, what we did after we heard it, and how everyone concerned felt. The personal relevance of an event affects this kind of recall, which is why more blacks than whites recall the circumstances in which they learned of the deaths of Martin Luther King, Jr., and Malcolm X. On days of great significance our individual stories are momentarily aligned with History itself, and we say, if only indirectly, "I was there."

Novel, consequential events often involve emotion, a third factor that makes memories vivid. Emotion can enter a particular memory at any time, when it first becomes a memory or years later when its significance is realized. One of the most tragic memories I've heard—it was unique, consequential, and emotional—involved a nine-year-old girl who wanted to drop in on her favorite aunt. She had to wait all day because her aunt was getting some badly needed sleep. Finally, when evening came, she, her older sister, and her brother were given the key to the aunt's apartment and told they could wake her up. The older sister unlocked the door and the girl squeezed into the apartment ahead of the others. It was dark, so they turned on a light. There, hanging from a doorway, was their aunt. She had committed suicide. The emotion at that time was overpowering, and it seems to have diminished only slightly in the years since. The girl grew up to fear betrayal: if her loving aunt had left her, why wouldn't anyone else?

Emotion has a paradoxical effect on memory, partly because there are so many different emotions. Much of the time it acts like a flashbulb, lighting up the autobiographical memory system so that it records a good many details. But there are occasions when emotion is so overwhelming, and everything happens so fast, that memory goes into a daze. Car accidents are an example; so are public performances. Events may become a blur because the emotions they arouse are painful or sad. We remember the day a loved one died but not much of the days that followed. There was too much happening during that time, and besides, we were just not ourselves.

The emotion of fear is especially uncertain in its relationship to memory. For everyone who says, "When you're scared, you remember," someone else says just the opposite. Fear can narrow one's focus of attention: if someone is pointing a gun at you, it's hard to remember much besides the gun. Psychologists call this the weapon focus effect; it appears in about a third of the experiments that test for it. As for the accuracy of highly emotional memories, the evidence is equivocal. Some studies show that emotional arousal (including a high level of stress) improves memory, others show that it makes it worse, and still others show that it has no effect. The flash that goes off at a highly emotional moment may burn details into your mind, but it may also blind you.

In general, cautions about the accuracy of memory remain in place for vivid memories. Within a week of the *Challenger* disaster in 1986, several dozen employees and students at Johns Hopkins University were asked how they heard about the event. Nine months later the researchers asked those they could relocate, twenty-seven in all, for a second rendition. Some of the new accounts were indeed inconsistent with the old ones. Right after the accident, for example, one woman reported that her husband had phoned with the news; nine months later, she recalled learning of the incident through a statement on television. Still, comparing all the details in all the reports, inconsistency was under 9 percent, which is not bad as far as accuracy goes.

But another study showed that time takes its toll. The day after *Challenger* exploded, a group of students at Emory University wrote an account of how they heard the news. Nearly *three years* later they were asked what they had written. Only 7 percent got everything right about their initial reports, while 25 percent got everything wrong. When shown the reports, the students were dumbfounded. "I still think of it the other way around," said one. "I have no recollection of it at all," said another. As far as the researchers could tell, the original memories had vanished.

A fourth and final reason why some episodes are so vivid is perhaps the most intriguing. It's that something in us has chosen them as symbols. Consider this woman recalling the birth of her first child: "I remember taking him to my mom—my mom had not seen him—and I'll never forget the look. It, she, just crushed me. She looked at him as if to say, 'Is that him?'" This woman knew that there was far more to this memory than the moment it captured. Her mother's look was the one she had always received as a child, her mother's attitude the one that had always met the things she produced. Nothing, in fact, could serve as a better metaphor for the extended nature of this mother-daughter relationship than the memory of that glance.

Instances where one episode stands for a pattern of repeated episodes have been called "repisodes" by memory researcher Ulric Neisser. Sandra's fire escape memory in Chapter Three is an example. She remembered that she had gotten away from family violence on one occasion by crawling out a window onto the fire escape and climbing from there to a neighbor's apartment. Years later she learned that she had done so not once, but many times. Upon examining testimony in the Watergate affair, Neisser concluded that John Dean's memories were likewise repisodic. In memory, more was packed into a single conversation with the president than had actually been said. The conversation stood in Dean's mind for a broad pattern of ongoing activities.

Symbolic episodes make it clear that we not only move up the memory hierarchy as times goes on, creating generic memories out of specific events. We also on occasion move down. We find a single concrete event that stands for a major theme in our life, that summarizes a whole cluster of meanings in the hierarchy above. We find the proverbial picture that's worth a thousand words.

Sometimes the picture is not of an event but of a thing. My wife and I once asked a group of older people to think of one autobiographical object from their past. They were to write it down in big letters on a sheet of paper, pin the paper on their chest, and walk around the room. Pretty soon they were sporting signs saying "buttonhook," "old-fashioned pen," "match," "fishing pole," "Hershey Bar," "tricycle," and much more. One person who had "violin" on his chest discovered someone else who had the same thing. A "red wagon" ran into a "pull wagon." A pair of "ice skates" met up with some "roller skates."

One of the women had written "coral elephant" on her piece of paper. She had come from a poor family that couldn't afford new clothes or jewelry for its children. Around the sixth grade, the girl became fascinated with a teacher, a young, attractive woman who always wore beautiful things. One day it was a piece of jewelry, a coral elephant pin, and throughout that day the girl couldn't take her eyes off it. After school she lingered to get a better look and tell the teacher how pretty it was. At the end of the school year, the teacher gave the girl that pin. "It was my most prized possession," the woman said with tears in her eyes. And yet, several years ago, she lost it in a move. All she has left is its memory, and a story that could symbolize her life.

Younger people, too, remember symbolic objects. A Lionel train set, laid out on a huge sheet of plywood on Christmas Day: "It was the first time my brother got something because he was a boy and I didn't because I was a girl." (You can bet there were other times.) A baseball bat, Babe Ruth style, black electrical tape on the handle: "The imagination I used with it! I could hit a rock and that bat made a sound like no other bat did. The entire bat was chipped from me standing on the driveway hitting rocks into the woods." A pair of faded blue jeans, size 5/6, brass snaps on the side pockets: "They symbolized my victory against weight. I finally fit into them after three years of literally starving myself. I think they fit for about three weeks." A writing desk, full of artist's supplies: "It was my mother's. She died when I was almost four and this desk was a link to her. My father never cleaned out her stuff, so she lived on for me in the desk. I can still remember how each drawer smelled."

How do you know an object is symbolic? Because it initiates a string of associations that can get you talking for hours. White gloves are that way for me, but so are baseball gloves, like the one I once got as a birthday present. I have a vivid picture of this glove sitting on the dining room buffet right next to the foldup cot I used to sleep in. It's night in the memory, and I'm in bed, and our family is about to go on vacation the next day. I can smell the neat's-foot oil that I've rubbed into the glove, and I can see it glisten in the rays of a streetlight outside the window. I know the memory isn't accurate because my birthday is in early April and our family never went on vacation until school was out, late June at the earliest. But accuracy doesn't matter. The memory fuses the best of April and the best of June, and once I start talking about the glove, it brings back images of playing catch with my father, of watching him play on his softball team, and of doing the same things with my sons. My memory of a baseball glove isn't vivid because it's a photograph but because it opens the door to one story after another. The more I tell the stories, the clearer the picture of that nighttime scene becomes.

On occasion, episodes at the bottom of the autobiographical memory system may point directly to the self at the top. Psychologists Jefferson Singer and Peter Salovey call such memories self-defining. They are the ones "that give shape to and are shaped by our lives, memories of our proudest successes and humiliating defeats, memories of loves won and lost—memories that repetitively influence our manner of intimacy or our pursuit of power—the memories that answer the question of who we are." They are also the memories that are such a help when it comes to repair. Therapists can use them to listen closely and diagnose wisely, and far more unobtrusively than with personality tests.

Can you think of a moment when you were most truly yourself? A Canadian educator of teachers once answered that request by remembering the day she read a poem to her students. Though not a literary masterpiece, the poem said in a few words what she had been trying to get across for hours. "The effect was electric," she said. "All around the room, eyes were lighting up with recognition and heads were nodding in agreement. Even before the ensuing discussion, I knew that they had finally understood." But understanding wasn't enough. After a visit to their teaching sites, the students returned. They had incorporated the poem into their lives:

> *They were full of stories of what they had seen done, of the times they or others had stifled and restrained the children's thinking, and of what they had done to try and change that. The poem wasn't just pretty*

words to cry over and then forget. It was something they were applying to their own lives. My satisfaction at that moment was immense and deep. I began to think that because of my course, maybe some of them really would be more sensitive to children's needs. That was one of those times when I felt closest to truly being a teacher educator.

Psychologist Dan McAdams refers to self-defining memories as nuclear episodes. His research confirms that they do indeed reflect aspects of our identity. Those in his studies for whom power was a dominant motive tended to recall nuclear episodes of physical strength or moral courage, times when they displayed some new understanding, influenced others, engaged in vigorous physical activity, or earned a measure of fame or prestige. A young gymnast wrote of a memorable performance she turned in on the uneven parallel bars:

From the tension of the mount until the flying dismount I put all my power into every move. . . . After my routine, my teammates smiled their approval and patted me on the back. I was stunned to see my score of 9.0. The coach cheered along with the crowd, and I felt a great sense of accomplishment. Today the score still stands as the highest on record.

Other of McAdams' subjects showed a preeminent concern for intimacy; it was matched in the nuclear episodes they recalled. This is the memory of a man of thirty-three:

Perhaps the greatest moment of my life was the time when [my daughter] was born since, unlike the birth of my two sons, I was able to be in the delivery room at my wife's side while she was being born. Her birth is a moment I will never forget, especially when she was placed on my wife's chest immediately after the birth and she just stared at the two of us without crying. I found myself crying instead, out of pure joy and happiness. Since that day three years ago, she has brought boundless love and happiness into my family life and has brought more love out of me than I thought existed.

The relationship between themes in the self and themes in nuclear episodes held even if the episodes were painful. People concerned with power were more likely to have "worst" memories of conflict, weakness, failure, humiliation, or being ignorant. For those concerned with intimacy, worsts usually involved another person, either a misfortune they shared or a rejection, separation, or a disillusionment they suffered. The relationship did not hold, and this is significant, when McAdams's subjects described routine episodes in their life. Memories of ordinary events did not provide a glimpse of the self at the top of the autobiographical memory system. Memories of extraordinary events did.

Prisoners who resisted the attempts of Chinese Communists to brainwash them in the 1950s illustrate in yet another way the connection between identity and self-defining memories. For it was identity that their captors ultimately wished to destroy, an old self such as "doctor," "teacher," or "priest." Prisoners who were able to resist the assault did so in part by finding a place in themselves where their captors could not go, a place where they could dwell on their life's most cherished moments. A professor from Europe would go off to a corner of his crowded cell and make drawings of standing before a Christmas tree, being in a university city, going on a romantic stroll with his fiancée, seeing a mother and a baby. He would write about the time in his life that each drawing represented. What he drew and wrote became so precious to him that he later smuggled them out at great danger to himself. Margaret Rathbun, an American prisoner-of-war in the Persian Gulf War, wasn't allowed pen and paper during her captivity, but she still managed to conjure up every memory she could from her entire life and play them over and over. These prisoners were protecting and reinforcing their very selves by living in memories of the past. They were forging a direct connection with who they once were in the hope of continuing to be that person.

It's fascinating to do consciously with self-defining memories what autobiographical memory does unconsciously. Could you build your life story around a few significant autobiographical objects? And what about episodes—could you pick half a dozen key moments? A Japanese student once told me of her mother's belief that life had only three such moments and that it returned to the place from which it came. So the path she was traveling formed a square, with one corner representing the point of departure and eventual return and the other three representing points of transition. Images like that remind us that it's not simply memory that is built around vivid episodes. Life itself rises to them and falls away from them.

As you select your key memories, ask yourself why each is so vivid. Perhaps the remembered experience was novel, something that broke the normal script. Perhaps it was consequential, the first in a chain of falling dominoes. It may have been connected with an event of great historical significance or engender great emotion. It may have been, and continue to be, symbolic, capturing a point in time when you were truly yourself. A memory may be vivid for one of these reasons, for several of them, or for all of them. And if it's truly self-defining, it will tell you who you are.

"It Seems Like Yesterday"

Vivid images introduce a time warp into the river of memory. When Clifford Pyncheon in Nathaniel Hawthorne's *The House of the Seven Gables* is given a fresh rose of a special variety, its odor brings back numerous associations. "I remember how I used to prize this flower," he says. "Long ago, I suppose, very long ago!—or was it only yesterday?" A ribbon of cassette tape keeps time evenly, methodically, one minute of actual time yielding one minute of recorded time. But memory time, the time of your life, is different.

If you were to take everything you could remember of your life, put the *when* back in, and lay it all out in chronological order, you would see that certain years claim more attention than others. Nearly thirty-five years after World War II, psychologist Howard Hoffman made an oral history of his wartime experience. When he and his wife plotted his recollections against available documentation, they found his vivid memories were subjectively longer, his dim ones shorter. Basic training, which constantly brought new experiences, claimed over eleven times the memory space per day than did staying in Germany at war's end. Howard, in fact, was astonished to learn from checking the calendar that he had spent a full six months doing the latter. After a year of harrowing combat, it had seemed like nothing.

Not only do we give vivid episodes more space in memory, we also bring them closer to the present. They seem to have happened only yesterday. The phenomenon is called forward telescoping, and doctors have known about it for years. "When was the last time you were in for a checkup? Had an EKG? A serum cholesterol test?" When patients' answers can be checked against medical records, they usually overestimate the recency of the occurrence. My doctor tells me he has rarely seen the opposite. I myself make the same miscalculation when something goes wrong with a car. "I just had that fixed," I say. But when I check old work orders I often find the repair only *seemed* to be recent. Psychologists became aware of forward telescoping in a series of surveys on crime victimization, when respondents were asked questions such as: "During the past six months has anyone attacked you? Tried to rob you?" and so on. In one instance, the answers given were checked against police records. About 20 percent of the reported incidents were included in the six-month reference period, when in fact they had occurred earlier. They had been telescoped forward.

What's behind this surge into the present? In some cases it may be that no similar incident has occurred between then and now. In some it may be a matter of how many associations the memory has acquired and therefore how vivid and accessible it is. One study found that when people were asked to estimate the dates of newsworthy events, they tended to telescope forward those they knew a lot about and to telescope backward those they were relatively ignorant of. "John Lennon dies" seemed more recent than it was. "Keith Moon of the 'Who' dies" seemed more remote.

When accuracy matters, it's possible to reduce the tendency to telescope. Elizabeth Loftus and Wesley Marburger suggest using the landmarks that autobiographical memory normally uses. In the state of Washington in 1989, the eruption of Mt. St. Helens was one of them. Loftus and Marburger found that the question "Since the first major eruption of Mt. St. Helens, has anyone beaten you up?"—asked exactly six months after the event— elicited more accurate dating than the question "During the last six months, has anyone beaten you up?" Personal markers, such as a birthday or wedding anniversary, helped to reduce forward telescoping. So did public reference points, such as New Year's Day. Simple dates ("Since February 3") did not. There were no associations that made them a landmark.

Of course, landmarks themselves are tossed about in the river of memory. Births, marriages, deaths—along with graduations, moves, retirements, and other major transitions—may change our lives so thoroughly that they seem vivid and recent:

> *My daughter is six now but it seems like just yesterday I was carrying her around. The memories are ones of joy, so they stay close to me.*

> *My wedding day was nearly four years ago. On that day I also gained two sons, ages six and three. So much has occurred in these past four years, yet it seems so recent.*

> *My dad died eighteen months ago, but as I was brushing my teeth I flashed back to the time when he told me to remember to put the toothbrush top back on. I stopped dead in my tracks because it seemed like yesterday that he said it.*

These memories reveal something else that is at work in forward telescoping. We want to keep a person or experience close in an emotional sense:

I cannot believe in any way, shape, or form that I graduated from high school five years ago. No way! I remember having lunch at my parents' house every single school day with about twenty or so friends. It seems like it was yesterday, hanging out and then pulling into a couple of cars and cruising back to school.

I remember when I would ride the Greyhound bus to visit my grandmother in St. Louis every summer. I felt very special riding a bus alone at twelve. It doesn't seem like it was around 1955 when I first started visiting her, but it was.

Our trip to the land of the Mayas. It seems like yesterday, yet it was in 1977. We went on a beautiful boat and everything was a first-time experience. It was wonderful. I went with my "date"—my wife.

At times, the telescoping in our memory points to the self. Am I the same person I once was? Am I different? Personal landmarks that come to the forefront of remembrance are often occasions in which we stepped into a new role and became a new person—a spouse, a mother, a soldier, a worker, a retiree. As a new self emerged, an old one receded into the past. When looking at the latter, memory turns the telescope around. Events seem smaller and more distant than they really are:

It seems like a thousand years ago that I was in high school. It was not even four years ago that I graduated, but I am a different person.

The sale of my company seems like so long ago, and it's only been two years. It was the selling of my dream and getting the money for all my hard work.

Memories from before I moved to California were from a troubled time. It seems like a lifetime ago, someone else's life. I am such a different person now, it is hard to believe.

Backward telescoping also occurs when we want emotional distance from certain experiences. Sometimes we actively try to create distance, burning letters, throwing reminders in the trash, and insisting, "That was then, this is now." But most of the time, telescoping occurs on its own:

> *It seems like a long time ago when my only daughter left for college, but it was only two years. I never really wanted her to leave so I try to forget that sad day.*

> *Two years ago I was in an automobile accident. A teenager lost control of her car and hit me head on at forty-five miles an hour. My mother was hurt badly. Both arms and one leg were broken, along with five ribs. It seems this happened a long time ago.*

> *When my cousin, who was only twenty-seven, died, he had brain tumors and was sick for eight months prior to his death. It seems like it was so long ago. You try to recover from the grief so you want time to go faster.*

As episodes at the bottom of the autobiographical memory system become more or less vivid, they advance to the present or retreat to the past. They do so in subjective memory time, not in objective calendar time. We may work bits of the calendar into our memory and experience some temporal fixity as a result. But there will always be occasions when we surprise ourselves with dreamy words like Clifford Pyncheon's, "Long ago, I suppose, very long ago. Or was it only yesterday?"

A Keeper of Archives, a Maker of Myth

It should not be surprising that autobiographical memories organize themselves in hierarchies. After all, the brain that contains these memories is showing itself to be organized, in part, in the same way. In the visual system, we know of cells at one level that recognize color, shape, and movement and cells at another that recognize what color, shape, and movement add up to—a face, for example. That's a kind of hierarchy. In the auditory system, we know of some cells that respond to pure tones and others, higher up, that respond to songs made up of those tones. Muscle movement is no different. There are "command" neurons that dictate the direction an entire limb takes, like the stretch to reach an approaching tennis ball, but not the contraction of particular muscles. The latter is the work of neurons further down the line. The more abstract or general a function, the greater the distance between the relevant neuron and eye, ear, or limb. Distance is measured in number of connections, and you need a lot to get to the top.

Face cells, song cells, and command neurons are about as high as scientists have gotten in their hierarchy climbing so far. There's a long way to go before they come in humans to cells of joy, cells of regret, cells of meaning, or cells of the self—the very pinnacle of autobiographical memory. And yet, work with split-brain patients may be pointing the way. This work is showing that there's a system of neuronal structures in the left hemisphere that monitors and synthesizes activity throughout the brain and tries to make sense of it. Psychologist Michael Gazzaniga calls the system the "interpreter."

A split-brain patient is someone who has had the nerve fibers connecting his two hemispheres severed in an attempt to control epileptic seizures. If you had a conversation with such a patient, you probably wouldn't notice anything out of the ordinary. But experiments by Gazzaniga and others have revealed things that are actually quite extraordinary. The experiments are based on the discovery that you can show a picture to one half of a split brain without the other half knowing about it. All you have to do is confine the picture to the left or right side of what the patient sees. Restrict a picture to the left visual field, for example, and it will be seen by the right hemisphere, and vice versa.

Suppose you were to show a picture of a chicken's foot in this way to the right hemisphere of a split-brain patient and ask him which of an array of pictures goes with it. You don't ask him to respond verbally, but simply to point to the picture with the hand the right hemisphere controls, which is the left. The patient will point to the picture of a chicken's head. Obviously: a chicken's head goes with its foot. You can do the same with the left hemisphere. Show the patient a picture of snow on the ground and he will point with his right hand to a picture of a snow shovel. No problem. It's as though the patient had two separate brains working simultaneously. *Almost* as though.

Things get interesting when the pictures of the chicken's foot and the snow are presented simultaneously, one to each hemisphere. Now you have the patient pointing to a chicken's head with his right hand and a snow shovel with his left—and wondering why. So you ask for a verbal interpretation: why do these things go together? A typical answer is, "The chicken foot goes with the chicken, and you need a shovel to clean out the chicken shed." What is noteworthy in the answer is the absence of the snow scene presented to the right hemisphere. That means it's the left hemisphere doing the interpreting. It knows about the chicken's foot, the chicken's head, and the shovel. (The patient can see both of his hands.) So it has to figure out how to weave these three into an explanation. Had the right hemisphere been the interpreter, you may have heard about finding a frozen chicken's head while shoveling snow. There'd be no reference to the foot.

The interpreter, then, is a maker of meaning. It uses language, but carefully designed experiments are showing that it's distinct from language. (Those patients who have some language capacity in their right hemisphere still interpret on the left side.) Despite its capacity to make meaning, however, it is premature to say that the interpreter is the new site of the Cartesian Theater. The interpreter is a system, not a single place. We do not know "where" nerve impulses become the subjective experience of consciousness, much less "where" the self resides, or even if "where" is the right question.

The interpreter works by night as well as by day. Every ninety minutes when we're asleep, it turns random bursts of brain activity into meaningful dreams. When the activity is in the visual system, we see scenes that shift, fade, and make sudden, bizarre combinations. If it's the vestibular system that's active, we experience something related to balance, perhaps the sensation of floating or spinning around. These random bursts of activity do not add up to dreams, however. Dreams include emotion and memory and meaning. The last is the work of the interpreter. Dreams, in this well-accepted neurological view, are brain activity in search of a good story, and it's the interpreter that provides it.

What concerns us who puzzle over memory is the psychological nature of the interpreter. What is the character of the self, the conscious representation of the interpreter, that is in charge of our autobiographical memory system? Is it a liar? A dupe? Or just plain sloppy? Is it an historian, a storyteller, or both?

After amassing a great deal of evidence, psychologist Anthony Greenwald concluded that when it comes to fashioning personal history, the self is a dictator, a "totalitarian ego." To begin with, he said, it's egocentric. Experiments have shown that people remember best their own contribution to a group effort and take more credit for the final product, if successful, than others in the group assign to them. People also overperceive themselves as the intended target of group action, just as leaders of nations often misconstrue the acts of other nations as intended to provoke them personally. Both as cause and effect, the totalitarian ego remembers itself as more central to events than it really was. It recalls the past "as if it were a drama in which [the] self was the leading player."

The self is biased in another way, says Greenwald. It remembers desirable outcomes, and being responsible for them, but not undesirable ones. In one study, Monday-morning college students said of their football team's victory on Saturday, "We won." But on Mondays after the team was defeated, students said, "They lost." I know that I remember every ill-advised tennis shot I've ever tried that proved to be a winner, all three of them. But I keep trying low-percentage shots because I've forgotten all the times I've hit the ball out. If I took the same approach to a slot machine, I'd be in deep trouble. Our willingness to disclaim responsibility for bad outcomes can go to humorous extremes. "The telephone pole was approaching," explained one driver to a police officer. "I was attempting to swerve out of its way when it struck my front end." Another driver, who had run a stop sign, said, "As I approached the intersection, a sign suddenly appeared in a place where a stop sign had never appeared before. I was unable to stop in time to avoid an accident."

Another memory distortion of the totalitarian ego is a kind of conservatism: the I-knew-it-all-along effect. It was demonstrated in an experiment in which subjects were given the correct answers to a test they were about to take. After completing the test, they overestimated their prior knowledge. "I knew the answers anyway," they said, but a control group proved otherwise. Any time we look back and discover a premonition that something was about to happen, we may be making the same distortion. How many premonitions have we forgotten once they failed to materialize? And how many prophecies have we revised after the fact? In a meeting with President Nixon, John Dean said of the Watergate coverup that "nothing is going to come crashing down to our surprise." That is what a hidden tape recorder revealed. But everything did come crashing down, and once it did Dean remembered just the opposite. His testimony nine months after the meeting was: "I also told him there was a long way to go before this matter would end and that I could certainly make no assurances that the day would not come when this matter would start to unravel." Hindsight revised his prophecy. In its conservatism, the totalitarian ego is like the politician who says she has *always* supported a position that has just recently proven to be popular.

But there's more to memory than distortion, more facets to the self than egocentrism. For one thing, it does a pretty fair job of monitoring what's "in there." Take what's called the feeling-of-knowing phenomenon. I've seen it torment students when they are taking tests. The students know that they know an answer— it's on the tip of their tongue—but they just can't think of it right now. They clench their fists, bounce in their chairs, look up to heaven, and even stare at me as if they could yank the answer that they know they know out of my head. Research shows that they're probably right about their intuition. Subjects with a strong conviction that a particular answer is "in there" come up with the answer more often than those with a weak conviction. And subjects who know they *don't* know something are usually right as well. Even when offered an extra incentive, they rarely produce the sought-after item. It's likely that a strong intuition about the presence of a memory leads us to search longer and harder for it, and a strong conviction about its absence leads us to give up. But more than motivation is involved. We have to give the self credit for being both vigilant and perceptive about what is going on in the hierarchy below.

Besides monitoring the presence of memories, the self also develops ways to judge their authenticity. It's not always deceived by the vividness of an image or the wealth of detail it contains. Is there something in your past that you wish were different? Take a moment to imagine it that way, making the fantasy as compelling and lifelike as possible. Now compare what you imagined with what you know to be true. How can you tell the two apart? Because of actual consequences in the present, said a young woman in a class of mine who was thinking of the death of her father. Because of what he remembers from the newspaper, said a former football player in the same class who had once stepped out of bounds on the eleven-yard line, nullifying a potential touchdown run. Because the imagined event violated a law of physics or some other kind of general knowledge, said subjects in a study that asked similar questions. The football player knew full well that the vividness of a memory was not the key. Long before I asked the question, he had scored that touchdown many times in imagination. In his mind, the fantasy was as clear as the reality, but he had no trouble distinguishing one from the other.

Not only does the self have ways of distinguishing fantasy from reality, it often goes to great lengths to do so. There are times when knowing what really happened in our life matters deeply, times when the fate of others depends on our knowing, times when we *must* know, even if it takes a lifetime to find out. So we consult external records, check our memories against those of others, and, if necessary, revise our mental pictures, if only by removing them from the category of "memory." And once we know the truth, we want never to deny it.

The puzzling nature of the remembering self stems from two opposing elements in its character. On the one hand, it has the temperament of a librarian, a keeper of memory's most important archives. It can be fastidious in that role, guarding its original records and trying to keep them pristine. The keeper of archives represents the conscience of memory, doing what memory is supposed to do, and trying to do it perfectly. Memory is supposed to distinguish between what is true and what is false, between fact and fantasy, between that which is authentically repressed and that which is artificially implanted. It is supposed to strive for accuracy and revise itself to conform to historical truth. Nor is this simply a matter of conscience. We humans have to stay in touch with the reality of the past in order to survive.

But memory's archivist by day has a secret passion by night: to fashion a story about itself, a story that some of us call the personal myth. A myth, in the sense that we use the term, is not a falsehood but a comprehensive view of reality, a different kind of reality than a librarian knows. A myth is a story that speaks to the heart as well as the mind, seeking to generate conviction about what it thinks is true. We think of myths as belonging to a culture, to a group of people. But there are also personal myths. When a myth is personal, it seeks to know the truth and generate conviction about the self, about who I am.

As a maker of myth, the self leaves its handiwork everywhere in memory. With the passing of time, the good guys in our lives get a little better and the bad guys a little worse. The speeds get faster, the fish get bigger, the Depression gets tougher. Things we did a few times as children we remember doing a lot of times as adults. Sometimes we say we "always" did them, always played the alphabet game on a family car trip, always got a dollar from our favorite uncle, always got thrown out of science class, always went to the same bar on Friday nights. Whether we loved it or hated it, it existed forever. All the distortions of memory, all the reconstructions, all the phantom implants—so out of place on a witness stand—appear in a different light when seen as narrative embellishments. Does the totalitarian ego put the self at the center of things? That's what storytellers do with their main characters. Does it put premonitions and prophecies where there were none? That's how storytellers get listeners to stick around for the ending. Such alterations are not the edicts of a dictator, but the signs of a mythmaker. They tell us who it is that's doing the remembering.

Nor is it merely narrative passion that explains the presence of myth. Once again, it is a matter of survival—the psychic survival of the self. A growing body of research now indicates that "positive illusion" is essential to mental health. The very kind of distortion that Greenwald attributed to the totalitarian ego has been found to characterize motivated, well-functioning individuals and to be missing from the thinking of those who suffer from depression. "Mastery-oriented" children who persevere in the face of challenging tasks remember their successes better than do helpless children, even when their performances are no different, and seem not to remember their failures. Adults with the same memory bias have overly positive self-evaluations, exaggerated perceptions of control, and unrealistic optimism. Less accurate than people who are depressed, they often create self-fulfilling prophecies that eventually lead to success. Even cancer patients adjust to their condition better if they believe they can personally prevent the disease from coming back. The key is "a belief in one's self as a competent, efficacious actor behaving in a world with a generally positive future," say researchers Shelley Taylor and Jonathon Brown. The key, in other words, is a life-affirming myth that gives the self strength as it looks to the future and interprets the past.

"I" and "Me"

When a woman described for me the very first memory of her life—it was of looking down a laundry chute—I asked her what she saw. She said, "I don't see the laundry chute. I see me." In the memory she was looking at herself from a position outside herself. Only a small minority of our memories adopt this visual perspective, but the system as a whole does something very similar. It creates a portrait of the self, something we can look at from the outside and say, "This is me and this is how I got to be the way I am." The remembering self, both as keeper of archives and as maker of myth, fashions a remembered self. *I* establishes *me*. When someone brought a video camera on our family vacation for the first time, an interesting schedule developed. During the day we water-skied, played volleyball, adopted stray animals, and—if we were teenagers—chased and beat up on each other. In the evening we gathered around a television set and watched tapes of those very activities. Each of us was an *I* (the remembering self, sitting on the crowded floor) watching *me* (the remembered self, on the television screen). That is how the adult autobiographical memory system works, with the self in the polar positions of subject and object.

What you see changes when you go from subject to object, just as it does when you stop water skiing, load up the VCR, and start watching yourself ski. When you're actually skiing, you focus on the situation you're in. You see the hecklers in the back of the boat, the wake, the slack in the towline, the approaching curve. But when you're watching yourself on the television screen, you focus on *you*. You notice your build, your style, the aggressiveness with which you attacked the curve, the abandon with which you flipped over. This is a standard finding in social psychological research: people actually participating in an experiment make "situational attributions" to explain their behavior. They look to outer circumstances. If they fail at a task, they say, "That assignment was too complicated." Observers of those very people, however, make "dispositional attributions" about what they see. They look to inner traits. If they watch someone fail, they say, "That person was too stupid." An actor on stage is aware of the situation: this is a play, this is a role, I'm following a script. But if he's good at what he does, those in the audience believe that *he* is heroic or villainous. They believe his actions flow from his inner self—from his disposition—which is why Leonard Nimoy of *Star Trek* had to write a book called *I Am Not Spock*.

As time passes, we become more like those watching a play. We see our memories, and ourselves, march before us on a stage. If you've ever been interviewed about your life, you know how much self-reflection the process can engender. The same is true if you've ever put your memories into writing. When you're finished with your work, your *I* literally sees *me* on the pages in your hand. As you think about those pages, you begin to make dispositional attributions. "I must have been shy, or quick-tempered, or selfish," you say. "A hero or a villain." You're speaking from the position of an outside observer. And you're putting a little more permanence, a touch more eternity, into your story.

The tendency to see more of one's inner traits as memory time goes by is known as the dispositional shift. In one experiment, it took only three weeks to appear. In another, college students were asked to write about their first day of elementary school, their first day of high school, and yesterday. The further back they went in time, the more they referred to inner traits rather than outer circumstances. They also concentrated their dispositional attributions in the beginning of their descriptions. When the autobiographies of seventy-seven psychologists were sampled in a third study, the dispositional shift appeared again, and it made no difference at all what the psychologists' theoretical positions were regarding inner versus outer determinants of behavior. Though dispositional attributions never outnumbered situational ones, they appeared most frequently in the beginning of the autobiographies, less frequently in the middle, and least frequently at the end. Not only are our oldest memories the ones with the most out-of-body perspectives, they are also the ones in which the dispositional shift is most evident.

In the next two chapters we will follow the development of *I* and *me,* the remembering self and the remembered self, from birth to adulthood. Here, let me conclude by saying that the work done by the autobiographical memory system—all the keeping of records and all the making of myth—is aimed at establishing the main character in our story. An older student once told me about a friend of his who had nearly drowned in a scuba-diving accident. Before he was rescued, there was a moment when the man actually thought he was going to die. He thought of the money he had wasted on the equipment rental, and then he thought of much more. "I've been a tightwad all my life," he said to himself, "and now I'm going to pay for it." At that instant the work of the autobiographical memory system came to a climax. All the events of one person's life had been turned into a single dispositional attribution and a single picture of the self.

∞

Chapter Five

MEMORY IN THE YOUNG

She is a woman who suffers from multiple personality disorder and she is speaking of a time when she had been locked in a closet by her abusive parents. Suddenly an "alter" emerges. It's Jill, a three-year-old, and she's terrified of the mice that are with her in the dark. "They were running around me, and I was afraid because they were running around me." We are drawn to her story, but something about her language seems odd. It's hard to pin down, but then you realize that despite the tiny, high-pitched voice, this is an adult speaking, not a child. There are none of the mispronunciations that are rampant in the speech of actual three-year-olds, no grammatical errors of the kind that small children routinely make, no "mouses" or missing parts of speech. What's happening is what usually happens when people, even normal people, are age-regressed through hypnosis. They feel like children, act as they think children would, but usually outperform children of the targeted age. Even though they may print like a six-year-old, for example, they often do so with perfect spelling.

This curious mix of past and present in memory raises an

intriguing question. Is it possible to use a technique—hypnosis, therapy, prayer, drugs, or something of the kind—to go back and recover "the child within"? Authors of a number of self-help books believe it is. In the bestseller *Homecoming: Reclaiming and Championing Your Inner Child,* John Bradshaw recommends a meditative tour back to the earliest stages of life. "See the beautiful infant you were. . . . Hear your voice as you coo, cry, laugh. . . . Imagine you could hold your cuddly little self. . . . Who else is there? . . . Your mom? . . . Your dad? . . . What does it *feel* like to be born in this house to these people?" In this part of the meditation, the adult self is looking at the infant self. In the next part, there's a switch of subjects and objects. "Now imagine you are that precious tiny infant looking out at all of this. . . . Look up at the grown-up you." Through the eyes of the baby you once were, you can look upon developmental wounds suffered in the first year of life. You can tell your adult self what you longed for at that time but never received. You can recover more of these infantile feelings if you write your adult self a letter. Do it with your non-dominant hand (your left, if you're right-handed; your right, if you're left-handed). That will help you feel more like a child:

Dear John,

I want you to come and get me.
I want to matter to someone.
I don't want to be alone.

> *Love,*
> *Little John*

The meditation is complete and memories in infancy repaired when the adult self responds: "Welcome to the world, I've been waiting for you. . . . I will not leave you, no matter what. . . . God smiled when you were born."

Some therapists believe we can go back in memory to the first few months of life, easily recovering "one incident after another."

One psychiatrist even claims that some of his patients have relived their own conception. He himself remembers his: the egg opened up in a gentle way and welcomed the sperm inside, as if the two had chosen each other. He also remembers his trip down the Fallopian tube, especially pausing at several places and holding off on further cell division before deciding to go on with life. The journey ended when he implanted himself in the lining of his mother's uterus.

Not to be outdone, psychiatrist Brian Weiss claims he has elicited memories of previous lives from patients. Under hypnosis, a woman of twenty-eight who was suffering from migraine headaches and pain in her jaw recalled a past life in which she lived in a cave in Greece. She died when a warrior speared her in the face, creating the same kind of pain she was presently experiencing. A man in his late thirties came to Weiss because he often flew into jealous rages when he thought his girl friend was flirting with other men. Taken on hypnotic regressions, he discovered that he had killed her for being unfaithful in a number of previous lives. Under hypnosis, backache sufferers recall being lanced in the back during medieval battles; obese people remember dying of starvation in concentration camps. Many of Weiss's patients find their symptoms are alleviated after recovering these ancient memories.

All of these memories, whether they go back to infancy, conception, or a previous life, tell of legendary places where the self began. They are the work of the mythmaker, not the keeper of archives. The kind of mythmaking involved, a kind in which we all engage, is the subject of later chapters. Here the focus is different, the work preliminary. We're going to follow the development of autobiographical memory from the beginning of life to its end. Then we'll be in a position to see whether we really can back up and reexperience not just the content but the perspective of a previous stage. That, after all, is the essence of "recovering"— seeing with the eyes (the *I*, really) of a child.

Only recently have psychology and related sciences brought a life span perspective to subjects like memory. Even more recent is an interest in narrative, which is an essential feature of the kind of memory we call autobiographical. The emerging picture is rather simple. In the course of life we change thinking caps, and each time we lose what cannot be transferred from one cap to another. Some theorists speak of a given change as if it were the repro-gramming of a computer—one disk in, another out—but I like to think of it as a smaller river flowing into a larger one. When that happens, the water it bears becomes part of the new mix. As adults, we carry the contents of earlier stages, but we cannot swim upstream and reenter a tributary, no more than we can reverse the flow of life itself.

Infancy: A Stream Is Born

When in life does memory begin, and where? Not in the Fallopi-an tube, either at conception or a few days later when the fertil-ized egg is traveling down to the uterus. At that point in our development, no neurons have been formed that could possibly make a record of these events. But near the end of pregnancy things have changed. The auditory system is developed enough to hear, and sound waves can enter the fluid that surrounds the fetus. The sound is not as muffled as you might think. Microphones placed in the womb can register the sound of voices over the thumping of the mother's heart, well enough to tell the difference between men and women.

But how does one determine whether a fetus *remembers* any of the sounds it hears? Developmental psychologists Anthony DeCasper and Melanie Spence had mothers-to-be read aloud to their unborn babies twice each day during the last six weeks of their pregnancy. The passage was always the same: a three-minute excerpt from Dr. Seuss's tale *The Cat in the Hat*. When the babies were three days old, a pacifier connected to a tape recorder was placed in their mouth. Vigorous sucking kept a tape of the familiar story playing, but weak sucking brought on a tape of their mother reading an unfamiliar one. Babies seemed to remember the sound patterns of the familiar story. At least they adjusted their sucking to keep it playing, something that newborns never exposed to the prenatal story failed to do.

Experiments like this, and work with premature babies as well, make it clear that we humans come into the world with a rudimentary form of recognition memory. Newborns "tell" psychologists about it in a number of ways. After no more than twelve hours of direct contact with their mothers, they suck more rapidly on a pacifier to hear a recording of her voice, rather than that of an unfamiliar woman. Or they suck more slowly, if that's what the experimenter wants. Within two weeks of birth, babies can also recognize their mother's smell, at least if nursing puts them in close contact with her skin. To show this, researchers put a baby in a crib and place next to its cheek a gauze pad that had been kept in its mother's bra or under her arm. Next to the other cheek they place a pad from some other woman. Breast-fed babies usually turn in the direction of their mother's pad. Bottle-fed babies, who have not experienced the same close skin contact, do not.

Newborns can also retain sights in memory—checkerboard patterns, for example—and it doesn't take them long to recognize visually what they've experienced through touch. This sensory crossover is really quite spectacular. At three weeks, infants can be blindfolded and given a nipple with a distinctive shape, one they have neither seen nor touched before. After they suck on it for a while, experimenters remove it, take off the blindfold, and place the nipple next to another that is completely novel. The babies spend much more time looking at the nipple they had just been sucking. It seems as though they abstract from the touching mode enough of the nipple's shape to recognize it in the visual mode—a tough trick at any age.

But more is to come. At two months, babies can recognize situations well enough to act with intention. In one series of experiments, a mobile is placed above a baby's crib and a ribbon hung from it. When the ribbon is connected to the baby's ankle, she quickly discovers that vigorous kicking sets the figures swinging. Two-month-olds remember the contingency for a few days, three-month-olds for a week; as soon as the ribbon is tied to their ankle, they smile and begin to kick again. These babies are highly dependent on context, however, much more than the scuba divers who did a better job remembering what they learned underwater when they were again underwater. If the babies are tested in a different crib, or with different bumper pads, or if a few of the figures on the mobile are changed, their retention is almost completely disrupted. They seem unable to screen out irrelevant stimuli.

By the time infants are six or seven months old, recognition starts to make a lasting difference. Instead of smiling at strangers the way they do at family, babies now grow uncomfortable and may even cry. The ability to distinguish a familiar face from a foreign one sets the stage for forming a lasting attachment to mothers and fathers. At ten months, recognition memories are already forming a hierarchy. After viewing fourteen different faces for a period of five seconds each, babies this age treated a generic face derived from the fourteen as if it were familiar, even though they had never seen it before. They looked at the composite for a shorter period of time than they did a novel face, which is what they typically do with something to which they've grown accustomed. In an experiment that used schematics, ten-month-olds did a better job of remembering a generic animal than they did the original eight from which it was averaged. Even younger infants will create generic memories if the stimuli are simple enough.

None of these infant memories are autobiographical, however. For that babies must be able to recall events, not simply recognize them. They must also be able to put them into words and relate them to a self. Recall comes first: there is sketchy evidence for it at six months, much better evidence at nine. If you put a toy in front of a five-month-old, then cover it with a cloth, he will lose all interest in it. But a seven-month-old will search for it under the cloth, at least if he is not made to wait before doing so. Recall is clearly present when an infant imitates someone else after that person has stopped performing an action. In one study, nine-month-olds were able to do so after a delay of twenty-four hours, fourteen-month-olds after a week.

The test of the fourteen-month-olds illustrates the rigor of these studies. Each of them arrived at the laboratory with its mother and sat on her lap next to the experimenter. In front of them was a little table. One by one, the experimenter reached under his seat for half a dozen toys, did something distinctive with each, and repeated his action two more times. One of the toys was a little box with a translucent orange top. The experimenter set it on the table, leaned forward, and touched it with the top of his forehead. That turned on a light bulb inside the box and lit up the orange cover. When the babies were brought back to the lab a week later, eight of twelve leaned forward to touch the top of the box with their forehead. Of twenty-four babies in two control conditions, none made a similar move. Since the babies in the experimental condition had not been allowed to touch the toys on their first visit, they must have remembered what they were shown, not (as in the ribbon-and-mobile experiment) what they did. This was a solid test of imitation and solid proof of recall.

Besides recall, something else is needed for autobiographical memory—a sense of self. Babies are born without one. They possess neither *I* nor *me,* neither the self-as-subject nor the self-as-object. The *I* is the first to develop. In the beginning, infants have no idea where their bodies end and where the world begins, no notion of themselves as separate individuals who can make things happen. But gradually they learn about the regularities of the world, about the connection between their actions "in here" and what happens "out there." They move muscles "in here" and discover something "out there"—a touch, a voice, a mouthful of warm milk, figures on a mobile that dance. But sensations also appear "out there" on their own, with no corresponding movement on their part. These provide babies with a critical clue. Slowly they separate the internal from the external, drawing a line between *I* and the rest of the world. A self-as-subject comes into being. When is the line clear, the self born? It's impossible to say because the process is so gradual, but the schedule is close to that for recall: some evidence at six months, much more at nine.

The traditional demonstration of a baby's awareness of *me,* the self-as-object, involves some red rouge. Experimenters hand a mother a cloth with the rouge on it and have her wipe her baby's nose, leaving a smudge that the baby is unaware of. The mother then places her child in front of a large mirror that rests on the floor. Before they are a year old, babies seem incapable of connecting the red nose in the mirror with themselves. If they're intrigued by it, they pat the mirror, as if the person there were another child. Starting at fifteen months, however, a few babies realize that it's their nose that has the red spot and they reach not for the mirror but for their own face. By their second birthday, about three-quarters of the babies that are tested do so. Now they know who it is they're looking at in a mirror. They can also watch a videotape of themselves and say, "That's Clare" or "That's me." They can do the same with pictures in a scrapbook. Though they're far from being able to reflect on themselves in a *mental* mirror, they do have an *I* that can see *me.*

What humans are able to remember during their infancy should not obscure all that they forget. Many kinds of events that will register in just a few years never enter memory in the first place. Those that do rarely last very long; their life is so brief that they never seem to leave the "present" to become part of the "past." Many animals are as oblivious as we. Rats, whose brain is immature at birth, remember little in their early days, while guinea pigs, whose brain is well developed, remember a great deal. We humans are notoriously immature at birth. Our brains have all the nerve cells they will ever have, but those cells still need a lot of work. They have to be coated with a fatty insulation known as myelin, and most of them still need to be hooked up with each other. The work takes especially long in the hippocampus, which is vital to the long-term establishment of autobiographical memory. The hippocampus is probably not fully functional until the age of four or five.

Long before the hippocampus is ready for extensive long-term storage, however, another biological development brings an end to infancy. In the second half of the second year a language switch seems to come on in the brain. It closes the period of "not speaking," which is the literal meaning of the Latin *infans*. Though infants have used single words before this time, they now start producing original word combinations: "Daddy shoe," "milk allgone," "kitty falled," "car road," "many dirts." The combinations mark the beginning of truly human speech. (Some animals use the equivalent of single words but do not use grammatical rules to put them together.) Now language explodes, and all that babies remember will soon be saturated with words.

Childhood: Into the River of Language

> Car broke,
> The—Emmy can't go in the car.
> Go in green car.
> No. Emmy go in the car
> Broken. Broken. Their car broken,
> so Mommy Daddy go in their their car,
> Emmy Daddy go in the car,
> Emmy Daddy Mommy go in the car, broke,
> Da . . . da car . . .
> their, their car broken.

The speaker is Emily, a twenty-one-month old who is quite advanced in her language development. She has a habit of talking to herself in her crib before she goes to sleep, and her parents have just started to record her soliloquies. Right now they're out of the room and the record button is on:

> *So my Daddy went in the meeting in, in the, in the car.*
> *So Emmy put the [circles] in the, [w-] in the way.*
> *Daddy stop it, in the [circles] over there,*
> *Emmy put over there,*
> *So car broke,*
> *Car [name],*
> *Car broken,*
> *So have to go in the green car,*
> *The—then, green car broken,*
> *So my go to nap.*

Here is a wonderful snapshot of memory that has just flowed into language. Two months before, one of the cars belonging to Emily's family was being repaired, and she had to go to school in a different one. Now she speaks of the incident and refers it to herself. Did she originally store the event without the benefit of language and only later acquire the words to speak of it? We can't tell, but such a thing has been known to happen. It's also possible that Emily's parents talked about the repair some time after it happened, and that she is reproducing bits of their conversation. Whatever the personal and social mechanisms of preservation, Emily can now remember, "Car broke." Her soliloquy about the incident is not always coherent or consistent. Sometimes it's the green car that's broken, sometimes it's not. There are intrusions into the main theme—references to circles, for example. There is no time line in her account, but rather a good deal of recycling and rephrasing. Emily's words do not hang together as narrative, but it's clear what she is referring to.

Emily's parents were assisting developmentalist Katherine Nelson in her investigation of early childhood memory. Nelson was excited about this snippet of monologue, but she was just as enthralled by another one. It appeared at about the same age, twenty-one months:

Mormor says no,
So why my kids go sleep, my,
Mormor say night, have go sleep,
So why, uh, so why my k-, have to go sleep.
I can't go sleep.

In this segment Emily is trying to figure out the sleeping and waking routines in her life, what normally happens as opposed to what happened on a particular occasion. (Mormor, her grandmother, often puts her to bed.) Emily's working on a script, just like the ones adults have for going to restaurants. Though its form is embryonic, the script indicates that Emily is operating on more than one level of a memory hierarchy. In her first year she was capable of both generic and specific recognition, and now she proves herself capable of both generic and specific recall.

As Emily's already stunning use of words expanded, so did her memory for scripts. Just three months after she began to work on the rules for sleeping and waking, she put a whole day in proper sequence, even though some details were incorrect. She had just turned two:

I can't go down the basement with jamas on. I sleep with jamas.
Okay sleep with jamas. In the night time my only put big girl pants
on. But in the morning we put jamas on. . . . But, and the morning
gets up . . . of the room. But afternoon my wake up and play . . . play
with mommy, daddy.

At two years and eight months, Emily anticipated her normal Friday routine before going to sleep on a Thursday night. The excerpt below, amazing in itself, covers only the first half of the day, and it is entirely correct:

Tomorrow, when we wake up from bed, first me and Daddy and Mommy, you, eat breakfast . . . eat breakfast, like we usually do, and then we're going to p-l-a-y, and then soon as daddy comes, Carl's going to come over, and then we're going to play a little while, and then Carl and Emily are both going down the car with somebody, and we're going to ride to nursery school, and then we when we get there, we're all going to get out of the car, go in to nursery school, and Daddy's going to give us kisses, then go, and then say, and then we will say good bye, then he's going to work, and we're going to play at nursery school. Won't that be funny?

The scripts in a child's mind show that in the beginning of life memory is about the future more than it is the past. Children want some way of anticipating what will happen, some way of predicting and controlling it. So they focus on regularities in meals, bedtime, baths, trips to the day-care center or the doctor's. They learn what to do at McDonald's (order a Big Mac, pay for it, and eat it) or at a birthday party (give presents, sing "happy birthday," have cake and ice cream, and play games). The scripts they create will shape what they remember and introduce distortions, just as they do for adults. When children retrieve a memory of a particular birthday party, they may add some things that didn't happen (the birthday cake that was thrown at another party) and leave out some things that did (the game of ringtoss).

Emily was far ahead of the typical schedule for the development of language and scripts. At two years and eight months, she rattled off a typical-Friday script with over fifty elements in proper sequence. The norm for three-year-olds is four to eight elements. But no matter what an individual's schedule, the length and complexity of her scripts will grow over time, as these samples of cookie making illustrate:

Well, you bake them and eat them.

—A three-year-old

My mommy puts chocolate chips inside the cookies. Then ya put 'em in the oven. . . . Then we take them out, put them on the table and eat them.

—A four-year-old

Add three cups of butter . . . add three lumps of butter . . . two cups of sugar, one cup of flour. Mix it up . . . knead it. Get it in a pan, put it in the oven. Bake it . . . set it up to 30. Take it out and it'll be cookies.

—A six-year-old

First, you need a bowl, a bowl, and you need about two eggs and chocolate chips and an egg-beater! And then you gotta crack the egg open and put it in a bowl and ya gotta get the chips and mix it together. And you put it in a stove for about 5 or 10 minutes, and then you have cookies. Than ya eat them!

—An eight-year-old

In her bedtime talks Emily hardly mentioned unique events such as Christmas and the birth of her baby brother, but she went over and over her routines. This is typical of most children and an intriguing phenomenon. In the very first stages of memory development, youngsters focus on the general at the expense of the specific. Knowing the regularities of life is just that important. One two-year-old who had learned the sequence of dinner-bath-bedtime became distressed one evening when her routine was upset. She was bathed before dinner and thought she wasn't going to be fed. Once scripts begin to stabilize, children can monitor and accept variations in them. Emily's early recollection of the family car being broken is an example. She is really puzzling over a variation: why aren't we going in the car that we normally go in? In a way, then, scripts become hooks on which children hang their memories of specific events. They help children comprehend these events and provide the background against which unique events, like a trip to the zoo, stand out. Without a framework of generic memories, we may not have specific ones.

Once the language switch is on, and it normally is by the age of two, the narrative switch is ready to go. On the heels of words come the first attempts to put the components of an event in chronological order. In fact, an instinctive sensitivity to order probably predates language. In any case, children do rather quickly what Emily did: begin to talk about the past and the future. In the first half of their third year, they typically do so in conversations with parents, who actually teach them how to remember and how to narrate what they do remember. In the second half, they are less dependent on adults. By the age of three many children can produce event narratives on their own. They have trouble fashioning make-believe stories, and will find that difficult for several more years, but they can pass on real accounts from their life. Several months before her third birthday, Emily had gone on a shopping trip with her mother, and she had manipulated her into buying a doll she wanted. Later, she spoke of what happened:

> *We bought a baby . . . cause . . . the, well, because, . . . when she, well, we thought it was for Christmas, but when we went to the s-s-store we didn't have our jacket on, but I saw some dolly and I yelled at my mother and said "I want one of those dolly." So after we were finished with the store, we went over to the dolly and she bought me one.*

This brief account builds to a climax ("I yelled at my mother and said, 'I want one of those dolly'") and then resolves it. Much more typical of three- and four-year-olds' stories is leapfrogging, a structure in which the narrative jumps from one event to another and often leaves certain parts to be inferred by the listener. The following rendition of an accident was made by a girl of three years and eight months in response to an interviewer's questions. She goes from a sister's broken arm to her own spanking and then back to the broken arm, which is in a cast at one moment, out of it the next, back in, and then back out:

GIRL: *My sister had, she's had [to have a cast on]. She broke a arm when she fell in those mini-bike. She broke her arm. She had, she went to the doctor, so I, My dad gave me spanking, and I . . .*
INTERVIEWER: *Your dad gave you what?*
GIRL: *A spanking to me.*
INTERVIEWER: *A spanking?*
GIRL: *Yeah, and she had to go to the doctor to get a cast on. She had to go get it, get it off and, and it didn't break again.*
INTERVIEWER: *And then it didn't break again?*
GIRL: *No. She still got it off. She can't play anymore. . . . She can't play we, she can play rest of us now.*
INTERVIEWER: *Oh good. . . .*
GIRL: *Mm, she has cast on. When she was home, When she came back and she, and she, and she hadda go back and take off the cast.*

Though individual children vary a great deal, the norm for the onset of autobiographical memory is normally between the ages of three and four. All the pieces are in place by that time. A self has been present since the end of infancy, and now it has a vague intuition that its thoughts are private and not transparent to others. Also in existence is a simple hierarchy that includes both generic and specific recollections. By three or four, the hierarchy has been penetrated with enough language that children can put their recollections into a primitive narrative. Their autobiographical memory will go through significant transitions in the ensuing years, but by this age all the components are present.

For memories to be considered autobiographical, one more thing is necessary: they have to be capable of lasting a lifetime, or at least to the age when people put together a life story. This is simply a matter of definition, an autobiography being the story of a life. None of Emily's memories, remarkable though they are, meet this final criterion. Even though some of them lasted for months, none survived to her seventh birthday, at least none that researchers could elicit. Most adults are like Emily in this regard. They can

retrieve no memories from before the age of three or four, a phenomenon called infantile or sometimes childhood amnesia.

After their fourth birthday, children's memories and their narrative abilities continue to grow. In a study of over 1,000 oral narratives told by close to 100 chldren, Carole Peterson and Allyssa
McCabe found that five-year-olds were becoming more confident
of their chronology but still ending most of their narratives before
they were resolved. At six, they understood climax and resolution
and were adjusting their stories accordingly. They were also doing
a much better job of orienting listeners to who, what, where, and
when. Between five and seven, the incidence of "complete
episodes of motivated behavior" increased dramatically in these
children's accounts.

The children in Peterson and McCabe's study were all white.
When researcher Sarah Michaels observed both middle-class
white and working-class black children relating experiences during "sharing time" in elementary school, she noticed a difference
in the typical narrative structure they used. The white children
told short, concise stories with a clear beginning, middle, and
end. Black students tended to juxtapose anecdotes that were the-
matically linked; their stories were longer and included shifts in
time, place, and key characters. Teachers recognized the white
story structure but not the black, and they steered students in the
direction of the former. What Michaels observed was the tendency of the schools of a dominant culture to homogenize the diverse
narrative traditions that enter them.

Throughout the school years children's memories are shaped
by the narrative style espoused by their culture. Their experiences
are grafted onto the meanings and markers of that culture. As they
learn how to read and write, they discover new mechanisms and
new models of memory. They learn a calendar of events, historical
and mythical, on which they can pin their memories. When a
first-grader asked his mother, "What's April?" she corrected him:
"You mean, *when's* April?" "No," he insisted, *"what's* April?" Sep-

tember, he explained, was starting school, October was Halloween, November was Thanksgiving, December was Christmas, January was going back to school, February was Valentine's Day, March was St. Patrick's Day. So what was April? Must be Easter, said his mother. This is just an inkling of what happens when a young memory is swept into the collective memory of a culture, be it national, ethnic, religious, or all three combined.

How accurate are children's memories? The question is critical because more and more youngsters are being asked to testify about secret acts, often sexual, perpetrated on them by adults. As I write these words, local newspapers are following two separate cases of children between the ages of three and eleven who say they were sexually assaulted by Sunday-school teachers. In one of the cases, many of the charges had to be dismissed by the judge because she could not qualify preschool-aged children as witnesses. In the other, the sole accuser, an older boy, eventually confessed that he had fabricated his story because he was angry at his teacher and wanted some attention from his mother. These are some of the extremes that the legal system has to work with.

Recently there's been an outpouring of research on the eyewitness testimony of children. Though the research can never tell us what actually happened in a particular case, some general themes are emerging. The first is that children's memories seem to respond in a unique way to trauma. Adults who survive catastrophes like tornadoes, airplane crashes, fires—even in one case the collapse of a hotel skywalk—often show significant memory impairment. They experience either partial or total amnesia for the event or recurrent unbidden recollections—too little memory or too much. Children suffer the emotional consequences of such catastrophes, but their memories seem unaffected. No problems in recollection were found, for example, among children exposed to lightning strikes or an especially traumatic kidnapping. Even children under three who were not able to verbalize their memories of trauma did reenact aspects of them in games. They showed whatever signs they could of remembering. Among children, it appears to be *chronic* exposure to trauma, not single instances of it, that lead to memory impairments such as dissociation.

Accuracy is a different matter. A second theme emerging from the research is that preschoolers are usually more suggestible than older children and adults and because of it make less reliable witnesses. One of the reasons is that they have a harder time keeping track of the sources of their memories, so they claim to remember seeing things they were only told about. With only a rudimentary sense of a private self, they also have trouble believing that they know anything that an adult questioner doesn't already know. Then too, they are more affected than older children by the manner of their questioner. In a recent study, three- and four-year-olds were interviewed about receiving shots at a medical clinic, a mildly stressful event. Half were questioned by a warm, supportive interviewer who gave them juice and cookies and half by an interviewer who remained distant and unsmiling. All were asked leading questions such as, "She touched your bottom, didn't she?" or "How many times did she kiss you?" The three- and four-year-olds were twice as inaccurate in their replies with the intimidating interviewer as they were with the one who built rapport. Older children, five to seven years of age, were unaffected by the style of their interrogator. They generally knew that they had not been hit or kissed, that their clothes had not been removed, and that that their bottoms had not been touched. It took ideal conditions of support for the younger children to do as well.

A third general finding is that young children are more likely to make errors of omission than errors of commission when first being questioned about sensitive events. Their reports will be incomplete rather than inaccurate. Preschoolers in one research investigation were told by an interviewer that it was naughty for adults to kiss them while their clothes were off. They were then asked to report if they were ever kissed while being bathed. Not surprisingly, they said no when in fact they had been—an error of omission. To get young children to include in their reports what they would otherwise omit, you have to ask very specific questions. But being specific introduces an old problem. It increases the risk of implanting false memories and creating false accusations—errors of commission. And children are more susceptible to this kind of contamination than are adults.

A fourth theme from contemporary research is that repeated questioning gives children, as it does adults, more opportunity to speculate when they really don't know an answer. In an actual case of abuse, there will be plenty of questioners—family members, police, nurses, social workers, psychologists, attorneys, and perhaps others. Some of them will be shocked; some will be outraged; and some will have a particular agenda that motivates them, consciously or not, to influence the child's memory. If children speculate in response to such influence, repetition of their story will given them confidence in what they say, just as it will adults. When they finally get to a witness stand months or even years after an alleged incident, that confidence will be quite convincing to juries, even if it has no basis in fact.

Recommendations for obtaining accurate reports from children are not that different from those for adults. From the very beginning, interviews about an incident would have to be free of intimidation and free of suggestion. In each, the child would have to be encouraged to tell his or her story in free narrative form, without interruption, before being asked about specifics. The trouble is that it is very difficult to maintain ideal interviewing conditions from the time of an incident to the time of a trial. And child molesters are well aware of the difficulty. They often target the youngest of children precisely because their testimony will not be admissible in court.

As children get older they become less suggestible as witnesses because their autobiographical memory becomes more independent of the adults who originally shaped it with language. Not only do children learn the many uses of memory—understanding what's going on in a strange new world, fitting into a family and a culture, getting what you want ("But you promised, remember?")—they also learn that they're supposed to tell the truth. All these developments take place as the self at the top of the autobiographical memory system, both the *I* and the *me,* becomes established in a whole new way. Let's see what happens.

"I" and "Me" Together

By the age of five, the brain has attained 90 percent of its adult size, even though the body, at 40 percent, lags far behind. The hippocampus, which is vital to the establishment of long-term autobiographical memories, is fully operational. These neurological developments set the stage for cognitive changes so dramatic that theorists like Jean Piaget claimed they produced a new thinking cap, a qualitatively different way of seeing the world. Others disagreed: it was the same *kind* of thinking cap, only bigger, with more "information-processing capacity." However you picture it (I'm partial to the idea that it's a new cap), the change is recognized around the world. Across many cultures, perhaps across all, there is a consistent pattern of children taking on adult-like responsibilities between the ages of five and seven. They are now trusted to carry messages across hilly fields from one village to another or to go alone to the store for small purchases. They begin preparing meals or taking care of very young children. They are given responsibility for the cattle, driving them long distances, supervising their grazing, and keeping them out of the crops. They go to school. English Common Law assumes that by the age of seven children have a working knowledge of right and wrong and may be tried for a crime. Catholic Canon Law operates on the same timetable: seven is the beginning of the "age of reason," when children become capable of sin and confession.

The mental transition that enables children to take on new responsibilities can be illustrated by one of the famous "conservation" experiments of Jean Piaget. If you pour some liquid from a short fat glass into a tall skinny one, preschoolers believe that the amount of liquid suddenly expands. Why? "It's higher," the children say, pointing to the level of the water in the glass. If you then pour the liquid back into the short fat glass, the children now believe there's less of it. Why? "It's lower." Preschoolers do not realize that the amount of liquid stays the same—is "conserved"—because they focus on the changing height of the liquid and fail to notice the corresponding changes in width. Older children can monitor both height *and* width, two dimensions at the same time. They realize that the quantity of liquid stays the same no matter what the shape of its container.

The ability to grasp two aspects of a situation affects much in the lives of children. Three- and four-year-olds do not distinguish their own emotions (one aspect) from those of someone else (a second aspect). Ask one with a toothache if it hurts, and she may say, "Yes, can't you feel it?" Children this young believe that the things that make them sad are the very things that make grownups sad, like not being able to stay up and watch their favorite show on television. Older children realize that someone else's emotions can be different from their own, that two sets of feelings can coexist. I can be sad and you can be mad at the same time. Two cognitive perspectives can also exist simultaneously. When I asked a five-and-a-half-year-old if she had any brothers or sisters, she replied, "I have a sister, Stephanie." "Does Stephanie have a sister?" I asked. "Nope." Another girl had a brother named Brendan, and Brendan had nine fish, two hamsters, and a cat—but no sisters. These children could not see themselves from the perspective of someone else. Older children could. They realized that you can be a sister to me *and* I can be a brother to you.

The new thinking cap that enables children to see two points of view at once makes them more competent storytellers, for they can now monitor the reactions of both themselves and their audience. It also has a profound effect on the self at the top of the autobiographical memory system. The typical six-year-old, says developmentalist Susan Harter, does not have the capacity for self-awareness. Though he has been recognizing pictures of himself since he was two, his *I* cannot see *me* in a mental sense. Nor can he see himself as others do. But as he acquires the ability to take another's perspective, he learns to see himself as someone else would. "I am a brother to my brother." He discovers that others have unique emotional reactions to him, and he begins to see the *me* that they do. The self that is an object of observation to them becomes an object of observation to him.

You can tell that *I,* the self-as-subject, is starting to observe *me,* the self-as-object, when children become self-critical. In the first grade, at age six, children are able to find fault with others but not with themselves. Three years later, at age nine, they are also criticizing themselves. Before, they checked out other children only to make certain that no one was taking advantage of them, that no one was getting more holiday presents or a bigger piece of birthday cake. But now they compare themselves for purposes of self-evaluation. They notice whether they read better than their classmates, solve problems more quickly, hit balls farther, or run faster. When they stack themselves up against other children, they can be quite harsh on themselves, tossing off remarks such as "Am I ever dumb!"

When Harter asked children what the words "ashamed" and "proud" meant, she caught another glimpse of the mental *me* in the making. Children between five and seven focused on how others could be ashamed or proud of them. "My mom was ashamed of me for doing something I wasn't supposed to do," they said, or "Dad was proud of me when I took out the trash." They were aware of another's perspective but had yet to internalize it. At eight they were responding differently. "When you throw milk at someone, the next day you're ashamed *of yourself,*" or "Like when you pass a test or do a good deed, you feel proud *of yourself.*" First

I see the perspective of someone else toward me and and then I see myself.

As children internalize outside perspectives, they begin to do what outside observers do: make dispositional attributions. Earlier, they described themselves in terms of physical characteristics. They were tall or short, black or white, boy or girl, five or six years old. They could run fast or slow. By the age of nine they are going beneath the surface and saying they are shy or friendly, lazy or hard-working, loud or quiet, quick or slow to lose their temper. And they are seeing these inner traits as enduring. They conserve them the way they conserve the amount of water in glasses of different sizes. Five years before, they weren't even sure that their gender would stay the same; they even thought that kids might turn into animals. But to nine-year-olds, even something as abstract as honesty can be a constant, a lasting disposition that is part of one's personality.

And so what happened in the second year of life in front of a physical mirror repeats itself in the ninth or tenth in front of a mental mirror. The self-as-subject starts to see the self-as-object. It would be fascinating to know if some memories flip into an out-of-body perspective at this age, but the relevant research has not been done. A missing detail, however, should not detract from the broader significance of a major development in autobiographical memory. With a mirror in its mind, the self is now in a position to interpret itself. It is moments away from the time when it can write its first life story.

Adolescence: Wider Waters—and the Story of a Life

Right now I'm looking at a little book called *My Story*. It's four pages long, handwritten with ink from a fountain pen. The cover of the book is made of thick green paper that's faded with time. The title's in black crayon. So are the curved lines on the spine that are supposed to make the book look like a Harvard classic. The author's picture is right on the cover, a happy-looking kid about twelve years old, hair combed, shirt and tie—not a hint of puberty anywhere. *My Story* was written for a school assignment over forty years ago, and the kid in the picture is me.

It's interesting to look back on an author just before the beginning of adolescence. Page one: introduction and birth, the move to our new apartment, and the birth of my younger sister. I was "disgusted" it was a girl. (Sorry, Mary.) Page two: the beginning of school. When I got to fifth grade, the story notes, I felt like I was on top of the world. "Well, I was on top of the first grade anyway." (Architecturally, this was true at St. Margaret Mary's, so this must be an attempt at humor.) Then comes some nun-pleasing stuff on becoming an altar boy and getting confirmed, and then on page three we get to what we've all been waiting for, the story of "the first really big fish I caught."

This fish devours the entire second half of my autobiography. We begin by setting the scene. It's summer vacation; my father, my older sister, and I are fishing for bluegills; and I'm practically falling asleep in the boat. Then I feel a tug on my line. Pretty soon the "old boy" is almost breaking my rod in two, but I still manage to land him. It's a northern pike, but (the climax) is he big enough to keep? Turn the page and . . . yes, just barely, and good-bye reader, that's the end of *My Story*.

At the age of twelve, half of my "autobiography" came from a minute of my life. The truth of the matter is that in the twilight before adolescence I could barely conceive of autobiography. The story *of* my life was mainly a single story *from* my life.

If you've ever canoed a river, you can appreciate what happened to my mind in the years that followed. On a river you may find yourself rounding a bend in a forest without knowing what lies immediately ahead. All of a sudden the vista expands: you've entered a lake. On all sides, the shoreline recedes, and you see before you perspectives longer and wider than any you've ever

imagined. You experience the dramatic cognitive changes of adolescence, and yet, because so much else is going on in your life,
you barely notice.

Other people fail to notice too. But as the change comes to
completion, they look at you and notice a new interiority, saying
that you've acquired "depth." That's the view from the outside.
From the inside, "depth" is "height," a view of your life from the
air rather than the ground. You now have a vantage point that
enables you to see how discrete episodes in your life interconnect,
how stories *from* a life become the story *of* a life. You can also think
about your own thinking. You can say, "That's not the way things
are; it's only the way I've been looking at them." With the new
thinking cap of adolescence, we all become potential biographers
of the self—a self with beginning, middle, and end.

What's behind this new thinking cap? Many psychologists
believe that it has to do with an increased capacity for information
processing—more working memory, if you will. Adolescents can
pull knowledge out of memory and compare it with other knowledge much faster than children. Relevant information springs so
quickly to mind that they have more mental energy to spread
around. Their thinking is more sophisticated because they have
extra attention to focus on the task at hand, just as a personal
computer with two megabytes of working memory can "think"
rings around a computer with only one megabyte.

The change in their conceptual apparatus frees adolescents
from the concrete and allows them to explore an abstract world of
possibility. Psychologists can demonstrate the change with a simple experiment using poker chips of various colors. The experiment begins when the psychologist tells the young person seated
across from her that she is going to say several things about the
poker chips. The youngster is to decide whether the statements
are true or false, or whether there's no way to tell. Then the psychologist picks up a chip that the youngster can't see, hides it in
her hand, and says, "Either the chip in my hand is red *or* it is not

red." Ten-year-olds look at the closed fist and say they can't tell. But adolescents say, "True." They know that the question has nothing to do with the visibility of the chips and everything to do with the logic of the words. If the psychologist now conceals another chip and says, "The chip in my hand is red *and* it is not red," ten-year-olds still focus on what is visible. They say, "I can't tell." And again adolescents respond to the unseen logic of the statement and say, "False."

The younger children in this experiment stand on the solid ground of reality and see what *is*. Adolescents soar into the realm of the hypothetical and see what *could be*. The new ability of teenagers to think about the possible opens the door for them to the world of ideals. They experience their first "crush," attributing ideals of beauty, intelligence, and compassion to some unattainable lover. They imagine the ideal parent, usually a composite of whatever they like in their friends' parents, and realize how deficient their own mothers and fathers are in comparison. Suddenly a parent who had always seemed powerful, good, and even perfect now seems unable to walk, talk, dress, or eat properly. Adolescents also envision the perfect world, one without hunger, war, or injustice, and say of the one they're in, "It doesn't have to be this way."

Nor do *they* have to be this way. With their newfound ability to consider possibilities, teenagers can ask, "What if *I* were different?" Now they turn to the principal psychological task of adolescence, which is forming an identity. We often answer the question "Who am I?" with a list of characteristics. But it can be answered just as well with a story, the story of a life.

A student of mine once spent many hours interviewing a high-school sophomore in order to piece together his life story. The *me* in the story, at least the one that a fifteen-year-old boy wanted to show to the world, was both a wild man and a ladies' man. His story was a paean to both themes, a grade-by-grade litany of achievements. In preschool, he and and a friend beat up a fat girl because she always got to the tree house first. In kindergarten, he and another friend would force Jason Myers to give them his pretzels. In first grade, he was always raising his hand to go to the bathroom. The teacher wanted his bladder checked, but his mother knew better. In second grade, he had to go to the principal for screaming in front of Denise Scott that someone has just kicked him in the balls. He even got to say it again for the principal—and show her where his balls were. In third grade, he stole the stars the teacher gave out as awards and tried to cash them in for treats. Most students cashed in five or six at a time; he walked up with 120. In fourth grade, he placed a thumbtack straight up on Mike Heston's chair. When Mike jumped up you could see the tack sticking in his butt. In fifth grade, he had to cool it because the teacher wouldn't stand for his nonsense. She happened to be his mother. In sixth grade, though, he was back to his old self, getting suspended for breaking into Jennifer Eccles's locker. Seventh and eighth grades he just blew off, like totally. In ninth grade, the stakes were higher. He started to steal chewing tobacco and shoplift shoes and clothes.

That was the wild man. The ladies' man was born in kindergarten, where he met Denise, the first love of his life. He liked her for a couple of years and even protected her from the (other) school terrorists, but she never paid any attention to him. In third grade, his friend Ronnie sent him a secret note with his Apple Jacks decoder. The note said, "I want to have babies with Angela Woodward." The next year he got interested in Angela and impressed her by getting the tack stuck in Mike Heston's butt. In fifth grade, a year before he broke into her locker, he had an ongoing relationship with Jennifer Eccles, although they never talked to each other. The entire affair was conducted through a mutual friend who regularly asked him if he still liked her and her if she still liked him. In seventh grade, on January 14, 1987, on a freezing Wednesday night with the snow blowing, he kissed Linda Jones behind the school. At the end of the year they broke up. When he got the letter that dumped him, "I was like, dang, I could've gone to soccer camp!"

The names in this real-life version of television's *The Wonder Years* have been changed, but you get the idea. In early adolescence autobiographical memories continue to have a social use—here, they entertain—but they also acquire a personal use. They begin to answer the question "Who am I?" with the descripton of an identity. This fifteen-year-old's was one for public consumption.

There is a private side to identity as well. Early stories of the self, such as those found in adolescent diaries, often contain mythic elements that psychologist David Elkind calls the Personal Fable. The Personal Fable is a positive illusion that reflects the young person's belief that her experiences are of universal significance. No one has ever experienced the world the way she has. No one has seen what she's seen or done what she's done. No one is destined for the greatness or the tragedy that she is. When she loves, she loves with her whole being; and when her love is unrequited, she is destroyed. How could anyone, a parent in particular, understand? For all its melodrama, the Personal Fable is a prelude to serious identity formation. It represents an impulse toward uniqueness, telling the young person how special and different she is. Although it is a story full of fantasy, later versions will become more realistic.

Later versions will also be given a background of belief and value, what psychologist Dan McAdams describes as an ideological context. Between fifteen and nineteen, he says, we are preoccupied with coming up with answers to fundamental questions about right and wrong, about relationships among people, about God. We want to get our ideology squared away. During these years you can almost see ideological context moving into a teenager's room. Gradually the rock, sitcom, and sports stars whose pictures cover the walls are replaced by abstract symbols of good and evil, by posters with slogans like "Dream the Dream" or "Follow Your Bliss," even by poetry and lengthy philosophical discourses. Gradually, the intimate surround of the young person's life changes.

The ideological context of one's autobiography will provide higher levels of meaning for the autobiographical memory system. Earlier, children thought about social institutions in terms closer to the ground. To them, "law" was the police officer or the judge, whose purpose was to punish. "Government" was the governor or the president or buildings or highways. "Education" was the teacher, "religion" the preacher. By late adolescence, however, young people are thinking abstractly about social institutions. They can understand the laws and conventions that hold societies together and appreciate the hopes and ideals they embody. They can take moral and religious positions that are their own, not their parents'. Doing so, they form a new relationship with the people they identify as their own.

In early adulthood, the Personal Fable will become what developmentalist Daniel Levinson calls the Dream. It's a more realistic vision of ourselves in the adult world. A young man may see himself as a great artist or a star athlete, a business tycoon or a superb craftsman—some kind of hero performing magnificent feats and receiving special honors. He may also see himself as the father of a family or a highly respected member of his community. A young woman's Dream is more likely to be "split," giving equal play to the competing demands of occupation and family. Not everyone entering adulthood has a Dream, says Levinson, but those who articulate one generally do better than those who do not. The Dream gives expression to our identity and energy to our plans, but it also enables us to separate in an emotional sense from our family of origin. With it we can say, "It's my life, not my parents'."

When we first put our memories together in the wide waters of adolescence, we first put ourselves together. Integrated memories give us an identity—a sense of personal stability over time, a *me* that stays the same. By the end of our teen years, our autobiographical memory system is as tall as an adult's. It has all the layers that an adult system has, and the *I* that presides over it can reflect on itself with depth as well as breadth. The content of the system will change over the years, sometimes dramatically, and so will its perspective on time, but its basic structure will evolve no further. Any *My Story*s written in the future will be true autobiographies, not stories *from* a life, but stories *of* a life.

The Adult-erated Child

Let us now return to this chapter's original question. Once the autobiographical memory system is fully grown, can it still see the way a child would? Can it recover the child within?

People who suffer from multiple personality disorder, or MPD, recover the child within in very convincing ways. That child may be one of a number of hidden personalities, or "alters," who come to the surface from time to time, speaking in different voices, having different brain wave patterns, requiring different eyeglass prescriptions, having different chemical compositions in their urine, and responding differently to the same medication. Despite these compelling signs of genuineness, however, there is a nagging puzzle about MPD. It stems from abuse in childhood, yet hidden personalites are rarely found in children. They present themselves, rather, in adulthood. Data from a recent survey of all of Switzerland's psychiatrists are illustrative. The average age of patients being treated in that country for multiple personality was thirty-eight; the range, fourteen to seventy-four.

Age is part of a larger puzzle. Thirty-nine percent of the psychiatrists in the Swiss study *had never heard* of multiple personality disorder! The reason is that they didn't need to know: outside of

North America, the condition is exceedingly rare and almost nonexistent. MPD has also had an irregular history. Though scattered cases were reported early in the nineteenth century, it was not recognized as a medical concept until 1875, in France, where it was called "double personality." Interest in it waxed and waned over the ensuing decades, with the next significant event being the case of "Eve," which was popularized in the United States first as a book and then a movie. But Eve was considered to be an isolated case. In 1968, when the American Psychiatric Association (APA) published the second edition of its taxonomy of mental disorders, the so-called *DSM-II,* multiple personality was not included. Then in 1973 came the case of "Sybil," which was also published as a book and a movie. Interest in multiple personality skyrocketed. In 1980 MPD was recognized in *DSM-III,* the third edition of APA's taxonomy. In 1982, the number of cases that were appearing was said to constitute an "epidemic." Six years later the journal *Dissociation* was launched to help respond to it.

The vagaries of this history have led some to argue that the phenomenon of many personalities inhabiting the same individual isn't real, that it's a creation of clients and therapists. Skeptics note that the number of personalities being discovered in any one person seems to be growing. Therapists are multiplying the multiples, so to speak, to the point where cases of over 100 alters in a single individual are now being reported. And patients seem to be able to make faster transitions from one personality to another, flipping back and forth as easily as they might switch television programs with a remote-control device.

It's clear that hidden personalities can be implanted through suggestion. "How many of you are in there?" a therapist might say. "I want you all to be listening, even though you haven't declared yourself." This seems to have happened in the case of California's "Hillside Strangler," Kenneth Bianchi, who revealed an alter during the course of hypnosis:

HYPNOTIST: *I've talked a bit to Ken, but I think that perhaps there might be another part of Ken that I haven't talked to, another part that maybe feels somewhat differently from the part that I've talked to. . . . Would you talk with me, Part, by saying "I'm here"?*

Bianchi answered "yes," and the hypnotist followed up:

HYPNOTIST: *Part, are you the same thing as Ken, or are you different in any way?*
BIANCHI: *I'm not him.*
HYPNOTIST: *You're not him? Who are you? Do you have a name?*
BIANCHI: *Steve. You can call me Steve.*

Steve went on to say that it was he who had murdered the women for whose death Ken was on trial. His hypnotist believed his was a genuine case of multiple personality, but others specialists disagreed. One thought Bianchi was consciously faking in order to save his skin. Another thought the creation was unconscious but very recent, probably occurring during the hypnosis. Bianchi was eventually convicted of murder.

Whatever advantage or recognition MPD might bring a patient or therapist, the suffering that leads to it is quite real. In nearly all cases, it is physical, sexual, or emotional trauma in childhood. Horrendous, uncontrollable assaults on one's very being lead to extreme attempts to distance oneself from the agony. This is what is meant by dissociation. One woman reported that when she was eleven years old, she would deliberately induce anesthesia in her hands to avoid the pain inflicted by an incestuous stepfather. She remembered "looking straight into his eyes and holding her breath so that this time she wouldn't cry, telling herself not to feel her hand." Dissociation is rarely so deliberate but every bit as real.

But why does dissociation in children not take the form of multiple personality? One reason, as we have seen, is that children's memories respond differently than adults' to trauma. It's also possible—remotely—that some children do have hidden personalities, and that therapists are not yet knowledgeable enough to uncover them. It's more likely that traumatized children have not yet been exposed to MPD models in the media and have not yet learned this way of channeling dissociation. (We now know that the famous Sybil had done extensive reading on MPD before it was diagnosed in her.) But I think something else is going on: a dissociated element in a child's mind simply may not take on a separate identity until that time in life when identities are constructed. That time is adolesence. Unable to create a single identity with a single voice, teenaged and adult sufferers create many identities with many voices.

Although the resulting construction is clearly culture-bound, it is not necessarily fake. The physical changes that accompany the emergence of alters are quite real. But when a three-year-old child suddenly appears in a thirty-three-year-old adult, we cannot assume that the child has been hiding out for thirty years. She may have been born just last week.

The timing factors involved in the construction of multiple personalities shed light on the broader question of the "child within." Is this child, or any other earlier self, discovered in memory? Or is it created? Does it date from childhood or adulthood? To answer these questions, we can compare the memories that adults have of childhood with the ones that children do. Do the memories that adults have contain visual perspectives impossible to children? Are there anachronisms, the voice and eyes of later stages imposed on the memory of earlier ones? Is there an understanding of language or narrative that is too advanced? There are few hard-and-fast rules, but there are some general guidelines.

Let's begin with memory claims that reach back farther than infancy, farther than birth, farther even than conception. What are we to make of recollections from previous lives? Many such recollections come when people who believe in reincarnation are hypnotized. The memories they produce are rich in detail but full of logical problems. For example, too many individuals claim to have been someone famous in the past, not someone commonplace. Too many, in fact, claim to have been the same famous person. The person they remember being is normally of the same race as themselves, unless they have been cued that different races were common. In addition, rememberers do not know things they should have known in their previous life, things anyone at that time and place would have known, such as who was the ruler of their country or whether the country was at war. It has not been difficult to discredit remembrances from previous lives, which is not to deny that some people have been helped by believing in them.

Memories from the womb are equally suspect. Only the most primitive kind of recognition memory exists at birth, and it is far from the kind of recall that is presumed in accounts of prenatal memory. We should also exclude from the realm of possibility the recall of events from the first half-year after birth. If babies up to six months show no evidence of recall (as opposed to recognition), why would adults gain the capacity in retrospect? I have run into a few people who say they remember being taken home from the hospital as a newborn or being passed around as a small baby from one relative to another. These are visual memories, but there's always something off about the pictures. The baby in the memory may take for granted that he is separate from the adults holding him. He usually recognizes the faces of his mother and father, and even some of the relatives. In adult memories of the first six months of life, the remembering and remembered selves are nearly always too old for the memory in question. The *I* is taken from a more advanced stage of development and projected backward in time.

Nor is it hard to find something that's off about memories from later in infancy. In them there may be an out-of-body perspective that's not true to original experience. The eye level of the viewer may be too high for an infant who has begun to toddle around.

The infant may be doing something beyond her years, like understanding adult conversation, or in some cases understanding language at all. Flashbulb memories of historical events often show these characteristics. "My first memory was the day President Kennedy was shot," said a young woman. "I was only eighteen months old, but I remember my mother saying, 'Oh my God, the president's been shot!' There was shock and pain in her voice." What's off about this memory is clear: understanding adult words and emotions, grasping concepts such as "president," and appreciating historical significance are all anachronistic. They are beyond the capacity of an eighteen-month-old. I once thought I remembered hearing on the radio about the Japanese attack on Pearl Harbor. I had a clear picture of myself on someone's lap in the front seat of a car, going over a bridge in Evanston, Illinois. But then I calculated that I was only twenty months old at the time, so I started asking around. Now I attribute the memory to cryptomnesia. I probably heard about the incident at a later age, created a picture of it in my mind, and then forgot that I was told.

The most credible adult memories of infancy that I've encountered are those of the Russian memorist Shereshevskii, which were recorded in his middle age by the psychologist Alexander Luria. Here is an example in which Shereshevskii describes an early sense of his mother:

Up to the time I began to recognize her, it was simply a feeling—"This is good." No form, no face, just something bending over me, from which good would come. . . . Seeing my mother was like looking at something through the lens of a camera. At first you can't make anything out, just a round cloudy spot . . . then a face appears, then its features become sharper.

My mother picks me up. I don't see her hands. All I have is a sense that after the blur appears, something is going to happen to me. They are picking me up. Now I see their hands. I feel something both pleasant and unpleasant. . . . It must have been that when they wiped me, they did it kind of roughly, and it didn't feel good. . . . I'm scared, I cry, and the sound of my own crying only makes me cry harder. . . . Even then I understood that after "this" feeling there would be noise, then stillness. Right after that I could feel a pendulum, a rocking back and forth. . . .

From somewhat later, Shereshevskii describes an experience of wetting the bed:

First a pleasant feeling, a feeling of warmth, then of cold, then something that doesn't feel very good, it burns. I start to cry. . . . They didn't punish me. . . . I remember one time—it was when I slept in the bed with my mother, but I'd already learned how to climb out. I remember Mother pointing to a spot on the bed. I can hear her voice. Most likely I could only babble then. . . .

There is no way, of course, of verifying the details in these memories. It's their *quality* that stands out. Years later, working quite independently, researcher Daniel Stern described an inner world of infancy that was amazingly similar to Shereshevskii's. His description was based on the direct study of babies. The most striking similarity was synesthesia, that sensory mix in which sound, taste, touch, and feel are not yet distinct from one another. About what he assumed was a smallpox vaccination, Shereshevskii remembered "seeing a mass of fog, then of colors. I know this means there was noise, most likely a conversation or something like that." Babies, said Stern, experience the world precisely this way. They sense patches of sunlight that pull like a magnet, bars on a crib that sing in harmony, hunger that sounds like an approaching storm, milk that cools like water on a fire. In the diffuse world of early infancy "memory" isn't separate from anything else. An image from the past simply lives in the present with a different kind of life.

What Shereshevskii remembered of his infancy seems to have

bypassed the river of language. Or, rather, it seems to have maintained its special character within that river, as if it were a time capsule bobbing along on the surface. Those of us who are not Shereshevskiis find that our earliest memories lose their character once they are saturated with language. Tiny fragments may survive—smells, tastes, sounds, feelings in the body—but they become part of something larger and something later. Other than that, there is no memory of infancy. There are influences from our first years, to be sure—the temperament we're born with, marks left by illness or accident, the particular social environment of our family—but it would be wrong to call every kind of influence a memory.

In the movie *Look Who's Talking*, actor Bruce Willis draws a lot of laughs by dubbing his voice over shots of a fetus and later a baby at various stages of development. The fetus says, "Hey, yo, let's get a little apple juice down here," and soon the mother-to-be is drinking apple juice. Seconds after his birth, the baby is screaming, "Help! Help! Put me back in! Buddy, let go of my head and put me back in!" The doctor does not oblige. As he grows, the baby turns out to be a wisecracker who's smarter than the adults taking care of him. There's no pretense in the film: the experience of infancy is clearly adult-erated. That's what makes it so funny. It's also what makes it a fine metaphor for what happens when adults remember their infancy. In all such memories we have to look at who's talking. Ninety-nine percent of the time, it's the adult.

When it comes to memories of early childhood, it pays to look not only at who's talking but also at how he's telling the story. In a study conducted by developmental psychologist Allyssa McCabe and her colleagues, only 12 percent of four-year-olds created classical narratives in which a story was built to a climax and then resolved. In a related study of adolescents looking back to their earliest years, over 50 percent did so. Adolescents also projected back into early childhood an understanding of multiple perspective that they didn't have at the time. Here is one of them recalling the thoughts and feelings of an entire family:

I can remember a Christmas time when we didn't have much money. And I can remember wanting a Christmas tree, and my parents were real upset about not getting a tree. And then my dad came in and tried to walk through the door pretending like he had this huge tree and he had this little bitty tiny tree, and everybody was so happy, you know. It's just the thought behind it. But I can remember everyone, you know, teasing him and everything. Well my mom was mad about it. She thought that he was, you know, making fun of Christmas, you know, bringing home something like that when we all wanted a big tree, but we were all happy with the tree we got.

The dad was pretending and trying to do his best, the kids were teasing and loving it, the mother was mad—all at the same time. An adolescent can understand that multiple perspectives can coexist, but a young child cannot. McCabe's research has shown that when adults remember childhood incidents the narrative structure of their remembrances comes from adulthood, not childhood. There is a "voice of experience" blended into the account. Sometimes there are specific references to the age difference between then and now, sometimes an awareness of a changed physical perspective. Once we learn to narrate events in chronological order, to build in climax and resolution, to take multiple perspectives, we can no longer *not* do so—unless, of course, we are deliberately trying to imitate children. We have simply forgotten a previous storytelling perspective.

The conservation experiments of Jean Piaget illustrate as well as anything I know how difficult, if not impossible, it is to recover the eyes of a child. Whenever I tell a class about them for the first time, the students are astonished. Pour liquid from a short, fat glass into a tall skinny one and the child really believes there's more of it? It's a revelation. Yet why should it be? Not that long ago those students believed exactly what the children in the experiments do. The students had simply lost touch with a previous perspective. Our forgetting of former *I*'s is what makes the world of the child seem ever fresh. In the early days of television, it's what made Art Linkletter's interviews with children so charming. It's what makes children's art so appealing. It's why we have an entire field of child psychology. Unable to remember what we once thought as children, we explore childhood as if it were virginal land.

As adults it's easier to recover the eyes of adolescence, and especially late adolescence, than it is those of children. We are, after all, operating with the same autobiographical memory system. I can connect up rather easily with some of the feelings I had in high school, with the interiority and love of solitude, with the fascination I had with psychiatry. Some of these feelings seem so recent that they could be mine today. Yet I find it much harder to reach the "inside" I experienced when I was wearing the thinking cap of a child.

To say that our memories of infancy and childhood are adulterated does not mean that the events they depict did not happen. Nor does it mean that the memories are unimportant. Far from it. The very distance of early memories summons the presence of myth, inviting the kind of truth it tells. So does the mystery of prenatal life. But in this chapter and the next we are giving the keeper of archives its due, advocating skepticism and using the strictest standards of evidence. The mythmaker's time will come later, after we have completed our journey through the stages of life.

Chapter Six

MEMORY IN THE MATURE

In the first two decades of our life, we acquire the mental tools that enable us to write our story. In the years that follow, it's no longer the tools that change but the story we tell. We go through adulthood like artists, continually painting over the portrait of ourselves that we first made in adolescence. In centuries past, painters literally did just that. Changing their mind about what was on a canvas, they would cover a tree, say, with the figure of a woman, a body of water with dry land. Sometimes they would paint an entirely new composition over an old one. The change was called "pentimento," because the artists had "repented" of their earlier work. When they were done, the new portrait looked like an original. It looked like it had always been there, the only one on the canvas.

Memory's repentances come about when the course of our adult life changes. Some psychologists who study human development believe these changes are highly predictable. Daniel Levinson, for example, thought that transitions came to everyone between the ages of seventeen and twenty-two, twenty-eight and

161

thirty-three, and forty and forty-five. The most tumultuous of the three transitions was the last, which involved the fact that our life was half over and perhaps not turning out as we had wished. Levinson called it the Midlife Transition; it's been popularized as the midlife crisis. Research other than Levinson's suggests that it isn't men alone who experience difficulty during these years. When nearly 100 women originally studied in their college days were contacted again in their early forties, they too were found to be in a period of turmoil. Ten years later, they were more sure of who they were, more confident and decisive. Their lives had stabilized.

Findings such as these support the idea of a normative timetable to the life cycle. But other social scientists stress the importance of nonnormative events that make life unpredictable. These are happenings we have no control over or no way of anticipating: a war, an economic depression, a natural disaster, a plant closing, an injury, a spouse walking out. Good things come unannouced as well: you accidentally meet someone who changes the course of your life, you stumble into a rare business opportunity, you win the lottery. Studies of the impact of these changes have led one researcher to conclude that no more than one person in ten experiences a genuine midlife crisis.

Whether predictable or not, the changes in our lives lead to changes in our memory. On one occasion sociologists tracked down more than 300 men and women whose early lives had been so disturbed that they'd received treatment at a child-guidance clinic. They found that those who were still troubled tended to remember their early emotional problems, but those who were now well adjusted had great difficulty recalling them. In a kind of pentimento, they had painted one life story over another.

Nothing reveals more clearly how thoroughly an old story is forgotten once it is covered over than the way people use the word "always." I first became aware of it when I was editing transcripts of interviews I had conducted. During the actual interviews I hadn't even noticed the word, but going over written copies of what people had said, I saw it everywhere. In fact, I was constantly crossing it out. Old folks and young, rich and poor, formally educated and not, individuals from every ethnic tradition and walk of life: people always said "always."

What was behind this bit of forever? Most of the time, a generic memory. "Always" was another way of saying what a person "would" or "used to" do. My mother-in-law always complained about her life, our family always chopped down its own Christmas tree, the grandchildren always spilled food at the dinner table, and so on. "Never" was the occasional flip side of regularities like these, as in "My father always promised to take us to a restaurant after a movie, but he never did." Sometimes the generic memory behind "always" was from higher up in the hierarchy, closer to the self: "I always got blamed for what my sister did." On occasion, when I could verify that "always" was really a very few times, I knew that the mythmaker was creating a remembrance to keep especially close to the self (the swim we always took to the island on summer vacations) or one to push away (the times you always cheated me).

Often the generic memory involved in "always" stretched into the present. It denoted an unpleasant situation that had gone on far too long, as in the case of part-time students who felt they'd been going to school forever. Or it referred to an enduring disposition of the self, something that *I* saw in *me*. "I have always planned my life," said an older woman. When researchers are able to check on the accuracy of such statements, they find them deficient. They caution us that it is very difficult to remember how we once saw the world, to recover accurate records of what we used to believe—even as adults. Usually we err by projecting our present thinking backward. In 1973, respondents in one survey indicated their attitudes on such issues as welfare spending, affirmative action, and marijuana penalties. In 1982 they were again asked about these topics and also requested to recall what they had said nine years before. What they remembered of 1973 was more closely related to their attitudes in 1982 than to their actual attitudes in 1973. In another survey, respondents were asked for their political affiliation—Republican, Democrat, or Independent—in 1972 and again in 1976, at which time they were also asked to recall what they had said earlier. Of those who actually changed in the four intervening years, 91 percent reported *not* changing! In memory, they had "always" been Republican or Democrat or Independent.

The same effect has been found in studies in which people are recalling income level, substance use, personal traits, and even the level of headache pain. In line with the previously discussed conservatism bias (or I-knew-it-all-along effect), we alter the past to make it more similar to the present. Psychologist Michael Ross says that we operate under a presumption of continuity when reconstructing our personal histories. If we believe it now, we believed it then. Or, as developmentalist George Vaillant has put it, once a caterpillar becomes a butterfly, it doesn't remember being a caterpillar; it remembers being a little butterfly.

Vaillant's illustration points to the most important use of the word "always." Sometimes our life changes so dramatically that we seem to become someone else. A new self emerges, and "always" plays a role in giving it roots. I began to glimpse this function by analyzing descriptions of time seeming longer than it actually was. The rememberers weren't saying "always" just yet, but they were getting there. Their descriptions centered on feelings of comfort in a new living arrangement or relationship. "We bought our home just five years ago, yet it seems we've been living here for twenty." "It seems as if I've known my boyfriend for years, when in fact I met him only six months ago. We've talked a lot, and I just feel like I've known him forever." When my adopted daughter My-Linh arrived on a plane from Vietnam at the age of three, she didn't know a word of English. A few years later she looked at a picture of the arrival scene and made up a little story. In it, she gets off the plane and says, "Hi, Mom. Hi, Dad. I'm going to stay here forever."

It is easy to see the significance of "always" in cases like these. The feeling of forever is a mythical expression of a truth about our sense of ourselves and our place on earth. We're like the various oceanic peoples who, in the course of their history, have moved from one island to another. Without the benefit of written records, many of these people come to believe after three or four generations that their ancestors originated on the island where they presently live. We are as permanent here, their collective memory says, as the sun and moon are in the sky. When a new self arrives in the course of life, we want to make it equally lasting. So we begin to think that it was always there, if only in a dormant state, waiting to be awakened. The new self seems uncannily old.

A forty-five-year-old woman, well on the road to recovery from alcoholism, told me that sobriety had been in her even during her darkest days. She could look back and see that a better self had always been there:

As I got sicker and sicker something in me had been saying you can do better. Something was saying alcoholics are not bad people. I remembered my grandpa drinking and cursing, but he wasn't a bad person. He was very thoughtful and very responsible. Part of me was saying I'm not my best person when I drink but I'm not a bad person.

"I was a piece of coal, but I had a diamond inside," said another woman, looking back on a troubled life. She discovered a new self after she had returned to college and realized how intelligent she was—how intelligent, in fact, she had always been. "I've always loved books," she said. From her new island she gained a fresh perspective. She came to believe that she had possessed a special talent, a "gathering potential," all along:

From every book, even a trash book, I got something. I learned how to spell a word or learned the meaning of a new word. I enlarged my vocabulary or found out there was a place called Capri. For a long time there were questions like, what is the meaning of life? Why am I

*here? If this is so horrible, why can't I croak? Believe it or not, I was
gathering in those years too.*

Establishing continuity and permanence for a new self isn't the
work of the mythmaker alone. Knowing of external records that
can be checked, some of us put memory's keeper of archives to
work. This is the statement of a thirty-five-year-old gay man who
came out eight years ago:

*I've got a high school journal downstairs. I just found it a few years
ago. Some of the details I'd forgotten though I did have a memory
that I had written, "I think I am a homosexual." There was this very
awkward language about how I had a date with Mary and it was time
for me to at least put my arm around her and I would try very hard to
do it, because you were supposed to. I was really madly in love with a
friend called Robert. I spent all the time I could with him, and I
described this in the journal.*

*When I was home in the spring I hunted up my high school year-
book, and there were two things in it that really leapt out at me. One
was from the teacher I was closest to. She wrote, "I have been pleased
at the value you place on three of your friendships. I think it indicates
the kind of person you are." That's ambiguous, but they all would
have to have been male friendships. I thought she knew something she
wasn't saying. The other comment was from Robert, who wrote a long
thing that included something like, "It's been so good being close to
you and having all this time with you. I feel I know you like a book
from cover to cover except that most pages are blank."*

He had "always" been a homosexual and now he had external
proof. Here is a case where history joins myth in establishing a
new identity.

But something else must be done to memories when we experience a new self. The old one must be cast off, as far away as possible—painted over, if you will. Some of the distancing is done

through backward telescoping, by making old-self memories seem as though they were from "a thousand years" or a "lifetime" ago, or even "from someone else's life." "Was that even me?" asked several Vietnam War veterans looking back on pictures of themselves in uniform. But we establish distance without a telescope too, by accentuating the contrast between past and present. Some years ago, I compared a sample of fifty young adults who were raised Catholic and who were still in the church with a closely matched sample of fifty who had left. Both groups had had sixteen full years of parochial education, from elementary school through college. When I asked them to think back to the end of their childhood and recall how important it was at that time for them to be Catholic, I found a contrast effect. Those who were now *out* of the church said it had been more important than those who were still *in*. They had magnified the difference between then and now. Those who had maintained their religious identity showed continuity in their ratings.

In memory research, contrast effects appear less frequently than continuity effects. When contrast does appear, there is normally a clear indication to the rememberer that he or she is now different. They were soldiers then but civilians now; Catholics then, ex-Catholics now. Or, in a fascinating study by Michael Ross and his colleagues, menstruating then but between periods now. Ross had women record in a diary their level of distress during a menstrual period and then recall that level two weeks later. Those who reported especially severe symptoms exhibited the contrast effect. Once they were free of discomfort, they overestimated its prior level.

Self-improvement programs convey the message that we ought to be different at the end than at the beginning, and similar effects have been found as people remember them. In a study of a pain management program, patients made ratings of their discomfort before beginning treatment. At the end of the program, after they *ought* to have changed, they amplified their estimates of initial pain. Exactly the same thing occurred in research on a study-skills improvement program. At the end participants overestimated how awful their skills were in the beginning. Such are the effects of concluding that one should have changed as the result of an improvement program.

We also conclude that we ought to have changed, either for better or for worse, simply as the result of growing older. In one longitudinal study, personal adjustment scores were obtained for subjects at the ages of twenty and forty-five. The scores remained quite stable over the twenty-five-year interval, but at forty-five subjects remembered being more poorly adjusted at twenty than they actually were. It was a contrast effect: I'm twenty-five years older, I ought to be more mature. In another study, respondents whose actual age was sixty-seven rated themselves as being healthier and having a better memory at thirty-eight than did a comparison group of thirty-eight-year-olds. Here the contrast effect went in the other direction: I've gotten a lot older, so I must be worse off.

Continuity and contrast effects are inevitable as adults paint over portions of their life story. Once in a great while, something else might happen too. As oil paint ages, it sometimes becomes transparent. Then old colors and contours that were once completely covered bleed through to the surface. A tree appears through the woman's dress that once hid it. A boat comes out on dry land. In memory too, old conceptions occasionally seep through to consciousness. Maybe you're visiting a home you haven't been to in decades. For a few moments you actually remember what you were thinking at the time you lived there, how you approached life, what your dominant concerns were. You open a time capsule like those that Shereshevskii seems to have carried from infancy. The experience may not last, and the contents of the capsule will surely change as they are exposed to the fresh air, but for a brief moment you will have seen yourself as you once were—even recovered someone within.

Middle Age and the Hill of Reminiscence

The idea of painting your life story on a canvas is a metaphor, but one scientific study took it quite literally. Researchers Susan Whitbourne and Dale Dannefer had adults of various ages "draw" their life. The subjects took a blank piece of paper, laid it down horizontally, and drew a line that represented the ups and downs they had experienced. Then they marked the line off into various segments to represent stages—grade school, high school, the Navy, family life, and so on. Whitbourne and Dannefer measured the amount of space given to each segment and divided by the number of years it represented. Proportionately, which stage of life claimed the most space? For subjects under forty, the odds were fifty-fifty that it was the present one. For subjects over forty, the odds were far less. The period to which they gave the most space was more likely to be in the past. Subjects in both groups maintained this temporal distribution of memories when a follow-up was done a year later—unless they had experienced a significant life change. In that case, they devoted more space to the present.

Though it's limited in scope, this study addresses an interesting question about autobiographical memory: what part of our lives do we remember best? We can't possibly recall everything that ever happened to us, every hour of every day of every year. So when we think of our life as a whole, to what stages do our thoughts instinctively turn?

Whitbourne and Dannefer's life-drawing method suggests that the answer depends on the current age of the rememberer. So does an approach known as the cue-word method. This method goes back over 100 years to Sir Francis Galton, who is better known for his innovations in statistical analysis and his obsession with measuring psychological traits. Galton's memory technique is akin to Freudian free association. Subjects are given a cue word—*window,* for example. They then report a memory that the word triggers. After several dozen cues are presented, subjects go back and date each remembered incident as closely as possible. You can try it yourself. Common cue words are *avenue, box, coin, flower, game, mountain, picture, storm, ticket,* and *yard.*

When memories are dated in this fashion and averaged across a number of subjects, an interesting pattern emerges. Piecing together the results of half a dozen studies, researcher David Rubin found that twenty-year-olds produce a high proportion of very recent memories and relatively few from the distant past. Thirty-year-olds aren't much different, once you allow for the fact that they are looking back on an additional decade of life. In general, the responses of both age groups fit the normal "forgetting curve." This curve looks like a slope for expert skiers. Most of our memories are of recent events, particularly those of the last few days. Then there is a rapid decline in retention until a point is reached where forgetting becomes more gradual: we've lost most of what we're going to lose. At this point the forgetting curve turns into a gentle slope that carries us back to the age of three or four, where we experience the dropoff of childhood amnesia.

All age groups show the same forgetting curve, but only in the second half of life does something else appear. Responding to the same cue words as younger people, subjects in their fifties and seventies (the only other age groups for which cue-word data are available) report a disproportionate number of memories from the early years, especially the second and third decades of life. This bonus of memories forms an extra hill at the bottom of the forgetting slope, just before the dropoff of infantile amnesia. Rubin called the hill "reminiscence," something over and above normal remembering.

The cue-word method for apportioning autobiographical memories may seem a bit artificial, and a lot depends on how you set up the experiments, but I have found that the results fit a surprising number of lifestorytellers. In some of them, the hill of reminiscence covers experiences even before the second decade of life. It goes back to somewhere between five and seven, when a string of continuous episodes, not just isolated fragments, can first be found in adult memories.

What is it about middle age that makes a hill out of our early-life memories? One factor may be the growing amount of content stored in memory and the corresponding need for condensation. Condensation seems to follow the so-called serial position effect: we remember what comes first and last in a series and forget what comes in the middle. Read these ten nonsense syllables out loud and in order. Do it just once, slowly: GAZ, YAT, FEX, WAB, NIF, SIZ, BOQ, PAZ, RUK, KIB. Now repeat the list from memory and see if what you remember does not come from the beginning and end of the list. The normal forgetting curve augmented by the hill of reminiscence shows the same serial position effect. The years middle-agers remember best are the ones early in life and the ones that have occurred most recently. The ones in between all run together. When researchers asked college students for a sample of autobiographical memories from the past year or two, they found that a large number of recollections came from the end of school terms, a smaller number from the beginning, and fewest of all from the middle. Within each term there was a for-getting curve and a hill of reminiscence.

The years that form our lifetime hill of reminiscence are also the ones in which novel events are concentrated. This is the peri-od of our first date, our first job, our first sexual encounter, the first home of our own, our first child, and so on. We're on the move, physically, emotionally, and intellectually—leaving home and neighborhood, trying out new roles and relationships, and gradually shaping our identity. Not only are we having an abun-dance of first-time experiences, we're processing them with con-stantly changing thinking caps. And, at the peak of the hill, we're processing them for the first time with an adult memory system. Virginal experiences seen with virginal eyes: it's a powerful com-bination that makes a lasting impression on memory.

Many of our first-time experiences also prove to be consequential, which adds to their vividness in memory. When researchers scoured the autobiographies of forty-nine eminent psychologists for "autobiographically consequential experiences," or ACEs, they found that the vast majority came from the years between eighteen and thirty-five. About two-thirds of the ACEs consisted of generic memories ("I realized that my not raising a family had given me freedom to make use of the opportunities that came my way") and about one-third of specific episodes ("My formal transfer to Teachers College . . . was 'decided upon' at a single moment, during my second year in New York"). But no matter what their level on the memory hierarchy, most of the ACEs came from the twenties and early thirties. That's a little later than the typical hill of reminiscence, but the psychologists being studied were professionals looking back on careers that took a long time to establish.

There's still more to the hill of reminiscence—the intriguing speculation that this is the period of life when major historical events have their greatest impact. When sociologists asked a national sample of adult Americans in 1985 to name one or two "national or world events or changes" that had occurred in the previous fifty years, most answers came from their respondents' late adolescent and early adulthood years. Older Americans named World War II, younger Americans the war in Vietnam. (It's the young who fight in wars.) Other respondents mentioned the Civil Rights movement, the assassination of John Kennedy, and the Depression. No matter what historical event was named, it was likely to come from a person's hill of reminiscence.

By the age of thirty most of us have had the experiences that count in our lives, and by the age of fifty we are beginning to see their long-range consequences. A number of studies have shown that we become more reflective in our middle years. We begin to wonder why our life has turned out the way it has—why we're living in this place, working at this job, sharing our life with these people, having this success or failure. What ACEs were we dealt, and how did we play them? In building a reminiscence hill, memory is bringing to the fore the years that contain most of the answers.

By the age of seventy, another factor is adding to the hill. We become aware that we are the last living witnesses to a particular piece of history or a vanishing way of life. Others become aware of it, too, and their curiosity and desire to make a record stimulates memories in us. "Tell us about when you were young, Grandpa." What was life like before television, before radio, before antibiotics? What was it like when you could actually be sent away to become someone's apprentice, when you had to be quarantined when you were ill, when marriages were arranged by parents? Scholars want to record oral histories of all manner of events—massive migrations, economic depressions, political revolutions, natural disasters, genocides—and they must make their recordings before all the survivors of the events have died. The history that only the oldest generation knows comes, of course, from their hill of reminiscence. Pressures from within and without turn up the spotlight on those years.

There is variation in all this timing, of course. Some hills of reminiscence come earlier, some later. Some cover more years than others. I have a hunch that when I finally look back on the contours of my life, my midforties will form a second peak of remembering. This was a time of great change for me, and not coincidentally, the moment when I finally "heard" the story of the white gloves. But no matter how different we all are, every one of us will look back on at least one period of especially vivid memories. The years we remember best will say a lot about who we are and why our life is turning out the way it is.

Old Age and the Life Review

A seventy-six-year-old man I interviewed some years ago—I'll call him Chris Vitullo—provided a clear example of the hill of reminiscence. Over a period of a month, Chris told me the story of his life. We would meet once a week, he would insist on feeding me, and eventually I would turn on the tape recorder. Chris spoke at great length of the tales his mother told him as a child, of his apprenticeship at the age of seven to an old barber named Antonino, of his trip, alone, to America when he was thirteen. Leaving his mother and father on the dock, "I had a lump in my throat as big as a fist." He remembered everything about the trip: the strange languages and foods, the way the boat listed so that Chris could see the ocean on one side but not on the other. Then someone spotted the Statue of Liberty. "*La libertà! Viva la libertà!*" From New York, Chris took a two-day train trip to St. Louis, got off at the wrong station, and then, with an incredible bit of luck, walked straight to the front door of his sister's home. All these events Chris recounted in great detail. Several years after arriving in St. Louis, he moved to Detroit and opened a barbershop with a friend. His father and mother came from Sicily to arrange a marriage to a girl named Gloria, and by the age of twenty-one the course of Chris's adult life had been set. Chris was full of energy as he described these events. But once he came to his marriage to Gloria, his narrative slowed to a crawl:

> When we got married, we were very happy after that with an exception that whatever comes along, you have to take, sickness or otherwise. We lived together forty-five years, Gloria and me. Yeah, we lived together forty-five years. We had a lot of good times together and a lot of bad times together. We worked, we paid our bills honorably, and we dressed well. We bought a house, we paid for the house, we had a little bit of money, whatever God provided, but we did it all in a good faith and honestly, and we arrived to the point that probably if God wouldn't want Gloria to pass away, maybe Gloria and I, we would be together today. But that's the way it goes in life, and we have to take what's coming to us.

After hours on his first twenty-one years, Chris spent only a minute or two on his next forty-five. In subsequent interviews I was able to learn more about Chris's marriage to Gloria and her death ten years prior to my interview, but it took a lot of questioning and checking. Chris wasn't resistant to speaking of this time; it was just that his memory had condensed nearly half a century into a single whole, with much of the detail forgotten. What Chris remembered best, and with the greatest joy, were the years of his life from six to twenty-one—his teens in particular. That was the location of his hill of reminiscence.

Chris's story also illustrates the major uses of autobiographical memory in old age. One type of late-life remembering has been called instrumental; it's the recollection of past planning, problem solving, and goal attainment. Chris had memories of this type from the time he was a grocer during World War II:

> I did a lot of maneuvering around. I was getting things that were hard to get. I had people coming to me for miles. If they needed onions, I had maybe three, four hundred bags of onions in the back room. The farmers wouldn't sell potatoes for three dollars a hundred pounds, but they would sell them for ten dollars. I bought them for ten dollars, I would sell them for ten dollars. I progressed from a little store to a nice market, almost a supermarket. I was selling fourteen sides of beef a week. I was selling hundreds of pork butts and pork loins. I had three butchers. We worked real hard, but I was able to earn enough money to buy a house and to buy whatever Gloria or my mother needed.

Instrumental remembering is used to underwrite a sense of competence in the present. As one older person said of surviving the Depression, "The lessons I learned in those years have really helped me in trying to live on my old-age pension." In a study of the oral reminiscences of 171 elderly subjects, psychologists Paul Wong and Lisa Watt found that those who had instrumental memories were almost always "successful" agers. Nearly all were living in their homes rather than in institutions, and they were far more likely to be well adjusted and in good health. They knew they could still cope. Their memories said in effect, "I have been and continue to be competent."

Another kind of remembering Wong and Watt called transmissive. Its purpose is to pass on to others one's cultural heritage or personal wisdom, or to bear witness to significant historical events. Often it takes the form of instruction in the values of a bygone era. As Chris said about the younger people in his life:

> *Whenever I get in contact with them, I tell them about obedience. I tell them they've got to be obedient to their father and mother. In the old ideas, obedience was something that had to be carried out. People obeyed the elderly people. I tell them about the Commandments. "Love thy neighbor." . . . If you haven't got that and you think you can do without, I think you're wrong.*

Perhaps the most important type of remembering in late adulthood is aimed at inner change. The product of a "life review," it serves the function of putting our lives in order in anticipation of death. Rememberers seek to affirm what was necessary in their lives and to reconcile themselves with what has happened. As Chris discovered, you have to come to terms with the road not taken:

> *While I was a young man, I felt a lot of times, deep down in my heart, that I was capable of doing other things than being a barber. I felt that I could have done better, but I hesitated to make sure. Before I took a jump, I wanted to measure the distance. I wanted to make sure everything was all right, and that hesitation . . . sometimes you got to take a chance. But I'm happy though. I don't miss nothing. I miss a lot of money, but money isn't everything. It seems to me that where there is money there is some of those guys that say, "Look, if you had another couple hundred thousand dollars, maybe you could do better business. Why can't we give it to you and be your silent partner?"*

Psychiatrist Robert Butler first coined the term "life review" in 1963, when he called it a "naturally occurring" and "universal" process. The life review is reminiscence plus—plus a final opportunity for repair and transformation. In Charles Dickens's novel *A Christmas Carol,* Ebenezer Scrooge meets the ghosts of Christmas Past, Present, and Yet to Come (that's the reminiscence), and he is also changed inwardly (that's the plus). The hero of Leo Tolstoy's story "The Death of Ivan Ilyich" is also changed at the end of a life review. A middle-aged man who becomes terminally ill, Ivan looks back on his life and sees it in an entirely new light. "What if my whole life has really been wrong?" he asks himself. With the little time he has left, he tries to rectify what he can.

In the course of a life review, some people may anticipate the judgment of their Maker and feel a need to be forgiven for their sins. Others may reveal hidden truths—a deep resentment they harbored toward a spouse, a love they were forced to abandon half a century ago, an affair they carried on all their married life. In the middle of his story, an old man once revealed to a student of mine that he had set fire to a building and unintentionally killed someone. Full of remorse, he resolved to turn himself in to the police, but as he was walking up the stairs to the station, he changed his mind. Instead of wasting his life in prison, he decided, he would use it to benefit others. He was never caught, and only at the end of his life did he reveal what had motivated a career of public service. And he chose to make the revelation to a virtual stranger.

Life reviews take many forms, spoken and unspoken. One New Year's Eve, a man in his eighties called a woman of forty who had once worked for him. They hadn't seen each other in over fifteen years, and he asked her to visit him. She did so the following August and found him suffering from emphysema. Speaking in a whisper and pausing frequently to catch his breath, he showed her all through his elegant home and grounds. He opened its private side to her—the basement and laundry room, the closets, even the drawers of his dresser. At every stop there was a story. Finally, when they sat down together, he let her know, indirectly but clearly, that he had never "known" his wife, had never in fact "known" a woman. Then he reached up and touched her on the breast. She allowed it. Then he lowered his hand as if something were complete.

A professor of social work once described another kind of life review. It involved an eighty-six-year-old Mexican-American named Mr. Garcia. He was a widower with no children and few friends, and he was homebound because of a leg amputation related to diabetes. A social work intern began to visit him on a weekly basis and tape his life story, which he told with great enthusiasm. Old memories came rushing back, and on one visit he spoke with great emotion of an incident that had occurred when he was eight years old. He had gone with his mother and his little sister to a large *mercado,* or shopping area, in a Mexican city. His mother told him not to let go of his sister's hand, but somehow the crowd pushed them apart. After days of searching, his family finally came to the conclusion that she had been kidnapped. All his life, Mr. Garcia carried the guilt stemming from his role in losing her.

On a subsequent visit Mr. Garcia told the intern that he had had an unexpected visitor. His lost sister had appeared to him in a vision. She told him to prepare for death, when the two of them would finally be reunited. After seeing that his sister wasn't angry with him, there was a profound change in Mr. Garcia. The burden of guilt was lifted from his memories. He eagerly drew up his will, put other affairs in order, and prepared the suit in which he wished to be buried.

When a life review is successful, it brings a sense of integrity, coherence, and completion to one's life. You realize you did the best you could under the circumstances, that you're a survivor if nothing else. Researchers Wong and Watt found that reminiscences containing marks of integrity were more characteristic of the healthy, well-adjusted older people they called successful agers. And a Thai researcher found that such remembering was associated with feelings of satisfaction about life among elderly in Thailand (all of whom were Buddhist), as well as among their counterparts in the United States.

The feeling of satisfaction from a life review may be augmented by seeing your life as part of a larger drama, as a variant of some archetypal tale. You may come to see your place in history. In the early 1980s, a fascinating project in the state of Washington brought 400 people to various county and city libraries. They ranged in age from twenty-nine to ninety-two, though most were retired, and they shared a desire to write their life story. Meeting weekly with a seminar leader, they learned the written history that related to their lives. The participants discovered that they were part of the twentieth-century shift from farm to town, part of their country's rise to world supremacy, part of the struggle to end racial segregation. They had gone from Depression child to affluent retiree, from prairie dweller to jet tourist. With their new perspective, the groups produced traveling exhibits of photographs and stories, a video program, and a play that was performed by professionals. They also published 110 autobiographies that now sit next to each other on library shelves, the same shelves that hold the official accounts written by historians.

One of the autobiographies is entitled *From Valdres to Moose Jaw*. It's the story of one family's journey from a poor village in Norway to a town in Canada. The writer, Ann Theberge, remembers the day her father left home to take advantage of a Canadian offer of land on its western plains. She was eight, and it was 1910, the year of Halley's comet. "The world was coming to an end," she wrote of her impoverished village's response to the spectacle. "The people gathered and prayed for forgiveness." Two years later she, her mother, and two smaller children were reunited with her father in a sod house surrounded by huge mounds of buffalo grass, seventy miles from Moose Jaw, Saskatchewan. Ann's young life was one of hardship. She had to leave home at fourteen to help another family in exchange for bed, board, and fifty cents a month. But she and her family survived, and years later she returned to visit her aging father. He felt guilty that he had not given her a better life, but she told him that he had done "the greatest and bravest act" by bringing his family from poverty into a land of opportunity.

Not all life reviews turn out so well, however. Some outcomes are mixed, and some may even lead to suicide. There are events in our lives that can never be undone, no matter how we rework them in our minds. There is damage that cannot be repaired, regrets that cannot be assuaged. Opening up what cannot be fixed may result in depression, guilt, anger, panic, and obsessional rumination, another kind of late-life remembering. Chris Vitullo experienced this too. For years after he lost his wife, he secluded himself in the house where they had lived:

> *I could have lost my mind thinking the same things. When it comes to thinking the same thing over and over and over and you don't forget the thing that you're thinking of, you don't forget the loss of Gloria. . . . Those few things were disturbing my life like you have no idea. I can't even explain how bad it was, but I saw the picture every minute as soon as I lay down in bed.*

Life reviews are not restricted to old age. Because death may threaten at any time, it may stir up memories at any time. In several studies of people who had been exposed to sudden, life-threatening danger, about a third reported an experience of "panoramic memory." They saw their whole life pass before them in an instant. A sixteen-year-old was riding a motorcycle on a poorly lit road when he came upon a stalled vehicle. He had no time to react:

> *I started seeing good and bad things in my life. They were scenes that flashed rapidly before my eyes like lantern slides in rapid succession.*

They started when I was about two years old. A funny thing, I remembered dumping a bowl of cereal upside down on my head. I remembered being spanked when I brought home a bad report card. I remembered high points like the first time I kissed a girl, the first time I got drunk and other things like that. With each one I had the feeling like I had then. It was like living them once again. With each one I, at first, found myself in the picture; but then I was detached, like one would sit and look at the pictures of himself in a family album. . . .

. . . I had no thought of why these scenes were flashing through my mind at the time; but, as I was attempting to figure out where I was after the accident, the thought occurred to me that I might have died and gone to heaven and that this was a judgment of my life or something like that.

Panoramic memories flow with a momentum all their own. They are distinguished from ordinary memories by the speed with which they pass and the amount of ground they cover. Time seems to stand still in them. Sometimes the smells and tastes of early childhood come back. Sometimes the future is introduced as people imagine friends and families receiving news of their death. And sometimes rememberers see themselves from an outside perspective as if they were actors on a stage.

Today, an army of mental health professionals, many of them social workers, are doing life-review therapy with the elderly. They're stimulating their clients with questions or music and having them write stories, paint pictures, or put on plays about the memories evoked. So the life review may not be as "naturally occurring" as Butler originally suggested. Nor is it anywhere as universal. Many studies fail to find evidence of it, though some do, and it is far from certain that successful resolution results in better adaptation to life. If the results of one study can be generalized, the odds are about two in five that you will never experience a life review. If you do, it will probably come before you reach the age of eighty. Only 5 percent of those in the study who were over that age were in the process of having one. In extreme old age, closeness to death is not the key.

Despite data such as these, the concept of "life review" may attain the stature of "midlife crisis" in the years ahead, so reified that everyone is presumed to have one, or worse, that everyone *should* have one. Just as people now attribute almost any dilemma in their forties to the midlife crisis, they may attribute any in their sixties or seventies to the life review. We psychologists have a knack for discovering an internal happening that may actually characterize only a portion of the population and turning it into something for everyone. We do so in blindness, however, oblivious to the great diversity that marks autobiographical memory not only in late adulthood, but throughout all the seasons of life.

"I Will Still Go On"

As we get older, changes in our organ of memory affect how we remember, and how well. It takes longer for information to reach the brain, longer for it to be processed there, and longer for it to return as instructions to the muscles. The change affects all kinds of physical and mental reactions. One is slower to "see" a tennis ball and slower to react to it, slower to put a memory into storage and slower to take it out, with recall suffering more than recognition. There is no single cause for this slowdown. Reduced blood flow to the brain, and therefore reduced oxygen, is probably involved. So is a reduced level of chemical messengers, which leads to a withering of neuronal branches. If branches fail, information has to find a longer, and slower, alternative route. Changes also occur in the insulation that covers nerve fibers, affecting the speed and efficiency with which electrical impulses are propagated. The net result for memory is slight, but noticeable. Older people cannot remember as rapidly as before, but they can remember nearly as well. And those who remain physically and intellectually active slow down far less than those who do not.

Overall, the brain loses weight as we get older, and nerve cells continue their lifelong habit of dying. In the hippocampus, which is critical to the formation of long-term memories, the cells die in the second half of life at the rate of about 5 percent per decade. But an anatomical compensation appears to take place, at least for a while. Sample neurons taken from the hippocampus of healthy humans show an increase in branching between middle age and early old age, up to about seventy-five. There are fewer neurons but they have longer, more complex branches. The net result is that neuronal losses have little practical effect on memory, bringing about some incidental forgetting, perhaps, but not much more. PET scans reveal that the brains of healthy eighty-year-olds are nearly as active as those of twenty-year-olds.

Serious memory failures, known as dementias, are another matter. One-half to two-thirds involve Alzheimer's disease, a malady in which the brain's nerve cells, especially those in the hippocampus, degenerate. The "plaques and tangles" that result are also found in normal brains, but to a much lesser extent. There are many theories as to what originally causes the problem. Researchers are looking at the walls of the brain's blood vessels for an excess of one substance and at the connections between neurons for a deficiency of another. Causative agents might include an accumulation of environmental toxins or a slow virus contracted in childhood but held off by the immune system until old age. It has also become clear that some forms of Alzheimer's, especially those that appear during middle age, have a genetic origin. Two defects associated with the disease have been found on the same chromosome implicated in Down's syndrome, and a third has been identified elsewhere.

Another kind of senile disease is caused by obstructions in blood vessels that temporarily prevent oxygen from getting to the brain. The blockages result in tiny and sometimes unnoticed strokes whose damaging effects are cumulative. Unlike sufferers of Alzheimer's, victims of multiple ministrokes have periods of lucidity in which memories are fully available. Still other dementias are related to Parkinson's disease, chronic alcoholism, emotional depression, excessive medication, or some combination of causes. But dementia is far from a normal condition of old age. The incidence for all types, including Alzheimer's disease, is estimated to be only 2 percent among people in their late sixties and 6 percent among those in their late seventies. The rate climbs to 22 percent for those in their late eighties and 41 percent for those over ninety. These figures are based on studies done in the United States, Japan, Australia, New Zealand, Britain, and Sweden.

So the chances of any of us having meaningful memory deficits are slim all the way through our seventies. The odds grow in the eighties, but even in the nineties they do not reach 50 percent. Through all these years, however, we experience loss and the fear of loss, which is really the fear of losing the self that is supported by the autobiographical memory system. It's the fear of becoming what my father has become, a man without a story and therefore a man without a self.

In late adulthood, the state of the self follows the state of the body. When people still have vigor and health, their *I* sees *me* as youthful. At eighty-three, retired journalist Bruce Bliven wrote, "I don't feel like an old man, I feel like a young man who has something the matter with him. I have now found out what it is: it is the approach of middle age, and I don't care for it." Years after they have retired, most old people still think of themselves as the teachers, postal workers, electricians, lawyers, or nurses they once were. And those who keep on working past sixty-five feel even younger than those who do not. If we have our health, we maintain a youthful self-concept, no matter what our age. We are what gerontologists call "young-old."

Researcher Sheldon Tobin believes that people know full well when they cross a threshold and become "old-old." They give up a youthful self-concept and say simply, "I now feel old." Less introspective than before, they no longer focus on the imminence of nonbeing but rather on the practicalities of dying. Will there be pain? Will I have control? Will I be alone? The transition ushers the elderly into a unique psychology of advanced old age and a final use for their autobiographical memories. In the face of increasing loss and the prospect of death, memory in the eighties and nineties is needed to preserve the self, to sustain images of the person we have always been.

Tobin tells the story of an eighty-four-year-old widow who was referred to him for treatment. A tiny woman revered for her bright disposition, she had recently lost her eyesight and become depressed. She was having uncontrollable fits of crying. Initially, she expressed a concern about being unable to put on her makeup properly, but said little else. Then Tobin asked about her earliest memory of life. She described being two years old and having her father ride on a great white horse into the center square of the Eastern European *shtetl,* or village, where she lived. In the memory he scoops her up and puts her on his huge shoulders so everyone can see how beautiful she is. Told by Tobin that she is still admired for her beauty, she replied, "Maybe, but I'm not sure they can see my eyes. My eyes were always the best part of me." It wasn't her blindness that troubled her as much as her fall from the white horse. She feared she was no longer the beautiful person she had always known herself to be.

It is difficult for an outsider, especially a young one, to look at a frail eighty-four-year-old woman and see her as a two-year-old on a white horse. But that's the *me* the woman sees in her mental mirror. Were she to look at a photograph from the past, she wouldn't say, "That *was* me," but rather, "That *is* me, even though I may have changed a bit." Tobin has found that young people validate self-descriptive statements such as "I enjoy being in charge of things" by drawing on examples in the present: "Right now I'm organizing my club's picnic." But old people draw on the past as well as the present. If they claim that they enjoy being in charge of things, they illustrate not only by saying, "I tell my children when they can come visit me," but also by remembering, "We had a small jewelry store and I ran it." For an eighty-year-old, the self-as-object is the two-year-old who is the apple of her father's eye, the fifteen-year-old dreaming of boys, the thirty-year-old mother of three, the fifty-year-old grandmother, and the seventy-year-old widow—all of them at once. Autobiographical memory has the assignment of keeping all these identities alive, and it does so by searching the bottom of the memory hierarchy for the vivid, symbolic events that make the identities concrete.

Over a period of several years, social worker Austin Lyman conducted reminiscence groups with Navajo elderly who were spending the cold winter months in an extended-care facility. At each session the groups discussed a theme from the past and then created a poem about it. At least one line of the poem was contributed by each person in the group. Put in scrapbooks, the poems became a focal point of discussion between the old people, their families, and the staff at the care facility. Here is an excerpt from one of the poems on the theme of herding sheep, a skill that most of the participants had learned as children:

I have survived in the past.
I can do it again now.
I've gotten over things before.
I can do it again.

I've faced bad weather, bears, wolves, and white men.
I can also face old age.
No matter how bad things were I still went out with the sheep.
I will still go on regardless of my age.

As the end of life approaches, the challenge for the self that first emerged in infancy is to exchange a picture of *me* as old for a picture of *me* as ageless. "I'm a person," insisted one woman. "I'm not an old person, because there are many things about me that are not old—besides my years and the difficulties I have physically. Whatever I am, it has nothing to do with age." An extraordinary sense of continuity can be created through the use of remembrance, and an extraordinary sureness about the self. As losses mount late in life, we need to marshal whatever memories remain to preserve our ageless self, to say, until our very last breath, "It's still the same me"—still the same self that was there in the beginning.

Chapter Seven

"IN THE BEGINNING"

As a psychologist, I've always been interested in dreams. Terrifying, comforting, amusing: no matter what their mood, they have such a sense of immediacy that it's often a jolt to leave them for the world of waking "reality." And the wisdom one sees in them . . . there are dreams from long ago that I never want to lose the memory of, so I repeat them to myself and to the most important person in my life. Sometimes I wonder if I could tell the story of my inner journey by touching on the dreams that came at the turning points, dreams that are mythic landmarks along the way.

I also stand in awe of those occasions when dreams keep track of time better than conscious memory. In one of the dreams I want never to forget, I'm standing in the backyard of the house in which I used to live. It's a frame house, white on the bottom, dark brown on top. As I look at it, I see a large room spanning the rear of the second story. Why haven't I noticed it before? Then I'm in the room, and I see a circular staircase leading upward. It's made of a solid, light wood with a blond finish. The stairs are covered with a light film of dust, and one or two of the treads have come loose from their supports, but the room is remarkably well preserved. There's no rot in the wood, the finish beneath the dust is perfect, and repairs could be made in an instant. I suddenly realize that I haven't been in this room for thirteen years. I climb the stairs slowly and discover I'm inside the steeple of a church. When I get to the top, I look out through clear glass windows at a view that is so broad and welcome I know I must return.

The meaning of the dream seems as clear to me now as it did then. So does the significance of a room that had "always" been there. But why the thirteen years? As I write these words, I suspect I'm mistaken about that number, but when I originally had the dream—it must have been in my mid-to-late thirties—I was struck by the accuracy of whatever number it was. I remember calculating backward and realizing that exactly *that* many years before I was entering a very secular university after leaving a very religious seminary. In the years following the transition I had closed off, but not destroyed, a spiritual side to my personality, and now a dream was calling it back. What amazes me today is the precision of the counting. Chronology is supposed to be a weakness of autobigraphical memory; how much more should it be a weakness of dreams! Yet here was a case where a dream was as good as a calculator.

"I've dreamt in my life dreams that have stayed with me ever after, and changed my ideas," says Miss Catherine in Emily Bronte's *Wuthering Heights*. "They've gone through and through me, like wine through water, and altered the colour of my mind." I call such experiences dreams of a lifetime: they are extraordinary, they are about patterns and transitions in one's life, and they are never forgotten. They may not be woven into the story of your life, but they could be—and in my opinion should be. I am not speaking simply of dreams you remember from long ago, the childhood space aliens with glowing eyes that knocked at your bedroom window, or the mummies that chased you around the house. These are not dreams of a lifetime unless they are also *about* a lifetime, or at least a significant portion thereof. Recurring dreams in adulthood often have this characteristic. Throughout her twenties, one woman dreamt of getting lost in reform school: "I was always looking for a way out of the school but could never find an exit. It was as if I was a rat in a maze who could never get to the end." In her seventies, another woman has a recurring dream of finding herself in a home with many pianos: "I always wander into an enormous room where there is a beautiful grand piano. I never see anyone there. I seem to live there but I have no idea why."

Dreams of a lifetime deal not only with major periods of one's life, but also with the transitions between them. A woman remembers that when she was about to give birth to her ten-year-old son, she dreamt of a little nude baby talking to her: "Mummy, I am a boy. My name is Michael. Please love me." The death of a loved one is also a frequent theme in these dreams. In her teens, an African woman had a dream that her father was going to die in a car accident. She woke up screaming and convinced him not to go to work the next day. She remembers the dream today because it was prophetic: on that very day, twelve people died in a car accident involving the vehicle he would have been in. When she was twenty, another woman had a dream about her father: "He seemed to be trying to tell me something that I couldn't hear. He was reaching for me, but our fingers could never reach quite far enough to touch." At noon the next day she received word that he had died during the night. Other people receive messages in dreams from loved ones already departed. Often the loved one helps with their grief by telling them that everything is all right.

Dreams may be remembered until the end of one's life for the same reason that vivid episodes are. They may be unique, consequential (proving to be prophetic), emotional, or symbolic. "Rehearsing" them, that is talking about them to others, not only keeps them fresh but keeps them stored in more than one place. People may feel that such dreams do not belong in their autobiography because they are too revealing or too open to misinterpretation or just too strange. But if the dreams speak of an extended state of mind or an inner transition, they surely do belong.

Just as fascinating as the nighttime dreams in our daytime stories is another category of mental life. It consists of the fragments of reality from our earliest years, the shards of remembrance that come just before the dropoff of infantile amnesia. What's the earliest thing in life you can remember? I've had an eleven-year-old tell me it was a "dippy" dress her mother made her wear—and a profound sense of embarrassment. A strong young man of twenty said it was being in the hospital, where he fearfully awaited a shot from a nurse. A man in his early fifties remembered trying to write the letter "A" in a red notebook and asking his mother if it was okay. And a man in his sixties recalled that he was just eighteen months old when he walked to the edge of the front porch only to be grabbed and pulled back by his mother. I've collected over a thousand first memories, and nearly all are experienced as veridical, as the work of the keeper of archives. There are no "special effects" in them (what Freud called the dream-work), no flying through the air, no objects changing before your eyes, no gross distortions that say this is only fantasy. Though they exist on the border between memory and dream, we label them one and not the other.

Several years ago my wife and I tried an interesting exercise with a group of retirees. We asked everyone who had a memory going back to their first ten years to stand up. We expected that everyone in the room would stand up, and everyone did, about forty people in all. Then we asked anyone who had a memory going back to their first nine years to remain standing. No one sat down. Then, remain standing if you have a memory going back to your first eight years. Your first seven. Six. By the time we got to their first five years, some people were sitting, but most were not. The majority had memories going back to when they were four or three. When we asked anyone who had a memory going back to their first two years to remain standing, only a handful did. And when we asked if anyone had a memory from their very first year of life, three people remained.

Well, this was a workshop with people who knew and liked each other, but these three individuals were greeted with a lot of skepticism. How could anyone remember back that far? It didn't take long for someone to ask, "Okay, what are the memories?" One of the three people still standing, a man, said he could remember being breast-fed on a streetcar by his mother. The second person, a woman, said she remembered her diaper being changed with several people looking on. The third, a man, said that his earliest memory went back to his first few *months* of life, but he wouldn't tell a soul what the memory was.

There were howls of laughter at each of these stories, friendly laughter, to be sure, but mixed with some hoots and catcalls. On the part of the three individuals, there was defiance. Each believed that they had a memory going back to before their first birthday, and they weren't going to be talked or hooted out of that knowledge. They took pride in the antiquity and accuracy of their earliest memory of life.

What happened in that workshop is typical of what research tells us. No matter what their current age, most people say their first recollection comes from the age of three or four, the time at which all the components of the autobiographical memory system are finally in place. Women generally assign a slightly earlier age to their first memory than do men. The average difference is several months, and the reason may be somewhat faster brain maturation and language development in girls. Several studies have found that higher IQ is associated with earlier memories. Perhaps the autobiographical memory system of the intellectually gifted wakes up sooner than most; perhaps as adults the gifted are more curious about memory, so they probe deeper, longer, and more efficiently. Age of earliest recall is also affected by the content of a memory. In a recent study of college students, hospitalizations and the birth of a sibling were recalled from the age of two, whereas deaths and moves to a new home waited until three. All of these findings speak to what is average, which means there's a lot of individual variation. So there will always be a few people who believe in recollections that go back to their very first year.

What is the typical content of first memories? Two studies that covered individuals ranging in age from the teens to the eighties found that most fall into the categories of trauma (a childhood accident, for example), transition (such as a move to a new home or the birth of a sibling), and trivia (such as receiving a particular gift or being dressed in certain clothes). A number of investigators report that early memories are predominantly visual, and several indicate that such memories are more likely than others to be seen from a vantage point outside the body. There seems to be no personality type (e.g., introverted or extraverted) or kind of episode (e.g., positive or negative, emotional or not) that is consistently associated with having an out-of-body memory. Nor is there any connection with having seen a photograph of the event. It simply seems to be a matter of how old the memory is. The majority of our autobiographical memories never shift into the out-of-body perspective, but those that do are likely to be among our earliest. Though data are sketchy, they indicate that perhaps 50 percent of us have at least one memory of this type.

These are the questions that science can answer. Others it cannot. Did the event portrayed in your first memory really happen, and did it happen the way you remember it? You will have to go to external records or to the memory of others to answer that question. All research can say about the memory itself is that vividness does not establish validity. Nor can any kind of research, scientific or personal, tell you whether your memory is direct (your own original perception) or indirect (a picture created by a photograph or something you were told). It is not true that an out-of-body perspective indicates that you were told about the incident, and that a normal, internal point of view is evidence that you were not.

And there's the ever-present problem of cryptomnesia. A young woman once described for me a first memory of sitting on the beach, playing with a sandpail. She remembered the birds, the warmth of the sun, a pail, and plenty of sand to dig up and throw around—all part of a generic "beach" script. But she also remembered something very specific: an older cousin running around in a red polka-dot swimsuit. When she told her aunt about the memory, the two of them were astonished. The cousin did indeed have a red polka-dot swimsuit, and she had it at an age that dated the young woman's memory: she had to have been only eight or nine months old when she was sitting on that beach. A similar case involves an older woman who had an early memory of being in a bedroom with double doors. When she asked her older brother about it, he said yes, a bedroom in one of the family's homes did indeed have double doors, and the family moved from that home when the woman was only two. The memory appeared to be both authentic and ancient. But even when unique details like red polka dots or double doors are verified by outsiders, we cannot rule out the possibility of cryptomnesia. Both women could have been told about these details and forgotten that they were told.

Questions about the historical accuracy of first memories are those of the keeper of archives. But unless you are about to face a court of law or need to settle some family dispute, the keeper's questions matter very little. What matters instead is the *meaning* of our earliest memories, what the self, as presently constituted, sees in them. What matters is the work of the mythmaker.

You can see this clearly when two different rememberers insert their own meanings into the very same image. One of Chris Vitullo's earliest memories was of receiving two silver dollars from his father at around the age of four. He had many similar childhood memories of finding riches, of digging up buried treasure, of being fed, of sources of life opening up to him. Chris's earliest memories touched upon an archetypal theme in mythic life. Fairy tales are full of similar images of finding food and riches. So, on occasion, are dreams, like ones of a house with a hidden room of spiritual treasure. The nourishment in these tales and dreams appears with the same feeling that the silver dollars appeared in Chris's memory of his father.

Now consider another memory of a silver dollar, this one from a woman half Chris's age. She recalls that on her fourth birthday her father carried her into the kitchen and gave her not just any silver dollar but the one he got while fighting in Europe during World War II. She remembers how shiny and heavy the coin was, bigger than the palm of her hand, in fact. She remembers how close she felt to her father at that moment, how proud and honored and special she was. Then comes *her* insertion of meaning, so different from Chris's: "I always wanted to live up to the right to possess that coin." What has happened in this woman's life has made her silver dollar seem especially heavy, less a source of nourishment than an impossible ideal. Despite a constant effort to make her father proud, the two of them have grown apart.

Or compare these memories of being in a baby carriage. In the first, the baby is lying on its back, "just being a baby," and people are looking at him. In the second, the baby is bored and restless and wants to get out. In the third, the baby is crying and crying, and nobody's coming. The first is from a man whose therapist reported that he was passive, wanted approval, and wanted to be the center of attention. The second is from a nun who felt confined through much of her training and who has ventured into areas like broadcast journalism. The third is from an alcoholic who has felt alone and helpless most of her life. While the age and accuracy of early memories is of interest to us, what really counts is the meaning we put into them. And if you look closely at meaning, if you approach these memories almost as though they were dreams, you discover something quite extraordinary. You begin to realize that even though the memories are from infancy and childhood, they're really about a person's entire life.

The Tense of Early Memories

When Freud came upon his patient's earliest recollections, he viewed them as he viewed all memories. They were, first and foremost, disguises that covered up conflict in the distant past. Freud called the disguises screen memories because he thought they concealed more than they revealed. One of his favorite examples came from the autobiography of Johann Wolfgang von Goethe. Writing in his sixties, Goethe described the circumstances of his birth in 1749 and then turned to the first episode he could actually remember. He was, perhaps, a little younger than four, and he was playing in the front of his house with some miniature dishes. He tossed one of them out of the window, and when it crashed on the street he clapped his hands in delight. Three boys outside were so amused they encouraged him to do it again. He did, and soon a whole assortment of crockery was flying out of the window and shattering on the pavement. The boys continued to egg him on, so little Johann Wolfgang went to the kitchen, got every plate he could get his hands on, and threw it in the street. Finally, someone put a stop to what was happening, but by then the damage was done. In place of all the broken crockery, Goethe wrote, he ended up with a wonderful story.

Freud saw nothing deeper in this memory until a twenty-seven-year-old male patient reported a nearly identical recollection from the same age. The young man, who had been sick as a child, described his earliest years as a paradise of unrestricted love and concern from his mother. Then a brother was born, and he had to share her. He became intensely jealous and even tried to kill the baby in its cradle—at the time he threw the dishes out of the house. Freud dug deeper into Goethe's life and concluded that for him, and for his male patient, throwing out the crockery was a symbolic act. Both men wanted to throw out a new arrival to preserve their relationship with their mother. In Goethe's case, the crockery episode served as a screen that covered a more disturbing memory.

Since my experience of delving into memories has been with individuals outside of therapy, I've run into less camouflage than Freud. More typical is the directness of a woman in her late fifties who also had a first memory of a brother's birth. "Throw him in the garbage!" she remembers saying. No conflict there, no remorse, and certainly no screen. But there's more that separates my thinking from Freud's than the matter of disguise. There's also the matter, and this may seem an odd way of putting it, of *tense*. What is the tense of early memories? For Freud, it was generally the past: the significance of early memories lay in childhood. But for me, as for most current interpreters of early memories, it is generally the present: their significance lies in adulthood, or whatever stage of life the rememberer is in. To put a finer edge on it, the tense of early memories is really present perfect. It's "I have been" rather than "I was."

The opening scene in one woman's autobiographical memory is of running lost and terrified through tall grass, but there are critical moments throughout her story when she feels small, unnoticed, and frightened, and has no idea where to turn. She *has always had* these episodes of terror. Another woman's earliest memory is of sitting in the lap of a fatherly man and grabbing his pipe. It's a memory with an apt Freudian screen: her life *has been*, and continues to be, one of seeking protective sexual relationships with far older men. Memories of famous people are interesting in this regard. Dwight Eisenhower's first memory was of being frightened off by an aggressive gander and then routing him with a broomstick. "This all turned out to be a rather good lesson for me," he wrote, "because I quickly learned never to negotiate with an adversary except from a position of strength." The earliest recollection of Golda Meir was of her father barricading the entrance to their home against a pogrom that never materialized: "It was a feeling that I was to know again many times during my life—the fear, the frustration, the consciousness of being different and the profound instinctive belief that if one wanted to survive, one had to take effective action about it personally." The earliest memories of Seymour Papert, the creator of the LOGO computer language for children, center on wheels and figuring out mechanical puzzles; Albert Einstein remembered receiving a magnetic compass as a small boy and being awed by the needle's urge to point north. Memories that have significance only in the past are dead memories. To live, they have to be about a past leading to the present.

Genes are one of the influences that lead us from past to present, and they may have an effect on early memories—not on what happened in the past, of course, but on how we remember it. The impact of genes was demonstrated in a study of over 500 pairs of Swedish twins whose average age was fifty-nine. Identical twins in the study were found to have memories of their childhood family environment, particularly of its warmth or coldness, that were more alike than those of fraternal twins. This was true not only of twins who had been raised in the same household, but also of twins who had been separated early in life. The latter is mind-boggling: even though they were reared in different homes by different parents, identical twins had surprisingly similar recollections of family relations more than fifty years before! Whether we remember our childhood through rose-colored glasses seems in part to be a function of genetic nudges that last a lifetime.

Sometimes the accent in the present perfect tense is on the present, on who I am now and what my life is like these days. When I interviewed a man of fifty-three who was living in dread of a second and fatal heart attack, he declared his first memory to be of his grandmother's death. He remembered in particular how the family dog that had been lying on her bed stepped down the moment she passed away. But another man, also fifty-three, had a first memory of births. He recalled watching baby chicks hatch and then go into "brooders" that provided them with heat. One Sunday he crawled under the brooder and fell asleep in its secure warmth. When he awoke, baby chicks were crawling all over him. As he spoke of this memory, a toddler tugged at his sleeve, another sat in a high chair, and a baby rested in his lap. Having raised one family, he had divorced, remarried, and begun a second.

There have been some impressive studies relating the content of early memories to the present condition of one's life. The studies have found, for example, that college students in different phases of identity formation tend to have early memories corresponding to whatever phase they are in; that adults who are anxious or depressed or who feel out of control have early memories related to their condition; that alcoholics do too. On the basis of early memories, the dangerously insane can generally be separated from the insane who pose no threat. Psychologists Sharon Davidow and Arnold Bruhn were able to make a sharp distinction between the early memories of young men being held for delinquency and those of a matched sample of nondelinquents. Besides obvious differences (delinquents were the ones who remembered incidents of serious rule breaking, setting fires, etc.), delinquents had far more early memories of injuries and illnesses, of parents being unavailable for help or actually causing injury, of being alone in unpleasant situations. In their memories they saw themselves as weak and vulnerable—as victims. Nondelinquents, on the other hand, had memories of receiving adequate nurturance and protection, of success rather than failure, and of being pleasantly alone. Three college seniors trained to look for these differences were given a set of four early memories from each of 142 subjects and asked to guess whether it came from a delinquent or nondelinquent. They were right 89 percent of the time. Davidow and Bruhn's research squares with other studies showing that well-adjusted individuals have more pleasant memories than those seeking help from clinics. It reminds me of an old woman whose first memory of life was of "demented" entertainers. She turned out to be in the process of losing her mind herself.

If our earliest memories are about the present, and the past that leads to it, what happens to them when the present changes? Gerontologists once followed a sample of old people from four

months before to two months after they had been institutionalized. They found that, after the move, their subjects' earliest
memory of life contained more themes of loss, mutilation, and
death than before, and more than a matched sample of elderly
who had not been institutionalized. Usually the memory change
was brought about by recalling a different incident, but sometimes
there was a subtle shift in the same memory. While on the waiting
list for a nursing home, one woman reported the following as her
earliest memory:

> *I remember my mother. She had hair like braids, open and falling upon
> her shoulder. She was sitting up in her bed and near her on her table was
> a bottle of honey and I remember asking her for honey. That's all I
> remember—nothing before and nothing behind. I still can see her sitting
> in bed. I must have been two years, two or three. Closer to two, I guess.*

After admission, the memory was now about dying:

> *I remember my mother's death. I remember at least one moment of it.
> She had honey on her bed and I wanted some of that honey. I didn't
> really understand that she was dying. I was almost three years old.
> That's all I remember. I can see her face clearly even now. She had two
> braids hanging down.*

So natural are alterations like this that some therapists won't
consider their work with clients complete unless their earliest
memories have changed. "Jane," for example, was a nineteen-
year-old who began weekly counseling sessions at the beginning of
her first year of college. Her problems were not unusual: conflicts
with her roommate, excessive dependency on her boyfriend, an
inability to compete with older siblings, being spoiled as the baby
of the family. By the end of the academic year she had become
more confident and outgoing, less self-centered. Her earliest
memories of life had also changed. Samples collected at the beginning and end of therapy were rated by evaluators who did not

know their source. The evaluators judged the second set to be more positive than the first. Some evaluators, in fact, thought they had come from entirely different people.

Memories can be made relevant to the present because of their open spaces. One set of meanings can be squeezed out, another drawn in. My own first memory of life goes back to when I was three or four and my family was looking over an apartment that we eventually moved into. It was the one I grew up in. In the memory, I am sitting in one of the dining room windows and my older sister is sitting in the other. Our knees are up to our chins. I look at her and say, "This is my window, and that's your window."

The first meaning I remember seeing in the memory was facilitated by its out-of-body perspective. My focus was on the frame of the window. I liked the way the frame contained me; it defined who I was and who I was not. Since that time I have written a little piece on looking out that window and seeing passersby walking down the path of life. Today, I see in the memory a wish to be settled into something, to have a single place that will forever be mine. My wife, however, sees something else. Spouse and clinician that she is, she says I'm controlling a relationship. I'm telling my sister what's what and whose territory is whose. I reply in defense: "I never tell you (er, my sister) what's what. I don't control. I just articulate what the present reality is." "Sure," she says, and on it goes.

And it *does* go on. The symbol of the window lives on because I can pour a succession of meanings into it, and because someone else can too. The spaces in our earliest memories, indeed in all of our memories, allow us to bring them to the present, where we can use them.

Where I Began

Of all the psychologists who have been captivated by early memories, no one put more emphasis than Alfred Adler on the memory that is chronologically the earliest. To Adler, a memory that is *the* first was something more than one that was merely one of the first. *The* first memory, he said, is a person's "subjective starting point, the beginning of the autobiography he has made for himself." As the memory that had survived longer than any other, it was the one that showed the fundamental meaning of a person's life. His own first memory is an example. Adler remembered being a little boy sitting on a bench, incapacitated by disease, watching his brother play. As an adult that same little boy became a psychoanalyst who coined the term "inferiority complex" and built a theory of personality around it.

Few psychologists today agree with Adler's emphasis on *the* earliest memory. One reason is that it's often difficult to determine chronological antiquity. It's like asking which ray of the sun actually breaks the darkness on a particular morning. In a study of high-school students, over 40 percent reported a first memory that was different, and earlier, than one they had reported just three months before. But despite the changing nature of early memories, most psychologists who work with them concur that they are indeed "subjective starting points" that provide a foundation of meaning in our lives. They are the first in a series of self-defining episodes at the bottom of our memory hierarchy.

The subjective starting points established by our first memories are like the creation stories that humans have always told about the origins of the earth. In some of these stories, the earth developed from a mother who sacrificed herself so that we might live off the nourishment of her body. In others, our world came from the intercourse of Father Sky and Mother Earth, or from a cosmic egg, or from a turtle rising like an island from the sea, or from the Word of a purposeful deity. The myths differ but they have something in common. They represent a people's efforts to say what their identity is, where they belong, and how they ought to live. "This is who we are," the creation stories say, "because this is how and where we began." In stating what happened at the beginning of our remembered lives, our earliest memories do something similar. They establish the place where we began—not a geographic place, but one that exists solely in the recesses of our mind. It's a mythic place where we are loved or not, lost or not, a victim or not, able or not. It's a place of silver dollars that nourish or set impossible ideals, of baby carriages that are either havens or prisons.

When thinking about your earliest recollection, it's important to be mindful of memory's tendency to establish contrast or continuity. You may have left your mythic place of origin or you may still be there. If your first memory is bad, contrast means that you have overcome a handicap, proven your parents wrong, gone from rags to riches, or grown in some other way. An old man's earliest memory is of his first day of school in 1926: "Mother left me to the tender mercies of Mrs. Grady and went home. I started to cry my head off. Mrs. Grady took my hand and led me to the front of the room, sat me on a high stool, placed a dunce cap on my head, and said now you have a reason for crying." The dunce didn't remain one. It took a long time to overcome his bad start, but he finally did, receiving his college degree at the age of seventy-three. (Take that, Mrs. Grady, wherever you are.)

If our earliest memory of life is good, contrast means that we have fallen from grace, lost our innocence, been betrayed, failed to live up to an ideal, or something of the kind. We have been banished from an Eden in which we were at one with a parent. "I don't think I have ever felt closer to him," said the woman whose father gave her a silver dollar on her fourth birthday. She was describing the moment she received it, a moment from which she subsequently fell. For a man in his forties, Eden was the one time his father showed up. In his first memory of life, he is a little boy, sick in bed. But he doesn't feel pain or distress. Instead, he's excited because he's going to see his father. He's actually going to touch the man, feel him, smell him—and ride in his big, black shiny Plymouth on the way to the hospital. Everything that followed in this man's childhood was a betrayal of that memory. In the summer the other kids would be out with their dads polishing the car or going for a spin. His father would be gone. At the age of twelve he asked his father if he could come to the garage where he worked every Saturday, just to learn a trade. His father said, "Hell, no, you can't come. You talk too much. You'll ask too many questions." The boy swore he wouldn't say anything, but the father said, "Just don't come back." It's ironic, but not uncommon, that this man's first memory establishes a mythic place where he was united with his parent and from which he was expelled.

A woman of forty-four has a first memory of standing behind a glass door, watching an angry mother walk out on her:

> She opened the front door and closed it behind her, and left me standing behind those little panes of glass, looking out, just crying. My heart was broken because my mother was leaving me. And she walked down the sidewalk and out of sight. I can still see the sidewalk that she walked down, and the cracks in the sidewalk. That had a real lasting effect on me. It was like, "You do what I say or I'll leave you."

In this story there is a Fall, an original sin, but the parent doesn't expel the child. The parent simply leaves, taking Eden with her. But the effect is the same. It has taken the daughter many years to realize that her life does not have to end in the same mythic place where it began. She doesn't have to be afraid of people walking out if she fails to do their bidding.

There is a particular poignancy about early memories involving separation from a parent. You can sense the fear in them:

> I was in the back seat of my parents' car at night with my dad driving and my mom beside him in the front seat. The three of us were coming home from my grandparents' house. I felt overwhelmed with this feeling that they were going to stop and leave me forever in the middle of this large field.

And the loneliness as well:

I was in the yard on a bright, sunny spring day. The wind put a chill in the air and I lay down on the ground. It seemed as though the cool air passed over me as I absorbed the warmth of the sun and the ground below. I lay there for a long time watching the sky when I experienced an overwhelming sense of being alone—totally alone in the world—frightened and almost panicked to reestablish contact with someone.

It is also poignant to hear or read memories in which an adult's sin is defined as the child's. One person, for example, remembers being dropped "accidentally" by her father while she was still a baby—and then being yelled at as if it were her fault. This is the definition of the situation that often prevails in memories of sexual abuse.

Some of us experience continuity with our earliest memory, whether of an Eden or a more hellish place. One man remembers yelling for his father from the top of some monkey bars where he had frozen in terror. It seemed like an eternity before his father arrived in his police uniform—powder blue shirt, navy pants, and hat. "He carried me all the way home, saying, 'Everything will be all right.'" His father's arms were a good place to be, and today that man is a police officer, "helping people and saying, 'Everything will be all right.'" My own first memory is of a good place as well—it's *my* place, in fact—and I draw from it feelings of comfort and security. Others are not so fortunate. Experiencing continuity with a bad memory, they find their lives recycling themes of abandonment and loneliness. "I can't remember any good, happy, or enjoyable first memories, to which I attribute my inability to trust people whom I love," says a woman who was a victim of sexual abuse at the age of two-and-a-half. "I easily crumble under what I believe is rejection." Another woman recalls a fleeting image of a dead sparrow in her back yard. "Ever since that day," she says, "I have formed a fear of being alone, violence, hurting others, and the unknown." When people's lives play out the theme of their first memory, they often feel that the memory *caused* their present state. It "led to" or "determined" the shape of their life today. It had a "lasting effect." It "made me" what I am.

Once in a great while this is true. A person may have a physical disability today because of an accident he suffered as a small child, and that accident may well be the first thing he can remember. A person may have difficulty in sexual relationships because of an early incident of molestation. But most of the time no single episode shapes the kind of person we become. A woman does not become submissive "because" her mother once left her crying behind a glass door. She becomes submissive because throughout her childhood her mother's actions declared, "Do what I say or I'll leave you." Ninety-nine percent of the time one incident didn't "do it" for life. But often enough one incident in the beginning symbolizes all that did.

"The First Time I . . ."

There are other beginnings that serve the same mythic function as our earliest memories, establishing how themes in our stories and aspects of our selves develop. They are life's significant firsts, most of which come from the hill of reminiscence. They begin in childhood:

The first time I tied my own shoes. It happened when I was five years old. I was at home and my brothers showed me how.

The first time I lit a match I was with a group of kids from the neighborhood. They dared me to do it and I did.

The first time I spent the night at a friend's house. I was excited beyond belief. However, I missed my parents so much that I made myself sick and had to go home.

The first time I performed in front of an audience. I was in a dance recital. I remember being so terrified, I thought I was going to be sick.

In adolescence they are of a different nature:

The first time I saw a dirty magazine. I was surprised to find it in our basement. I was awestruck and nervous at the same time because I knew it was wrong.

The first time I had a real kiss. This guy I liked asked me if he could walk me home and on the way home he stopped me, put his arms around me, and kissed me. I was embarrassed, scared, and excited all at the same time.

The first time I got in trouble with the police. I was with some older friends and we were drinking beer. We were parked in these apartments and the cops drove by so we ducked down. They saw us and searched us, scared us, and then let us go.

The first time I drove a car. My father took me out to the farthest reaches of the country. It was a stick shift and I could not start out of first gear. My father was furious.

The first time that I was all alone in my freshman dorm. My parents had just dropped me off and were on their way back home. None of my roommates had arrived yet, and I was all alone for the very first time in my life.

They change again in young adulthood:

The first time my fiancée said, "I love you." We were in a small pub having a drink after a wonderful dinner. When he said it, I burst into tears and we had to leave. Everyone looked at us strangely and thought he had hurt me in some way.

The first time I drew my service revolver. My inexperience led me to index the cylinder, and I nearly fired. Minutes later, when things were under control, I was shaking.

The first time I held my daughter. I felt the miracle of her. I was scared, happy, overwhelmed, fascinated, confused about what my life would become. All kinds of things were going on at once. It was an awesome experience.

The first time my husband and I disagreed. It was terrifying, as we never raise our voices in anger.

The first day of kindergarten for my first child. Having had a bad experience myself, I expected him to be reluctant to go. He entered the school without even looking back or waving goodbye. Tears came to my eyes as I turned and walked home.

Fewer first times come from middle and late adulthood:

The first time I walked into a college classroom as a student—at age forty.

My first trip abroad. I was newly divorced and felt I should get away. My children were old enough to be left alone so I booked a trip to Europe with a friend. We were gone almost three weeks and it was fantastic.

The first time I saw and held my first granddaughter.

The first, and only, time my husband had bypass surgery. I was scared to death!

Some of life's most memorable firsts come from any season of life:

My first awareness of a sunrise. It was at my grandmother's cottage with fishermen on the lake.

The first time I saw someone die before my eyes.

The first time I experienced an understanding of God's message.

The first time I realized why I am who I am.

The first time I started life over on my own.

The first time I was asked to remember my first memory. I couldn't!

Because memories of our first-time experiences are less remote and therefore less ambiguous than our earliest memories of life, their mythic content may be less. But you may still find in them veins of meaning reaching far into the hierarchy above.

Take memories of your first bike ride. One young woman told me that hers was on her brother's bicycle, a rusty old hand-me-down, "just like everything else I got." Another young woman had also gotten a hand-me-down, but she felt very differently about it. To her, the bike was something of value, her brother's at the beginning of the ride and hers at the end, a family inheritance she had earned. Parents in bike-ride memories can be like magnets, attracting feelings from the present as well as the past. Are they leery, in the memory, of letting the child take off by himself? Or do they stand back and say, "You're on your own now, kid?" Do they run alongside supportively? Refuse to let go? Push, even cause the child to crash? How were your parents in your life?

The first day of school is another beginning that produces self-defining memories. One woman recalled wetting her pants because she didn't know where the bathroom was and the teacher wouldn't listen to her. Another had to leave her classroom because her mother became ill, called the school, and had her come home. This girl went on to miss so much school looking after her mother, who had multiple sclerosis, that she didn't learn how to read or write until her teens. She now cares for two ninety-year-old grandparents and at times feels lonely to the point of suicide. Her life story is continuous with the memory of her first day of school.

First-time remembrances from later in life can also be self-defining. "Something about it felt good," said a forty-five-year-old alcoholic of her first drink, a shot of VO in a glass of Canada Dry. She was sixteen at the time. "I thought, gee, that's all right. I wonder what another one would be like. Someday I'm going to get all

I want of this." One researcher has shown that far more alcoholics than nonalcoholics remember their first drink. They recall it instantly and in great detail, and they regard it as one of their life's most significant episodes. The memory of that drink is a first time that stands for other times. It's a creation story that underwrites a present identity: I am an alcoholic.

Identity involves who we are not as well as who we are, and it is sometimes possible to find a first-time memory for each. A gay man remembers when he first had sex with his wife: "I went to bed and she came to bed afterwards. I had turned over facing the wall with the covers over me and was simply going to ignore her completely. Just absolutely rigid. She broke into tears." He also remembers his first sexual experience with a man: "I was ecstatic. I was in love with him. I wrote him letters daily, saying we would be together until the end of time, saying that everything marriage should have produced was here in this relationship." The first of these self-defining memories establishes contrast with his present identity, saying who he is not. The second establishes continuity, saying who he is.

As these examples illustrate, not all of the power of first-time experiences is the result of retrospective mythmaking. When novel experiences occur, they create what psychologists call a primacy effect—a mental set that sensitizes us to later experiences of the same kind. A terrifying introduction to sex steers us one way; a loving one, quite another. One woman remembers her first visit to a new church:

> It was as if the entire church came over to welcome me. I had never experienced anything like that before in my life. The people were so warm and friendly and helpful, and there was a spirit of such unity that I felt I'd like to be a part of this. That started my commitment.

A man's introduction to the Navy was quite the opposite, hardly warm and friendly, but it too sensitized him to what was to come. His group of Navy recruits arrived at their barracks at three in the morning on one of winter's coldest days. After a few hours of sleep, they experienced their first full day of military life:

> *They lined everybody up and gave us a cardboard box and said, "Okay, now you put all your personal belongings in that box, all your clothes, everything." So we did. You stand around in your birthday suit, and I mean it was cold, and then you get in line and the guy measures your head and writes on your head what size your hat is. Then they measure your chest, measure your waist, your inseam, your feet. By the time you get done you think, well, when in the heck are you gonna get some clothes? There's no lunch, no dinner, no coffee, no nothing. Then you step between these two tables and they swab both your arms and just start shooting the needles into you. Within the hour you couldn't even lift your arms over your head. Then you went and put on your dungarees and went to chow. It's a wonder everybody didn't die of pneumonia because it was so bitter cold.*

Last times may also be important in a life story. When people use the expression, "The last time I . . .," they may mean nothing more than "The most recent time I. . . ." They may also be remembering a resolution they once made: "The last time I drank I made a complete fool of myself, and I have not drunk since." But the word "last" also signifies the close of a season of life:

> *The last time I dressed up for Halloween and got rejected by everyone. "Ain't you too old for this!"*

> *The last time I visited my friend in North Carolina. As I got on the plane I realized we would never be college buddies again.*

> *The last time I played baseball. It was a bad experience because of my injury. I had a double or a triple but I couldn't throw the ball fast enough to get a guy out at first. I threw a floater so I knew it was over.*

> *The last time I saw my house in which I had lived for twenty-five years*

and raised my family. The house subsequently burned down to the ground and I never saw it again. Some of my happiest memories were part of that house.

The last time I went to work before I retired. Everyone was so nice. I had flowers on my desk from accounting and a surprise in the lunchroom. They gave me a clock (that I never put out) and other gifts to open.

Last times also involve loss, separation, and death, which may be a reason we think of them less readily:

The last time I saw my best friend, when we left California. She was standing in the driveway watching us drive off. I cried for hours as we drove along Big Sur.

The last time I saw my father he was in a semicomatose state, lying in his hospital bed. Although he couldn't speak, as I said goodbye to him, I told him I loved him. He gently squeezed my hand. He died the next day.

The last time I saw my grandfather alive, he was at home. He had lost his eyesight and when we went into his room I was unable to say anything and he never knew I was there. He died a couple days after that in the hospital.

The last time I saw my husband alive. We said we'd see each other about six. He dropped dead of a heart attack at one, and I didn't know about it until I came home in the evening. It was terrible because I never had a chance to say goodbye.

Among the vivid memory episodes of our life, first times outnumber lasts by a wide margin. There may be several reasons for this. Last times are often painful and sad, and we prefer not to dwell on them. There's a labeling problem too: we know that a first time *is* a first time, but often we're not sure if a last time is truly going to be the last, so we don't think of it as such. Sometimes last times are buried in first times. Your first day alone in a college dorm is not only the beginning of a new stage but also the end of an old one. Most of life's transitions have the same mix of opening and closing.

In their religious life, humans periodically return in memory to their points of origin. Jews do so during Passover, Christians at Christmas, Muslims in the course of a pilgrimage to the city where their Prophet first received his message. In an annual ceremony, men of the Australian Arunta retrace the journey of their clan's divine Ancestor. They fast, carry no weapons, and avoid contact with women or members of other clans. They stop at all the places their Ancestor stopped and repeat the gestures he performed. They become his contemporaries, present at the time of their creation. We may describe these commemorative events as "returning to the beginnings," but that reflects a linear view of time, time that has a beginning, middle, and end, time that is going somewhere. If time is cyclic, as many people on this earth believe, we don't go back to the beginnings; the beginnings, rather, return to us. At the end of each year the world returns to chaos, and a new year is created afresh. By participating symbolically in the destruction and rebirth of the cosmos, humans themselves are born anew.

There is a similar movement in many healing ceremonies. Among the Na-khi people of southwest China, therapeutic ritual begins by regressing to preexistence, "at the time when the heavens, sun, moon, stars, planets, and the land had not yet appeared, when nothing had yet come forth." Then comes an orderly account of creation, of the appearance of evil, and finally of the coming of the First Healer. "Unless its origin is related," it is said in the ritual, "one should not speak about it." In autobiographical memory, we return to the founding events of our lives by commemorating events like birthdays and anniversaries, but the beginnings also drift back on their own. Joy in lovemaking elicits memories of the first joyous time—an experience of continuity. A fight in the present calls forth a memory of something in the beginning that has been broken or betrayed—an experience of contrast. Not only do we search our memories for origin myths that explain our present condition, we seek some way of reestablishing contact with them. Even if the memory is painful, we may feel a need to return to it and repair it. So great is the power of getting a first time right—mythically right—that many forms of psychotherapy take this approach.

Choosing Your Origin Myth

Is it possible to look at a first memory and tell you what it means? When I'm asked that question I say no, not unless you and I have a long talk together. And even then, it won't be me who ends up telling you what the memory means; it will be you who ends up telling me. All I can do is point out themes in a memory and indicate how common the themes are. I can observe whether a silver dollar is nourishing or imposing, whether a baby in a carriage is simply lying there, or crying, or trying to get out. I can point out that a trivial memory, like seeing a dead sparrow, may hold more meaning than a dramatic one, like being taken to the emergency room of a hospital. The latter carries its own explanation for staying in memory, while the former does not. There is a written exercise I have students do in which I ask if they see a connection between their first memory and the rest of their life story. Some say no, they cannot, but most come up with a plausible interpretation. Was the meaning there all along or did they make it up on the spot? It doesn't make much difference because the self that created the meaning "already there" is the same self that fashioned it "on the spot." Sometimes I see an unconscious connection that students do not, some metaphor they may be using without knowing it. But it's impossible to relate a single early memory to an entire life story unless you have a thorough knowledge of the two elements you are relating.

So you, who know your memories and know your life, will have to make your own connections. When you do, think about the word "first." While "first" can mean the oldest memory you have, it can also mean the memory to which you ascribe primacy. What matters is primacy. No psychologist who works with early memories works only with the one that is chronologically the earliest. Psychologists work with a cluster of early memories and look for the one that is most important. Which of your early memories says it all? Which childhood event is at the same time the most prophetic mythically and the most accurate historically? *That* is your first memory.

I have a hunch, but it's only a hunch, that as we move toward the end of life, the two meanings of "first" coalesce. The most important memory is the one we establish canonically as the beginning. It's the one we feel stretches farthest back in time *and* the one that is prime. Over the years your autobiographical memory may actually take the event that means the most to you and slip it into the position of earliest—*the* first, not one of the first. But if that doesn't happen, you can still take matters into your own hands. As you see how your life story is ending, you can consciously set up its beginning. You can choose your most important myth of origin. You can create the story of how the person that is you began.

∽

Chapter Eight

MEMORY INSPIRITED

Interesting things happen once you begin to hear the mythmaker in memory, once you learn to distinguish its voice from that of the keeper of archives. You no longer wish to purify remembrance of distortion, even if that were possible. You seek, rather, to know what particular distortions mean, what deeper truths they lead to. Your thoughts turn again to *where* memory is. Eventually you begin to see it in a larger, collective context. You start to be aware of the immense ecosystem in which the memories of individual people move about. You begin to sense all the life and breath—and spirit—that myth brings to memory. And you begin to understand why a fleeting image of white gloves can have the power that it does in one person's life.

But first you have to hear the voice. Listen to a man in his seventies thinking back to the beginning of his life: "I got to tell you that in the old days the mother would chew the food and put it from mouth to mouth, just like the birds. This is not done anymore, but they used to do it in my time. This is a conception in my mind, that maybe my sisters and my mother, they chew the

217

things and they put it in my mouth." In this example, myth is heard in a "conception" of infancy, but that's not the only stage of life where it is found. Remembering her adolescence in Russia before the revolution of 1917, an old woman said: "It was perfect contentment. We followed the traditions without any pain, without any disappointment. It was happy, and we were gay, and we had all the freedom we wanted." And remembering her adulthood, especially a marriage of over fifty years, another old woman said: "I have only the most beautiful innermost thoughts. . . . There's nothing, nothing that I can think of in our marriage that would have made it any more wonderful for me."

You can hear the voice of the mythmaker not only in what people say but also in how they say it. Sarkis Hashoian was not a particularly religious man, but a point came in his story of escape from the massacre of Armenians in 1915 when he grew hushed and reverent. He was describing his mother's drowning of her own daughter, Sark's sister. The girl was blinded by measles and days from death. "My mother took her in the water and got out about this far and dropped her. But when she dropped her, my sister came back up and said, 'Ma-ma, what have I done to you? You gonna drown me.' My mother went back and picked her up and 'her flesh came all over me,' so she couldn't do nothing. She took her back out again and dropped her. My sister, she came up once again, and that was it." Each time Sarkis told me that story—he did so twice—he spoke the words of the girl in the same quiet, deliberate manner: "Ma-ma, what have I done to you?" In a moment that was holy, he repeated the words almost sacramentally.

Gerontologist Sheldon Tobin and his colleagues have tried to quantify the mythic level of recollections. Using a five-point scale, they scored one (no myth at all) for remarks like "my mother used to take me to a lot of concerts"; three (a moderate level of myth) for "mother was a good housekeeper, very meticulous, devoted to her children"; and five (a high level) for "mother was one of the most wonderful women in the world. Everyone loved her." Negative memories were scored as well. They ranged from "mother was a picky person, hard to live with" (no myth) to "I had a mother, the most selfish creature on earth" (a high degree of myth). Nor was it simply people who became mythic in memory. Events did too: "I remember a Christmas—my father coming home with an orange for each of us children. We thought this was the most wonderful thing in the world." And so did entire lives: "Lousy! Lousy in every way. I never had nothing."

When Tobin's research group compared samples of middle-aged and elderly subjects, they found that the elderly had higher levels of myth in their memories. They were more likely to see their parents and spouses as heroic, to describe them in terms of cultural symbols like "good provider" or "good hostess," to lend drama to their own earliest memories, indeed, to dramatize the whole of their lives. Both samples were largely urban, Jewish, and female. The middle-aged group ranged in age from forty-four to fifty-five, the elderly from sixty-five to 103. The latter were free of major incapacitating illness and mentally alert. This was clearly a circumscribed sample, but what happened in it was not.

In old age, the keeper of archives seems to relax its grip on reality. No longer are memories needed, as they were at the beginning of life, to create maps to find one's way in the world. There is little of the world left to find. No longer is it necessary to strip away illusions in order to cope, as it might have been in young adulthood. In old age, too, many of the important people in your life have died, and you no longer have to think so realistically about them. Once your mother is gone, you can forget about the daily battles and remember her as "one of the most wonderful women in the world." And after your husband has passed away, you can forgive him his faults and retreat to an island of "the most beautiful innermost thoughts." At the end of life, when memory is not needed to deal with reality, it can become the stuff that dreams are made of.

The myth in memory helps to preserve the self in the face of loss and diminishment. An eighty-one-year-old man recently placed in a nursing home kept bragging that he had beaten up his sergeant in the Army sixty years before. "And I could do it again if I wanted to, by God!" The rebellious hero of the past enabled him to say something in the present: "I'm still around, and don't you forget it!" Myth also helps the elderly prepare an identity for posterity. Wanting to be remembered as a warm, loving person, one woman in failing health began to close every phone conversation with, "I love you," and to give everyone a hug when she left them. Others select identities for preservation by making funeral arrangements or plans for the disposal of their body. "I want people to have a party and celebrate and have fun the way I like to," said one person. "I just want to be buried in the ground," said another, revealing quite a different self-image. She explained: "I am a practical person and I want the simplest, least expensive funeral possible." Still others make identity statements by indicating that their organs are to be donated to medicine or that their ashes are to be left in a special place. Or they gather treasured objects—photo albums, letters, jewelry, the family Bible, a stamp collection—and declare in a will who is to receive them. All these activities are meant to establish who the dying think they are and how they wish to be remembered.

While further research is needed to substantiate the claim that memories become more mythic as we enter late adulthood, I sense there is an important truth here. It's not that young people don't think mythically; it's that the myth isn't concentrated in their memories. Most likely, it's centered in their visions of the future, in what we called earlier in this book their Personal Fables and Dreams. Nor is it that old people give themselves over to illusion and distortion. The elderly subjects in Sheldon Tobin's study who were quite willing to idealize their parents (or make them cruel villains) were remarkably accurate in their perceptions of the living daughters who were their caregivers, more accurate in fact than the daughters were in reverse. The daughters were their link to life, and one is very realistic about such links. Very often old people feel freer than those who are still in the thick of things to speak candidly of their lives. They don't care as much what others might think. Myth is not falsehood, and when I speak of memories becoming mythic, I do not mean they are becoming less true.

What I do mean is that the good and evil in a person's life is being put into unmistakable categories, into outcomes as clear as heaven and hell. I mean that the self is being comforted and nourished in the face of loss, that it is being given a sense of "always" in the face of a forthcoming void. I also mean—and here we have to be aware of the entire ecosystem of memory—that our life experiences and our identities are being prepared for a final transformation into collective life.

A Family's Memories

Actually, our individual and seemingly private memories have been "in" collective life all along, much more than we realize. That's what I discovered by following my grandfather's white gloves and finding they were not only in the machines of memory, but in the minds of people as well. All throughout our lives we have shared memories with those around us, sometimes repairing them in the process. The families, neighborhoods, and nations that envelop us all have memories of their own that transcend any one individual's. So do the memories in the vast cultures we call Art and Science and Religion. We grow up in the context of collective memory, and over the course of life we breathe it in and breathe it out.

Family stories may be the most engaging collective memories of all. They're about the relatives who were there when the missionaries first came, about encounters with ghosts and spirits, about war coming to your front door, about practical jokes and pranks, about weddings and vacations. People fall in love in these stories: "I met your father on a blind date. I couldn't believe the pink

Cadillac!" There are fights in them, and drinking and cheating: "Your aunt deliberately got herself pregnant by my boyfriend and forced him to marry her. Later, the baby died." There is lost opportunity and regret, narrow escapes from death—and sometimes no escape at all. A family's stories may be invisible to outsiders, and even to those who grow up on them they may seem as insubstantial as air. But more so than the pictures on the wall, they convey the family's essence and spirit.

A family's collective memory says who it is, how it began, and what it hopes to be. The stories it contains nourish the idea that "we" are special, that we're made up of survivors, that we have a connection to history. The stories define our traits, saying that we're a practical lot, or stubborn or intelligent or troubled. Our children learn from the stories how the world works and what can be expected from it. They pick up our ethnic, religious, and social values.

Perhaps the most definitive family memories are its earliest, the ones about its most distant ancestors, the ones about founding events "in the beginning." I have found it interesting to ask about these memories. In the category of oldest ancestor, I've found heroes who were often a part of history—a grandfather who was a marvelous horse rider in the Polish cavalry; a great-grandfather who was a fur trapper on the Detroit River, living life on his own terms and doing it in harmony with nature; an aunt, many generations back, who was hanged during America's Salem witch trials. A woman I know is proud of the fact that the person at the top of her family lineage gave up legal rights to his land rather than fight in Germany's Seven Years' War. Another claims she is related to Civil War General George McClellan. McClellan kept putting off an attack on Confederate soldiers, and her family says that is why they're all a bunch of procrastinators.

I have also found it interesting to inquire about the oldest family story in existence. In my corner of the planet, that has led to tales about the drama of coming to America. The stories tell of life in the old country and the passage to the new. In one, a little Russian girl visits her older sister every Chanukah. Although they are all poor, the sister treats her with elegance, pouring her tea from a samovar and giving her a pair of warm gloves. This first family memory comes with a moral: if only young people today, who have been given so much, knew as well how to give. Stories of the passage to America bear the familiar message that our survival was precarious. Your great-grandfather almost fell off the boat coming to this country; if someone hadn't pulled him in from outside the railing, none of us would be here today. On the same trip his baby brother—your great-granduncle—got sick, died, and was prepared for burial at sea. When his mother asked to hold him one last time, she saw his eyes blink. He wasn't dead at all and in fact lived to be over ninety years old. Forebears who escape death tell you that surviving is in your blood and that ultimately you will survive—a theme that comes out strongly in family slave narratives such as Alex Haley's *Roots*.

Some of these American immigration stories establish that we were here first, either because we were among the original European settlers or because one of our ancestors married a native American. Whether that native was "a savage and wild woman," as in one family's myth, or a self-reliant fur trader, as in the one mentioned above, her or his presence in the family line is a matter of pride. This I find intriguing. It may be a way of establishing that even though we're a family of immigrants, we are still indigenous to America.

Often a family's earliest memory, just like an individual's, identifies a theme of long duration. It explains why we are who we are—why we have this name and not that, why one half of the family is Protestant and the other half Catholic. "Alcoholism runs in my family," declares a man in his late twenties. The oldest story of which he is aware concerns an alcoholic great-grandfather who once chased his wife out of the house with a knife. "We feel we are a little unconventional and very independent," a woman in her sixties tells me. Her family cherishes a "spunky" ancestor, its most remote, who went to court as a twelve-year-old and had himself declared illegitimate so he wouldn't have to turn the wages he earned over to his father. The oldest memory in my family involves the grandfather with whom I identify so strongly. As a child he had been forbidden by his father to go ice skating, but one day he went anyway and fell through the ice. He managed to climb out of the water and get home, but when he appeared at the door, he was very stiff, "with ice chunks hanging all over him." His father was extremely solicitous. He dried him off, warmed him up in bed, and then asked him how he felt. When the boy said fine, his father "gave him his lumps" for disobeying orders.

This story, which I chanced upon as I scavenged around in my father's taped memories, is the only thing I know about my great-grandfather. Yet the combination of love and discipline in this earliest of family memories has an uncanny feel to me. It's what I experienced from my father, what my sons experienced from me, and what their children, I am sure, will experience from them. The oldest Kotre story in existence speaks of a tradition of fatherhood that has "always" existed in my family. Now I know of its mythic progenitor.

Another kind of family memory defines its individual members. These are the origin stories that your family tells you *about you*— specifically, about the circumstances of your birth or the time in your life that is covered by your own childhood amnesia. "Before you came along, we had given up hope of ever having a child"—a powerful message of welcome, quite different from being told that you were the family "mistake," different again from being informed that you were adopted, and the polar opposite of being lied to about your parentage. Stories about you "before you can remember" are often pure entertainment. The first time your father ever changed your diaper, the litany begins, you sprayed him right in the face. When your uncle babysat for you, you cried so much that he swore he would never *ever* have children. We reminded him of that at his wedding. At one and a half, you made a dive for your mother's lap but hit the crossboard on the couch instead. It split open your head and required thirteen stitches. When you were two, you made breakfast for yourself. Everyone else was asleep, so you climbed on the kitchen counter, turned the stove on high, cracked open some eggs, and swallowed half a bottle of vitamins while you were at it. When you were three—don't you remember?—you used to stand on the couch, grab the dog's tail, and try to have her drag you around on your belly. You also said you wanted to eat a motorcycle for lunch. At four, you took a sand shovel and hit your brother on the head while he was sleeping in the hammock. He would have killed you if mom hadn't intervened. The same year, your father dropped a brick on your head while he was building the porch—which is why you're so dumb today.

All these examples are drawn from actual people, though not (thank goodness) from just one person. Full of affection, they cement bonds of intimacy. Other family stories of this type are far more serious. They emphasize threats to life and the precariousness of survival, a common theme in a family's mythic storehouse:

I was told I almost died in the hospital after being born because I had so much trouble breathing. I had to stay in for observation. Then when I came home, I turned blue because I was not breathing properly. My passages were blocked.

Mother told me that I cried day and night. Nothing helped. The doctor told her that I would never live. Wrong!

My mother told me that when I was very young, two or three years old, I had gotten ahold of a box of strawberries and ate almost a whole quart. It so happened I was allergic to them, and that night my face swelled up and my eyes were swollen shut. In those days very little was known about allergies, and my parents were sure that my eyes would remain shut. Fortunately, it only took a couple of days and I was back to normal, but I gave them quite a shock.

The family story was about the time when I almost drowned when I was wading in Clear Lake. My mother had watched her brother drown, and when this happened to me, she stood on shore, too paralyzed to act. My aunt ran in fully dressed and rescued me.

In still other accounts of what you were like as a child, the family is identifying and reinforcing the personality traits it sees in you today. Your own earliest memories reveal what *you* think of you; these stories reveal what *they* do:

My parents told me that when I was still in my crib, I would thump myself to sleep. I would lay on my stomach and kick my legs up and down. They used to call me "Thumper" from the Bambi movie. . . . I believe this story because it is very hard for me to sit still. I still to this day thump my feet or wiggle my knees back and forth.

I was told that as a baby, just under two years, when I was placed in my chair with wheels, I would race around the kitchen and adjoining family room. As my family cheered me on, I would increase my speed. I would stop abruptly at each corner, lift my chair, turn it, and continue with my course. Coming to the edge of the stairs, I would stop at the edge, quickly turn my chair in the opposite direction, and resume my activity. . . . I believe my mother was telling me that my running skills and agility were with me from a very young age.

My grandmother told me that when I was two years old I put on a play of "Me and Mommy" for my family. She said I acted both characters out so dramatically, she really believed me. . . . It opened my eyes to how I really am in life.

When I was four years old, I locked myself in the bathroom. My mom called the fire department. The fire chief came over and talked me into unlocking the door. . . . I think I was told the story to prove how stubborn I was.

In a fascinating study of family memories, journalist Elizabeth Stone suggests that men and women tend to hear different tales about their origins. Men are more likely to hear "golden boy" stories that tell them they were special, even sacred:

I came after two brothers who died at birth—a gap of ten years. So my birth, as I was told, was awaited with great anticipation. You know—"another baby may die." . . . I was the only one born in a hospital and much was made of that. It was like I was the one who was going to take on the modern role, I was the inheritor of the experience in America. The message was, "You're special, you're unique, you're going to make it in America." I knew I was going to make it big.

Men also tend to hear that they were hell-raisers:

My mother had taken me with her to the grocery store, and we ran into an elderly man whom she knew. 'My my, what a nice little boy,' he said, and patted me on the head. My mother said, 'Aaron, say hello to the nice man.' But I didn't say hello. Instead, I made a fist and socked hard. The problem was that my fist was at about the level of his groin."

Women, on the other hand, are more likely to learn that they were quiet, docile, and "good"—so "good," in fact, that it was easy to forget them. More than one heard about the time they were left somewhere:

I was a very good child, and when I was growing up, it was believed that children have to have lots of fresh air. They would put me outside in the carriage for two hours, then bring me in for lunch and then take me out again for another two hours. And I was such a good child that they forgot me once. They left me outside until ten o'clock at night.

I was a kid who could take care of myself. That's the way my mother tells it. She says that one afternoon she went to visit one of her friends. As she tells it, "I went there with four kids and I came home with three. You were so good about amusing yourself and taking care of yourself—you were off playing someplace by yourself in a corner, and I just forgot about you. I got home, and after I was home for a while, I realized that I didn't have you, so I went back to get you, and you were just fine."

The sex differences Stone found coincide with historical realities. In general, boys have been the preferred sex and the "sacred" children, and girls have been the ones to be disposed of because of their sex. There's a biological basis for her findings, too: little girls, on average, are indeed quieter than little boys, who tend to be less controlled and more active and aggressive. But historical and biological background do not obscure the fact that these stories were *told* to children as they were growing up, and there is a huge difference between being told that you were special and being told that you were forgotten.

Parents have a variety of reasons for telling children stories about themselves. Aside from entertaining, they may be steering, guiding, and warning. One of the men in Elizabeth Stone's study recalled a story that was used to admonish him. His family had gone to a parade and literally fought its way to the front of the crowd, but when they got there he refused to open his eyes because he was so scared. The admonition? Toughen up: boys aren't supposed to be afraid. How a story is told is critical. In one family, a tale of searching frantically for a lost child may say that she is special, but in another it may say that she wasn't worth very much in the first place.

The young, in their turn, may relish hearing things they never knew about themselves. But they may also cringe as they get older and realize what was going on in some of the stories. One of Stone's women subjects was told by her mother that she was

potty-trained at the age of one and that at two and a half she was
sent to the store on her own to buy a loaf of bread. As an adult,
she resented the compliance these accounts of her goodness and
responsibility fostered in her, because the only way she found to
be bad was to be mentally ill. Some young adults have told me that
they refuse to accept how family stories have defined them:

> *They told me that I was a broken record. It makes me rather sad. I*
> *was a smart child that had the urge to get things out. I think it was*
> *wrong to make fun of a child because she talked a lot.*

> *My mother said I was pampered and got a lot of attention from the*
> *older children. It made me laugh because I don't remember and I cer-*
> *tainly never felt pampered. I always saw my younger brother as pam-*
> *pered.*

> *My brothers told me that I cried all the time. I told them that maybe*
> *I wouldn't have cried so much if they had picked me up once in a*
> *while. The story defined me as a pain in the butt. I still believe that if*
> *he could have gotten away with it, my one brother would have done*
> *away with me at the first opportunity he had.*

Is it possible that stories we are told about ourselves eventually
become memories of our own? Yes, especially if we accept the
moral of the story. It's perfectly normal that when people enter a
new group they begin to have the kind of memories the group
encourages. Are these memories false? Not necessarily. Whatever
their mix of fact and fantasy, they are the means by which an individual's identity is grafted on to a group's. They are the glue that
binds a child to a family, a player to a team, a patient to a school of
therapy, a devotee to a religion, a citizen to a nation. It makes *me*
one of *them*. A young man who was adopted as a boy remembers
his great-grandfather being at his baseball games, even though the
old man had died before he was born. The young man's memories
are ostensibly inaccurate, but they reveal a deeper truth: how
much he values belonging to his family.

There are times when an urgency arises to separate what has been so thoroughly joined, to separate *me* from my family's definition of me, to know what I myself recall as opposed to what I was told. Those who have blanks in their remembered life story are sometimes desperate to have a direct memory of events they were told about, and they want proof of the memory's authenticity when it comes. A woman once wrote me to say that her sister was raped as a child but doesn't remember the rape as happening to her. She believes it happened to her sister, the writer of the letter. Another woman who had an early memory of nearly drowning subsequently learned that the incident involved not her, but her sister. So whose memories are whose? Unfortunately, there is no litmus test that can help, nothing that will turn a memory blue if it originates in you and pink if it originates in someone else. In families, my memories seep into you, and your memories seep into me, and after a while it becomes impossible to separate the sources.

Much of the time it doesn't matter whose memory is whose, and on occasion great power is generated by the fusion of the individual and the collective. The earliest recollection of a Jewish man in his fifties is of his father lying on top of him to protect him from machine-gun fire. The man is not sure if the memory is accurate or if it is truly his first, nor can he rule out the possibility that it's only a picture created by something he was told. But whatever its status, the mental image has all the power of something that happened "in the beginning."

What is remarkable about this individual memory is its confluence with collective memory. The incident it depicts would have happened when the man was three or four years old, at some point in his family's escape from the Nazis at the beginning of World War II. When he was five, his family came safely to America and immediately began telling their story of deliverance during Passover. It was now a part of ritualized family memory, fused with an even larger collective memory, that of the Jews' exodus from Egypt. At the very time that his autobiographical memory was being formed, a small boy lived with the sense of a protective father above. He had remembrances from his own experience, from hearing his family's stories, and from hearing his culture's stories. How could he separate these sources? And why would he want to, when the power of their synergy was so great?

I have often wondered from an historical perspective how long the idea of private memory has been in existence. When early humans lived together in small, face-to-face groups, did they even conceive of it? And how do twentieth-century children start out in life? Do they assume that their memories are visible to others (and so essentially collective) or hidden from them (and so individual)? In this section I have been emphasizing the collective nature of autobiographical memory, but perhaps it needs no emphasis at all. It may be the natural state of our remembrance, the way it was in the beginning.

Into the Air

How do an individual's autobiographical memories enter a family's? Let us consider just one way, by observing what happens at the time of someone's death. Here we resume the story of preparing an identity for posterity, but we do so now from the perspective of posterity. At this point, there are more twists and turns to the tale because successors do not always view the deceased the way the deceased viewed themselves. Besides, survivors are many and are likely to have conflicting memories of the one who has passed away. And those memories will change as time goes by.

Posterity's mythmaking often begins even before the death of a predecessor. Descendants may make of him a "living legend" or a "legend in his own time." A young woman I know thinks in this way of her great-grandmother, an old Polish immigrant who still speaks in broken English. "She knows things," says the great-granddaughter. "Lillian knows who will die and speaks with the spirits of the dead." On one occasion Lillian asked her husband to stay home from work, though she didn't know why she made the request. Lying down for a nap that afternoon, she was awakened by a vision of her father. He had come from his bedroom, where he lay ill, and he was wearing a pair of knickers, the kind of pants that young boys wear. His appearance was taken as a premonition of death, and it proved to be true. Her great-granddaughter isn't superstitious, but she cannot explain her forebear's power. "She tells this story with no mysteriousness at all. She tells it as if it were something that makes her just a little different from the rest of her family. She has many more stories of family members visiting her at the time of their death. She has stories of premonitory dreams and intuitions that almost always come true. Her brothers and sisters say, 'Lillian knows things.' My grandmother calls it a gift. My mother is not interested. I am afraid Lillian will leave this gift with me." Here is an identification across four generations with a figure who is becoming mythic. The family stories about this figure confirm an identity in a young woman who herself "knows things" and wants to use her gift as a psychologist.

At the actual time of a person's death, mythmaking is likely to intensify. A nun in her early fifties told me about the day her mother died. She was eight at the time and her father had kept her home from school because the death was imminent. The nun remembered bouncing a ball outside the house and going in from time to time to ask a nurse what was happening. On one of those visits the nurse told her that her mother had just passed away:

> I said, "Can I see her?" She said, "All right," and she brought me into the bedroom. A sheet was over my mother's head. I waited at the bottom of the bed, and I was looking up at a picture of St. Theresa on the wall. The nurse pulled the sheet down, and I looked at my mother and I looked up at the picture. There really was a resemblance! The nurse said to me, "Do you think your mommy looks like the picture?"

I said, "Yes," and she said, "She does." Whatever that meant, I don't know, except it was a beautiful picture and she was a beautiful woman. When she died, she didn't look ravaged by illness.

Whatever its mix of past and present, this forty-five-year-old memory contains many elements of myth. The sick mother has not only become beautiful, she has been linked with a saint who lives on in an extended culture. As the little girl looks up in the memory, you can almost see her mother's essence rising into the picture. It's a vivid symbol of sublimation, of an identity lifted into the air and transformed. This is memory inspirited—borne aloft so survivors can breathe it in.

A twenty-one-year-old woman who had lost her father two years before described what I mean by breathing in. Psychologists would describe what happened while she sat staring at his body as "identification" or "incorporation" or "introjection," and the young woman herself used a unique metaphor. To me, all these expressions are the equivalent of breathing in:

The night of the wake he was out in the living room and I couldn't sleep. I didn't know what to do, so I got up and washed my hair. My sister was sleeping. I came out, and the casket was there. I stayed away from it. I just sat there and said, "Well, you've got a lot of pull now, so do something. Send up signs. Do all these wonderful things." Then I'd say, "I'm really stupid! I'm sitting here talking to this dead body." So I'd run into the other room and I'd lie down, and come back out, and each time I'd get closer until finally I was just sitting there saying, "Well, you know you're going to be watching." And I had this great vision that he was going to be on my right-hand shoulder for the rest of my life. I thought, "Okay, I'm being watched over." And things got much easier then. . . .

Since then unbelievable things have happened. I'm a straight A-B student. Before it was C's and D's. I've finished a major and a half already and I'm going to finish two majors. I used to run away from everything, but now I say, "That's not the way to do it. You face

everything head-on 'cause you can beat it. You're bigger than it."
Sometimes I feel it's unfortunate he isn't seeing this progress. But he
is. He's on my shoulder, every day, every night. I feel I'm so much of
him, so much of him is me!

The transmission of identity across the generations is often
complicated by the fact that the dying person may want to leave
behind one version while posterity might want to receive quite
another. A grandson making a sculpture of his grandfather when
he was a very old man explained: "When you do a portrait, you
examine someone else and tell what you think they are. And
you're trying to get out of yourself whatever you feel you are."
During the long hours that his grandfather sat for him, the old
man kept spouting doom and gloom. It's not clear what lay
behind this harangue, but his grandson would have none of it.
"He was getting me so depressed I couldn't work anymore, so I
finally told him he either had to shut up or he had to leave." The
grandfather did leave, but he returned long enough for his grandson to complete the work—to put an identity in stone. "Grandpa
always looked like an avenging eagle to me. He has this tremen-
dously intense stare, and he cranes his head forward like a hawk
that's about to strike, but it's a completely defensive posture. He's
looking and examining the environment to protect himself, not to
go out and actually do something. So I was trying to capture that."

Such is the meaning of one man in the mind of one of his successors. But successors are plentiful, and if you listen to enough of
them it becomes clear that the deceased have multiple identities
and mean many things to many people. Another woman viewing
her father's open casket shed no tears despite the eulogies she had
heard. How sad, she thought, that all these people praise him,
when they don't know how cruel he was to me and to those closest to him. Sometimes conflict develops openly over which identities of the deceased are to prevail in collective life. After San
Francisco mayor George Moscone was assassinated, a furor arose

over a sculpture that had been commissioned to memorialize him. The sculpture rested on a pedestal covered with bullet holes, outlines of a .38 caliber pistol, spatters that looked like blood, and graffiti. The face had an empty expression that made it look like a mask. Moscone's wife, city officials, and most of the public were outraged. As sociologist David Unruh noted, the artist had chosen "to preserve the identities of assassinated public figure and plastic politician over the preferred identities of family patriarch, liberal Democrat, friend of the poor, and respected politician."

No family has made clearer to me the presence of multiple identities in collective memory than that of Sarkis Hashoian. Sark, you may recall, was the man who escaped the 1915 massacre of Armenians and told me in reverential tones about his sister's drowning. I had recorded his life story several years before his death. After he passed away, I spent some time with his family, remembering.

"He was the kind of a person that . . . you don't cry over spilt milk," said his wife of fifty-eight years. "He and I worked together for thirty years, side by side, and it's hard for a man and his wife to work together. He had his department. I had my department."

She was referring to a cleaning store he operated. "What was your department?" I asked.

"Mine was . . . I was the boss."

To his middle-aged daughter, Sark was several persons at once. Each depended on a remembered stage in her development. When she was a little girl, he was the tired father who came home after a hard day's work, lay down on the couch, and let her listen to his stomach gurgle. When she was a teenager, he was the strict but funny man her friends adored. "Whenever I'd ask him for the car to drive them home, he'd always go, 'What is this hocuspocus?' And they'd laugh because that was about the extent of his vocabulary." When she thought of her motherhood, Sark was the loving grandfather who played with her kids—and cheated at backgammon.

Sark's son, in his fifties, remembered the foreigner he thought his father was—a tough guy, harsh and emotionally distant. His grandson, in his late twenties, recalled his grandfather as "the wild man at the back of the store, cleaning clothes. Gramps always had to do everything himself, but he was kind of neurotic. He had to get it done in like five nanoseconds. Otherwise he sweated and freaked out." As collective memory flowed on that occasion, the many sides of Sark's personality emerged. So did his many roles: husband, co-worker, father, grandfather, senior citizen, American.

Sark's family showed me something else: how a person's identities change over time in those who memorialize him. When his children were growing up, Sark told them about his experiences in 1915, but his account came out in bits and pieces that were more like object lessons. "Finish your dinner, eat your vegetables, I had to eat grass, you wouldn't have made it." The reaction of the kids was predictable: they laughed it off. But after he died, his children thought for a second time about his story, and their father's life took on an entirely new meaning. "I think my dad was a great man," his daughter now said. "I want my children to know where they came from." The son who once found him distant and alien now considered him an anchor, saying, "This guy survived that great attack from the outside world. *I'm* going to survive." His grandson remembered standing at Sark's coffin with a relative named Jeff. These are his words: "When you're nineteen or twenty, driving a hundred miles an hour down the sidewalk, you figure you're not going to die. So Jeff was like, 'Geez, is this all there is? You go through your whole life, and you end up in the box?' I said, 'Turn around and look.' And here was this room full of people—kids, grandkids, Dana and all of Jeff's kids. And it was amazing to think from even a genetic standpoint how this one piece of a gene pool made it across the ocean." What became of Sark's story illustrates how memories of the deceased live on by addressing the developmental requirements of people at different stages of life. In death, Sark became the legend that he was not in life.

What happens to remembered identity over longer periods of time can be seen in the case of historical figures such as Abraham Lincoln. Lincoln was shot on Good Friday, April 14, 1865, five days after the official end of the Civil War. Sociologist Barry Schwartz points out that at the time of his death, Lincoln was not that popular a president, having been reelected by only a slim majority just six months earlier. While many felt sympathy for him, few thought his loss was irreparable. Sermons delivered throughout the North on Easter Sunday looked back on him as honest and well meaning, but far too merciful in regard to the Southern traitors, and far too merciful for his own good. Some preachers even said that God allowed the assassination to happen so that a stronger, sterner man would see to the righteous punishment of the Confederacy. Lincoln was just too insensitive to the cost of the war he had waged.

Subsequent generations abandoned this view of Lincoln and adopted another. People became genuinely fond of him, naming towns, streets, and businesses in his honor. Postage stamps began to bear his image. The identity preserved in collective memory at this point was that of "common man." Lincoln was the rail-splitter, the man of the soil, the people's president. It was stressed that he had come from a background of poverty, that he was simple and unpretentious, even awkward and homely. He loved to joke and tell stories. At the beginning of the twentieth century, the United States experienced a wave of egalitarian feeling known as the Progressive Movement, and Lincoln became its symbol. Numerous reminiscences were published by men who were young contemporaries of his and who were now in old age. The titles stressed his closeness and accessibility: "An Audience with Lincoln," "Intimate Personal Recollections," "Impressions of Lincoln," "Lincoln as I Knew Him," "A Boy at Lincoln's Feet."

In 1909, the centennial anniversay of Lincoln's birth, his likeness was stamped on the most common object imaginable, a penny. (It replaced the older Indian head.) A memorial to Lincoln was also commissioned, and its location showed a significant change in how he was remembered. "You must not approach too close to the immortals," said Congress. "His monument should stand alone, remote from the common habitations of man, apart from the business and turmoil of the city; isolated, distinguished, and serene." A huge statue of Lincoln was to be placed behind the pillars of the memorial, in the way the ancient Greeks placed statues of their gods in enclosed temples to secure their separation from the world. Lincoln was becoming something new: the Great Emancipator, the Savior of the Union, the Christ-like Man of Sorrows who sacrificed himself for us. In addition to a man people were fond of, he became one they revered.

Little was subtracted from Lincoln's identity across a century of rememberers, but a great deal was added to it. Indeed, the combination of simplicity and dignity, familiarity and remove made Lincoln a powerful symbol for enduring aspects of the American psyche, more powerful even than the country's first president, George Washington. In 1865 one of Lincoln's eulogizers had asked, "Who shall deny that Lincoln dead may yet do more for America than Lincoln living?" The eulogizer knew well how the memory of a person lives on by adapting to the needs of changing times.

To stress the role of myth in collective memory is not to say the keeper of archives is idle. Periodically, and in response to the needs of their own age, historians set about demythologizing a nation's heroes. On the 250th birthday of Thomas Jefferson, Americans were reminded that although he had written in the Declaration of Independence that all men were created equal, he had also said that blacks were inferior to whites, that although he had publicly opposed slavery, he had never freed his own slaves. On the 500th anniversary of Columbus "discovering" America, a huge debate erupted over who he was—a hero of great courage and vision, a greedy seafarer who stumbled upon a new land and exploited its native peoples, or a religious mystic who thought that the world had to be converted to Christianity before it ended in 1656. In 1992 the United States was uncertain about who its "discoverer" was because it was uncertain about who itself was. Did it want Columbus to be idealized or condemned?

Despite the presence of the archivist in collective memory, the primary force behind the preservation of identity is myth. Myth puts identities into a form that generations of descendants can be inspired by or recoil from. It creates heroes, heroines, and villains. It gives concrete image to abstract meaning, clarity to good and evil, archetypal resonance to isolated incidents. And it has the capacity to speak to successors at any stage of their life.

A small boy breathed in his forebear's identity some twenty years ago when he heard of his homecoming from World War II. His great-uncle Louis had joined the Marines at the outset of the war and spent most of his time in the Pacific. His father had missed him terribly and tried to keep track of his whereabouts through news and occasional letters. On a spring day in 1945, Louis's father was driving a team of horses when he spotted a school bus approaching in the distance. Seeing a uniformed figure inside, he began to tremble. The bus came to a halt and out stepped Louis with his shiny cap, sergeant's stripes, and medals. He had come home unannounced. His father got down from the wagon and embraced him, and soon the rest of the family was joining in. It was a hero's return in classic, small-town America.

The young man who tells the story today heard it from his father, who was there at the homecoming, a small boy himself. The story contains the very images for which a boy longs. Over the years, that boy learned everything that Louis had done during the war. When he came of age, he too joined the military; and when he was deployed in the Philippines in 1988, he thought of his great-uncle, who had fought his way through these very jungles. "To this day, I have a bracelet made from the metal of a downed Japanese Zero, which Louis made and sent to my father, who was four or five years old at the time." This story instilled pride in a young boy, along with a sense of patriotism. Its meaning has changed little over time.

Quite a different story greeted Chinese-American writer Maxine Hong Kingston when she reached puberty. It was about an aunt back in China who was carrying a child that the village knew was not her husband's. One night when the baby was about to be born, masked villagers raided the aunt's house. They slaughtered the roosters and pigs that were outside, even an ox. They broke into the house and smeared blood on the doors and walls. They found their way to the aunt's room, ripped up her clothes, and tore her weaving from its loom. In the kitchen they broke bowls, cut open rice sacks, and overturned great jars of duck eggs, pickled fruits, and vegetables, all the while screaming, "Pig! Ghost! Pig!" That night the aunt gave birth to her baby in the pigsty, and in the morning the two of them were found at the bottom of the family well. The aunt had killed her baby and committed suicide. "Now that you have started to menstruate," Maxine's mother said after telling her the story in secret, "what happened to the aunt could happen to you. Don't humiliate us."

It was a severe warning for a young girl about to become a woman. But the meaning of the story, unlike that of Louis's homecoming, changed over the years. When Maxine was in her thirties, the story began to haunt her, and she saw it in a different light. She started to imagine the man her aunt had had sex with. Had she sought him out? Had he raped her? Maybe he was one of the masked villagers who slaughtered the family animals and smeared the house with blood. Maybe he had organized the raid. Maxine put a new meaning into her aunt's death: she did not go quietly. No, she committed a spite suicide, poisoning the family's drinking water with her dead body. And now came a new identification: Maxine would become that aunt. Her mother had told her to tell no one of the incident, but Maxine would put it in writing and offer it to the public. She would restore the memory of her aunt, even if she too ended up in a well. At a particularly receptive time in Maxine's life, her aunt became a forerunner who offered "ancestral help."

It is cases like these that help me understand the power of my grandfather's white gloves. They were ancestral help that came at a particularly receptive time in my own life—not in my boyhood or adolescence, but in my middle age. I cannot become my grandfather, but I can put on his gloves and restore something in my family that died with him. I can breathe in his memory, let his story rain down. In all of our families, and in all of our lives, there comes a time when autobiographical memory completes a cycle, returning to the place where it began. Collective memory pours down on individuals, giving birth to new streams, filling rivulets already formed.

THE TACKLE BOX

I keep it under the workbench in the basement—a banged-up tackle box of pitted gray aluminum. Open it from the top, spread out the hinged shelves, and you get a smell of old metal, dirty cork, gas, oil, and who knows what else. To me it's a primary smell, not a blend, as basic and pure as that of a damp wind or a cup of hot chocolate. It's just "tackle box."

The box used to be my father's, and I remember that it was a step up when he first got it, bigger than anything he had had before. I brought it home six or seven years ago when it was clear that he was through fishing. The box held lots of memories for me, and it also held a lot of him. Pieces of inner tube for taking the kinks out of lines. A measuring tape. Little wrenches and screwdrivers, old prescription bottles of reel parts, spare rod tips and guides, tiny screws and nuts. Not that he had any of the equipment that these parts fit, but (I can hear his mind working) you never know. There were packets in yellowed plastic bags of cut-out newspaper articles and instructions that come with fishing line on how to tie various knots—the trilene knot, the sur-

243

geon's knot, the blood knot, the nail knot, the needle knot. There had to be twenty or thirty separate sources in that box for how to tie the improved clinch. Each time I dug into the box I'd toss out some of the junk, but for a number of years I kept just about everything. I wanted to preserve the tackle box just the way it was. I wanted to preserve him just the way he was.

My father, in the meantime, wasn't staying just the way he was. During the years I spent writing this book, his memory disappeared almost entirely. My mother moved him to the Alzheimer's unit in her retirement village, where she could check on him for a few minutes each day. After he was there for a while, he became incontinent and had to be diapered. He lost any ability to recognize people. On a visit last summer, my sisters and I walked into his ward and found him sleeping in a chair next to a woman patient. An attendant told my mother that the woman was "after" him. (They were, after all, sleeping together.) My mother told the attendant not to worry about it, which sounded a little like, "She can have him." Just a few days before, my father had asked my mother to marry him. She told him that they *were* married, and that they had been married for fifty-six years. She didn't exactly say yes.

As we walked the grounds and took pictures that day, my mother kept asking, "Do you know who these people are?" He said no. He did point out an airplane in the sky, and he did say something about the ducks in the pond. He walked slowly and probably would have fallen had we not been hanging on to him. Back in his room I gave him a shave and tried to tease him, but he would have none of it. When it was time to leave, he hugged my sisters but not me. They were women and I was a man.

Sometime that summer I got out the tackle box. I knew I couldn't preserve it any longer. Out went my father's old painted, cigar-shaped lures that we used to call plugs. Out went tiny metal lures with no mark other than "Al's Goldfish" or "Pat. Pend." Out went plastic worms, dirty metal leaders, spinners, loose jigs, a metal stringer with clips, and all the sinkers and swivels that covered the bottom of the center compartment. I kept the bobbers, big and little. I could use them. I kept three flatfish because of a memory of him telling me what a good lure it was. I never caught anything on one, and as far as I know he never did either. And now I remember the optimism he lavished on a little kid. Coming to a new place on the lake, he'd say, "There's gotta be one right there." How many times I heard it, and how many times it came up empty! But it was part of the ritual and had to be said. I saved the Johnson's Silver Minnow, tarnished now, because that was the first lure he had me cast. I saved two River Runts because I caught my biggest fish on a River Runt. That fish broke out of the water in the near-dark and scared me out of my wits.

I organized the box in different sections. On half of one of the shelves I left some of his tools and spare parts. I'd never use them, but this was the museum section. Next to it, the bobbers; in the shelf below, sinkers. Then I added some of *my* things. Some Rapallas, one or two of which I had already appropriated from him, a new plastic box of spinners and jigs, my growing collection of flies. My stuff is in the tackle box and so is his stuff, and I'm already beginning to forget whose stuff is whose. Just like my memory of my father.

I call him less frequently these days. At Thanksgiving his voice was dry and husky, and his conversation short. He had had several falls, breaking his knee on one occasion and bruising his shoulder on another. He recovered, but now he stays strapped in a chair for much of the day. My mother told me that he was starting to curse the nurses when he wasn't comfortable and had even let the dentist have it on one occasion. The last time I spoke with him, however, his voice was like a little boy's, as innocent and sweet as it was confused. *His* final words to *me* were "Bye, Daddy." Now that I've cleaned out the tackle box, now that I can use it, I can let him go.

☙

NOTES

Chapter One: The Whereabouts of Memory

p. 17. Proust, M. 1913. *Remembrance of Things Past.* Vol. 1. New York: Albert and Charles Boni.

p. 17. The expression "memorial container" comes from Casey, E. 1987. *Remembering.* Bloomington: Indiana University Press.

p. 17. " . . . close my eyes, and cry . . . " Gilbert, A., and C. Wysocki. 1987. Smell survey results. *National Geographic, 172,* 523.

p. 18. Melzack, R. 1992. Phantom limbs. *Scientific American, 226,* 4, 120–126.

p. 18. The human brain is described as the most complex structure in the known universe by Fischbach, G. 1992. Mind and brain. *Scientific American, 267,* 3, 48–57.

p. 19. On neurons firing in small clusters see Squire, L. 1987. *Memory and Brain.* New York: Oxford University Press.

p. 19. Zeki, S. 1992. The visual image in mind and brain. *Scientific American, 267,* 3, 68–76. (The hierarchy Zeki describes is functional, not necessarily anatomical.)

p. 19. On hierarchies of processing in the finch see Fischbach, Mind and brain.

p. 20. Regarding the representation of language in the brain see Damasio, A., and H. Damasio. 1992. Brain and language. *Scientific American, 267,* 3, 88–95.

p. 21. On amnesics with hippocampal damage, consult Squire, *Memory and Brain.* See also Kandel, E., and R. Hawkins. 1992. The biological basis of learning and individuality. *Scientific American, 267,* 3, 78–86. And: Sacks, O. 1985. *The Man Who Mistook His Wife for a Hat.* New York: Summit.

p. 21. Multiple personality disorder: Schacter, D., and J. Kihlstrom. 1989. Functional amnesia. In F. Boller and J. Graffman (eds.), *Handbook of Neuropsychology.* Vol. 3. Amsterdam: Elsevier.

p. 21. Damasio and Damasio, Brain and language.

p. 22. Kimura, D. 1992. Sex differences in the brain. *Scientific American, 267,* 3, 118–125.

p. 22. Lashley, K. 1950. In search of the engram. In *Symposium of the Society for Experimental Biology,* Vol. 4. New York: Cambridge University Press.

p. 22. Robert Ransmeier's experiment is reported in Gerard, R. 1953. What is memory? *Scientific American, 189,* 3, 118–126.

p. 23. Goldman-Rakic, P. 1992. Working memory and the mind. *Scientific American, 267,* 3, 110–117.

p. 23. This estimate of the sizes of pockets of neurons comes from Squire, *Memory and Brain.*

p. 24. Specific anatomical changes in the brains of laboratory rats were found by Greenough, W., J. Black, and C. Wallace. 1987. Experience and brain development. *Child Development, 58,* 539–559.

p. 24. Brain effects of stimulation in monkeys, and the complex wiring that results, are discussed by Kandel and Hawkins, The biological basis of learning.

p. 24. Stimulation and longevity of nerve cells: Fischbach, Mind and brain.

p. 25. In *Consciousness Explained* (Boston: Little, Brown, 1991), philosopher Daniel Dennett used the term "Cartesian Theater" to denote the hypothetical place where visual awareness is centered.

Chapter Two: Is Everything "In There"?

p. 27. Penfield, W. 1969. Consciousness, memory, and man's conditioned reflexes. In K. Pribram (ed.), *On the Biology of Learning.* New York: Harcourt, Brace, and World.

p. 28. Penfield, W. 1975. *The Mystery of Mind.* Princeton: Princeton University Press.

p. 29. Penfield, W., and P. Perot. 1963. The brain's record of auditory and visual experience: A final summary and discussion. *Brain, 86,* 595–696. The sample cases quoted here are from this article.

p. 29. " . . . no loss of detail": Penfield, Consciousness.

p. 29. Freud, S. 1930. Civilization and its discontents. In J. Strachey (ed.), *The Standard Edition of the Complete Psychological Works of Sigmund Freud.* Vol. 21. London: Hogarth.

p. 30. True, R. 1949. Experimental control in hypnotic age regression states. *Science, 110,* 583–584.

p. 30. Regarding the admissibility of hypnotically refreshed memories in Maryland courts see Scheflin, A., and J. Shapiro. 1989. *Trance on Trial.* New York: Guilford Press.

p. 30. Stump, A. 1975. That's him—the guy who hit me! *TV Guide,* October 4–10, pp. 32–35.

p. 31. Lamal, P. 1979. College student common beliefs about psychology. *Teaching of Psychology, 6,* 155–158. More documentation of common beliefs about memory is found in Loftus, E., and G. Loftus. 1980. On the permanence of stored information in the human brain. *American Psychologist, 35,* 409–420.

p. 31. *Déjà vu* experiences: Greeley, A. 1974. *Ecstasy: A Way of Knowing.* Englewood Cliffs, NJ: Prentice-Hall.

p. 32. Bartlett, F. 1932. *Remembering.* London: Cambridge University Press.

p. 33. Mann, A. 1959. *LaGuardia: A Fighter Against His Times, 1882–1933.* New York: J. B. Lippincott.

p. 33. Freud, S. 1910. Leonardo da Vinci and a memory of his childhood. In J. Strachey (ed.), *The Standard Edition of the Complete Psychological Works of Sigmund Freud.* Vol. 11. London: Hogarth.

p. 34. Loftus and Loftus, On the permanence. Also questioning Penfield's conclusions were Mahl, G., A. Rothenberg, J. Delgado, and H. Hamlin. 1964. Psychological responses in the human to intracerebral electrical stimulation. *Psychosomatic Medicine, 26,* 337–368.

p. 34. On replicating Robert True's results see Orne, M. 1982. Affidavit submitted to state of Pennsylvania. True told Orne that *Science* had abbreviated his questions when publishing his report.

p. 35. Laurence, J.-R., and C. Perry. 1983. Hypnotically created memory among highly hypnotizable subjects. *Science, 222,* 523–524.

p. 35. Loftus, E., and J. Palmer. 1974. Reconstruction of automobile destruction: An example of the interaction between language and memory. *Journal of Verbal Learning and Behavior, 13,* 585–589.

p. 35. Loftus, E., and K. Ketcham. 1991. *Witness for the Defense.* New York: St. Martin's Press.

p. 36. Weekes, J., S. Lynn, J. Green, and J. Brentar. 1992. Pseudomemory in hypnotized and task-motivated subjects. *Journal of Abnormal Psychology, 101,* 356–360. All the subjects in this study were selected for their hypnotizability, though not all were hypnotized.

p. 36. Piaget, J. 1962. *Plays, Dreams and Imitation in Childhood.* New York: Norton.

p. 36. President Reagan's memory of fiction as fact is discussed by Cannon, L. 1991. *President Reagan: The Role of a Lifetime.* New York: Simon & Schuster.

p. 38. Neisser, U. 1981. John Dean's memory: A case study. *Cognition, 9,* 1–22.

p. 39. Memory for a penny: Nickerson, R., and M. Adams. 1979. Long-term memory for a common object. *Cognitive Psychology, 11,* 287–307.

p. 40. Wiesel, T., and D. Hubel. 1965. Comparison of the effects of unilateral and bilateral eye closure on cortical unit responses in kittens. *Journal of Neurophysiology, 28,* 1029–1040.

p. 40. Weisel, T. 1982. Postnatal development of the visual cortex and the influence of environment. *Nature, 299,* 583–591. This article is about sutured eyes in young monkeys.

p. 41. Godden, D., and A. Baddeley. 1975. Context-dependent memory in two natural environments: On land and underwater. *British Journal of Psychology, 66,* 325–331.

p. 41. Young children at the park and in nursery school: Wilkinson, J. 1988. Context effects in children's event memory. In M. Gruneberg, P. Morris, and R. Sykes (eds.), *Practical Aspects of Memory.* Vol. 1. Chichester: Wiley.

p. 41. Bower, G. 1981. Mood and memory. *American Psychologist, 36,* 129–148. The effect Bower describes is less powerful concerning drunk and sober states than it is for happy and sad states. The reason is that alcohol interferes with getting material into memory in the first place.

p. 42. Bahrick, H., P. Bahrick, and R. Wittlinger. 1975. Fifty years of memory for names and faces: A cross-sectional approach. *Journal of Experimental Psychology: General, 104,* 54–75.

p. 42. On lineups with perpetrators absent see Malpass, R., and P. Devine. 1981. Eyewitness identification: Lineup instructions and the absence of the offender. *Journal of Applied Psychology, 66,* 345–351.

p. 42. Problems with relative judgments in lineups: Gonzalez, R., P. Ellsworth, and M. Pembroke. 1993. Response biases in lineups and showups. *Journal of Personality and Social Psychology, 64,* 525–537.

p. 43. Sources dealing with interrupted recall are Fisher, R., R. Geiselman, and M. Amador. 1989. Field test of the cognitive interview: Enhancing the recollection of actual victims and witnesses of crime. *Journal of Applied Psychology, 74,* 722–727. And: Neisser, U. 1988. Time present and time past. In Gruneberg, *Practical Aspects.* Vol. 2.

p. 45. Whyte, L. 1960. *The Unconscious Before Freud.* New York: Basic Books.

p. 45. Leibniz, G. 1981. *New Essays on Human Understanding.* Cambridge: Cambridge University Press.

p. 46. The conclusion that the existence of unconscious mental processes is "no longer questionable" comes from Loftus, E. (ed.) 1992. Science watch. *American Psychologist, 47,* 761–809.

p. 47. Kunst-Wilson, W., and R. Zajonc. 1980. Affective discrimination of stimuli that cannot be recognized. *Science, 207,* 557–558. Results of this experiment have been replicated by others. See Greenwald, A. 1992. New look 3: Unconscious cognition reclaimed. *American Psychologist, 47,* 766–779.

p. 47. Jelicic, M., A. De Roode, J. Bovill, and B. Bonke. In press. Unconscious learning established under anaesthesia. *Anaesthesia.*

p. 47. Ability to "see" without knowing: Weiskrantz, L. 1986. *Blindsight.* New York: Oxford University Press.

p. 47. Ability to choose the house that wasn't burning: Marshall, J., and P. Halligan. 1988. Blindsight and insight in visuo-spatial neglect. *Nature, 336,* 766–767.

p. 47. Hypnotic blindness: Kihlstrom, J., T. Barnhardt, and D. Tataryn. 1992. Implicit perception. In R. Bornstein and T. Pittman (eds.), *Perception Without Awareness.* New York: Guilford Press.

p. 47. Temporary blindness: Kihlstrom, J. 1987. The cognitive unconscious. *Science, 237,* 1445–1452.

p. 48. Consciousness and the brain's electrical activity: Crick, F., and C. Koch. 1992. The problem of consciousness. *Scientific American, 267,* 3, 152–159.

p. 49. Briere, J., and J. Conte. 1993. Self-reported amnesia for abuse in adults molested as children. *Journal of Traumatic Stress, 6,* 21–31.

p. 49. The widely read book on sexual abuse is Bass, E., and L. Davis. 1988. *The Courage to Heal.* New York: Harper & Row.

p. 49. The pamphlet: Spear, J. 1992. *Can I Trust My Memory?* Center City, Minn.: Hazelden.

p. 50. Regarding suggestions of abuse during therapy see Trott, J. 1991. The grade five syndrome. *Cornerstone, 20,* pp. 16–18.

p. 50. Loftus, E. 1993. The reality of repressed memories. *American Psychologist, 5,* 518–537.

p. 50. Dear Abby. 1992. Daughter's "memory" tearing her family apart. *The Ann Arbor News,* September 14, p. B2.

p. 51. Loftus, The reality.

p. 52. Paul Ingram's case is described by Wright, L. 1993. Remembering Satan—Parts I and II. *The New Yorker,* May 17, pp. 60–81, and May 24, pp. 54–76.

p. 53. Ofshe, R. 1989. Coerced confessions: The logic of seemingly irrational action. *Cultic Studies Journal, 6,* 1–15.

p. 54. Orwell, G. 1949. *Nineteen Eighty-Four, A Novel.* New York: Harcourt, Brace.

p. 56. Spence, D. 1982. *Narrative Truth and Historical Truth.* New York: Norton.

p. 57. On changing the memories you merely watch see Linton, M. 1986. Ways of searching and the contents of memory. In D. Rubin (ed.), *Autobiographical Memory.* Cambridge: Cambridge University Press.

Chapter Three: Like a River

p. 60. Neisser, U. 1982. *Memory Observed.* San Francisco: Freeman.

p. 60. Dr. Leyden's feat is recounted by Conway, M. 1990. *Autobiographical Memory.* Buckingham: Open University Press.

p. 61. Stratton, G. 1917. The mnemonic feat of the "Shass Pollak." *Psychological Review, 24,* 244–47.

p. 62. Shereshevskii's remarkable abilities are described by Luria, A. 1968. *The Mind of a Mnemonist.* New York: Basic Books.

p. 62. On the memorist Tomoyori see Thompson, C., T. Cowan, J. Frieman, and R. Mahadevan. 1991. Rajan: A study of a memorist. *Journal of Memory and Language, 30,* 702–724.

p. 62. Marek, G. 1975. *Toscanini.* London: Vision Press.

p. 63. The woman with the photographic memory is described by Stromeyer, C. 1970. An adult eidetiker. *Psychology Today,* November, pp. 76–80.

p. 65. Bjork, E., and R. Bjork. 1988. On the adaptive aspects of retrieval failure in autobiographical memory. In M. Gruneberg, P. Morris, and R. Sykes (eds.), *Practical Aspects of Memory.* Vol. 1. Chichester: Wiley.

p. 72. Linn, M., S. Fabricant, and D. Linn. 1988. *Healing the Eight Stages of Life.* New York: Paulist Press.

p. 73. Grove, D., and B. Panzer. *Resolving Traumatic Memories.* Audiotape produced by David Grove Seminars.

p. 74. Ramsey, D. 1976. *Grief Therapy.* CBS/Carousel Films.

p. 74. Bradshaw, J. 1990. *Homecoming: Reclaiming and Championing Your Inner Child.* New York: Bantam Books.

p. 75. Lifton, R. 1961. *Thought Reform and the Psychology of Totalism.* New York: Norton.

p. 75. Lam, T. 1991. Talking about rape. *Ann Arbor News,* June 9, p. A9.

Chapter Four: The Autobiographical Memory System

p. 86. Linton, M. 1982. Transformations of memory in everyday life. In U. Neisser (ed.), *Memory Observed.* San Francisco: Freeman. Linton, M. 1986. Ways of searching and the contents of memory. In D. Rubin (ed.), *Autobiographical Memory.* Cambridge: Cambridge University Press. In another diary study, Wagenaar found that *when* was almost useless as a retrieval cue. See Wagenaar, W. 1986. My memory: A study of autobiographical memory over six years. *Cognitive Psychology, 18,* 225–252.

p. 86. The World War II veteran is Howard Hoffman. See Hoffman, A., and H. Hoffman. 1990. *Archives of Memory.* Lexington: University Press of Kentucky.

p. 86. Remembering the hour of the day or the day of the week better than the month or the year: Friedman, W., and A. Wilkins. 1985. Scale effects in memory for the time of events. *Memory and Cognition, 13,* 168–175.

p. 87. Christie, A. 1968. *By the Pricking of My Thunbs.* Cited in Loftus, E., and W. Marburger. 1983. Since the eruption of Mt. St. Helens, has anyone beaten you up? Improving the accuracy of retrospective reports with landmark events. *Memory & Cognition, 11,* 114–120.

p. 87. Kotre, J. 1984. *Outliving the Self.* Baltimore: Johns Hopkins University Press.

p. 87. Linton, Transformations.

p. 88. Extendures: Linton, Ways of searching.

p. 89. Ericsson, K., W. Chase, and S. Faloon. 1980. Acquisition of a memory skill. *Science, 208,* 1181–1182. (The numbers were read at one-second intervals. Interestingly, the same student was unable to remember more than six letters of the alphabet at a time; he had no way of grouping them meaningfully.)

p. 89. Chase, W., and H. Simon. 1973. Perception in chess. *Cognitive Psychology, 4,* 55–81.

p. 90. Brown, R., and D. McNeill. 1966. The "tip of the tongue" phenomenon. *Journal of Verbal Learning and Verbal Behavior, 5,* 325–337.

p. 90. Students "remember" that the professor pointed to the blackboard: Nakamura, G., A. Graesser, J. Zimmerman, and J. Riha. 1985. Script processing in a natural situation. *Memory and Cognition, 13,* 140–144.

p. 91. Barclay, C. 1986. Schematization of autobiographical memory. In Rubin, *Autobiographical Memory.*

p. 92. The work on depression and people's memory hierarchies comes from Singer, J., and P. Salovey. 1993. *The Remembered Self.* New York: The Free Press.

p. 93. Three references on neurological flashbulbs: Gold, P. 1987. Sweet memories. *American Scientist, 75,* 151–155. McGaugh, J. 1990. Significance and remembrance: The role of neuromodulatory systems. *Psychological Science, 1,* 15–25. Squire, L. 1987. *Memory and Brain.* New York: Oxford University Press.

p. 93. Cohen, G., and D. Faulkner. 1988. Life span changes in autobiographical memory. In M. Gruneberg, P. Morris, and R. Sykes (eds.), *Practical Aspects of Memory.* Vol. 1. Chichester: Wiley. Using a very different method than Cohen and Faulkner, William Brewer found the same relationship between the vividness and uniqueness of memories. See Brewer, W. 1988. Qualitative analysis of the recalls of randomly sampled autobiographical events. In Gruneberg, *Practical Aspects.* Vol. 1.

p. 94. Linton, Ways of searching.

p. 98. Colegrove, F. 1899. Individual memories. *American Journal of Psychology, 10,* 228–255.

p. 98. On people's vivid memories of news events see Brown, R., and J. Kulik. 1977. Flashbulb memories. *Cognition, 5,* 73–99. Also see Neisser, U. 1982. Snapshots or benchmarks? In Neisser, *Memory Observed.*

p. 99. Steblay, N. 1992. A meta-analytic review of the weapon focus effect. *Law and Human Behavior, 16,* 413–424.

p. 100. On the accuracy of highly emotional memories see Egeth, H. 1993. What do we *not* know about eyewitness identification? *American Psychologist, 48,* 577–580.

p. 100. Accuracy of *Challenger* memories in Johns Hopkins University study: McCloskey, M., C. Wible, and N. Cohen. 1988. Is there a special flashbulb-memory mechanism? *Journal of Experimental Psychology: General, 117,* 171–181. An earlier study had found that memories of the day President Reagan was shot remained quite consistent over a period of six and a half months. See Pillemer, D. 1984. Flashbulb memories of the assassination attempt on President Reagan. *Cognition, 16,* 63–80.

p. 100. At Emory University: Neisser, U., and N. Harsch. 1992. Phantom flashbulbs: False recollections of hearing the news about "Challenger." In E. Winograd and U. Neisser (eds.), *Affect and Accuracy in Recall.* Cambridge: Cambridge University Press.

p. 101. Woman's memory of the birth of a child: Kotre, *Outliving the Self.*

p. 101. Neisser, U. 1981. John Dean's memory: A case study. *Cognition, 9,* 1–22.

p. 103. Singer and Salovey, *The Remembered Self.*

p. 104. Weber, S. 1990. The teacher educator's experience: cultural generativity and duality of commitment. *Curriculum Inquiry, 20,* 141–159.

p. 104. McAdams, D. 1985. *Power, Intimacy, and the Life Story.* Homewood, Ill.: Dorsey.

p. 105. Lifton, R. 1961. *Thought Reform and the Psychology of Totalism.* New York: Norton.

p. 106. Hawthorne, N. 1851. *The House of the Seven Gables.* Boston: Houghton Mifflin (1964 ed.).

p. 107. Hoffman and Hoffman, *Archives of Memory.* On a much smaller scale, witnesses to a staged crime estimated that it took two and a half times longer than it actually did. See Buckhout, R. 1974. Eyewitness testimony. *Scientific American, 231,* 6, 23–31.

p. 107. Garofalo, J., and M. Hindelang. 1977. *An Introduction to the National Crime Survey.* Washington, D.C.: U.S. Department of Justice.

p. 108. Regarding the telescoping of newsworthy events see Brown, N., L. Rips, and S. Shevell. 1985. The subjective dates of natural events in very-long-term memory. *Cognitive Psychology, 17,* 139–177.

p. 108. Loftus and Marburger, Since the eruption.

p. 111. On hierarchical organization in the brain see Fischbach, G. 1992. Mind and brain. *Scientific American, 267,* 3, 48–57.

p. 111. Gazzaniga, M. 1992. *Nature's Mind.* New York: Basic Books.

p. 113. Hobson, J. 1988. *The Dreaming Brain.* New York: Basic Books.

p. 113. Greenwald, A. 1980. The totalitarian ego. *American Psychologist, 35,* 603–618.

p. 114. These stories about disclaiming responsibility for bad outcomes come from the *San Francisco Sunday Examiner and Chronicle.* 1979. April 22, p. 35.

p. 114. John Dean is quoted in Neisser, John Dean's memory.

p. 115. Gruneberg, M., and R. Sykes. 1978. Knowledge and retention: The feeling of knowing and reminiscence. In M. Gruneberg, P. Morris, and R. Sykes (eds.), *Practical Aspects of Memory.* London: Academic Press.

p. 116. On judging the authenticity of memories vs. imagined events see Johnson, M. 1985. The origin of memories. In P. Kendall (ed.), *Advances in Cognitive-Behavioural Research and Therapy.* Vol. IV. New York: Academic Press.

p. 116. Personal myth: McAdams, D. 1993. *The Stories We Live By.* New York: Morrow.

p. 118. Taylor, S., and J. Brown. 1989. Illusion and well-being: A social-psychological perspective on mental health. *Psychological Bulletin, 103,* 193–210.

p. 119. The dispositional shift was first described by Moore, B., D. Sherrod, T. Liu, and B. Underwood. 1979. The dispositional shift in attribution over time. *Journal of Experimental Social Psychology, 15,* 553–569.

p. 120. The dispositional shift in college students' writings and in psychologists' autobiographies: Peterson, C. 1980. Memory and the "dispositional shift." *Social Psychology Quarterly, 43,* 372–380.

Chapter Five: Memory in the Young

p. 121. "They were running around me . . ." Chase, S. 1983. The people inside me. 20/20 (ABC-TV News) segment.

p. 121. Silverman, P., and P. Retzlaff. 1986. Cognitive stage regression through hypnosis: Are earlier cognitive stages retrievable? *International Journal of Clinical and Experimental Hypnosis, 34,* 192–204.

p. 122. Bradshaw, J. 1990. *Homecoming: Reclaiming and Championing Your Inner Child.* New York: Bantam Books.

p. 122. "One incident after another" Janov, A. 1970. *The Primal Scream.* New York: Dell.

p. 123. The psychiatrist who remembers his own conception is referred to in Linn, D., S. Linn, and M. Linn. *Healing the Eight Stages of Life. Stage 1: Infancy.* Audio tape.

p. 123. Weiss, B. 1988. *Many Lives, Many Masters.* New York: Simon & Schuster. Weiss, B. 1992. *Through Time Into Healing.* New York: Simon & Schuster.

p. 125. DeCasper, A., and M. Spence. 1986. Prenatal maternal speech influences newborns' perception of speech sounds. *Infant Behavior and Development, 9,* 133–150.

p. 125. DeCasper, A., and W. Fifer. 1980. Of human bonding: Newborns prefer their mothers' voices. *Science, 208,* 1174–1176.

p. 125. Cernoch, J., and R. Porter. 1985. Recognition of maternal axillary odors by infants. *Child Development, 56,* 1593–1598.

p. 125. Checkerboard patterns: Friedman, S. 1972. Habituation and recovery of visual response in the alert human newborn. *Journal of Experimental Child Psychology, 13,* 339–349.

p. 125. Sensory crossover demonstrated: Stern, D. 1990. *Diary of a Baby.* New York: Basic Books.

p. 126. Rovee-Collier, C. 1989. The joy of kicking: Memories, motives, and mobiles. In P. Solomon, G. Goethals, C. Kelley, and B. Stephens (eds.), *Memory.* New York: Springer-Verlag.

p. 126. Recognizing generic faces: Strauss, M. 1979. Abstraction of prototypical information by adults and 10-month-old infants. *Journal of Experimental Psychology: Human Learning and Memory, 5,* 618–632.

p. 126. Generic animals: Younger, B. 1985. The segregation of items into categories by ten-month-old infants. *Child Development, 56,* 1574–1583.

p. 126. Recall between six and nine months of age: Mandler, J. 1990. Recall and its verbal expression. In R. Fivush and J. Hudson (eds.), *Knowing and Remembering in Young Children*. Cambridge: Cambridge University Press.

p. 127. Five- vs. seven-month-olds: Fox, N., J. Kagan, and S. Weiskopf. 1979. The growth of memory during infancy. *Genetic Psychology Monographs, 99,* 91–130.

p. 127. Nine- vs. fourteen-month-olds: Meltzoff, A. 1988. Infant imitation and memory: Nine-month-olds in immediate and deferred tests. *Child Development, 59,* 217–225.

p. 127. The test of the fourteen-month-olds: Meltzoff, A. 1988. Infant imitation after a 1-week delay: Long-term memory for novel acts and multiple stimuli. *Developmental Psychology, 24,* 470–476.

p. 128. On the appearance of the self-as-subject see Harter, S. 1983. Developmental perspectives on the self-system. In E. Hetherington (ed.), *Handbook of Child Psychology*. Vol. 4. New York: Wiley.

p. 128. The self-as-object: Lewis, M., and J. Brooks-Gunn. 1979. *Social Cognition and the Acquisition of Self*. Plenum Press.

p. 128. Infant rats and guinea pigs: Campbell, B., and X. Coulter. 1976. The ontogenesis of learning and memory. In M. Rosenzweig and E. Bennet (eds.), *Neural Mechanisms of Learning and Memory*. Cambridge, Mass.: MIT Press.

p. 129. Regarding the maturing of the hippocampus see White, S., and D. Pillemer. 1979. Childhood amnesia and the development of a socially accessible memory system. In J. Kihlstrom and F. Evans (eds.), *Functional Disorders of Memory*. Hillsdale, N.J.: Erlbaum.

p. 130. Emily is quoted from Nelson, K. 1988. The ontogeny of memory for real events. In U. Neisser and E. Winograd (eds.), *Remembering Reconsidered*. Cambridge: Cambridge University Press.

p. 133. The samples of cookie making are quoted from Nelson, K., and J. Gruendel. 1986. Children's scripts. In K. Nelson (ed.), *Event Knowledge*. Hillsdale, N.J.: Erlbaum.

p. 133. Two-year-old's routine is upset: Hudson, J. 1990. The emergence of autobiographical memory in mother–child conversation. In Fivush and Hudson, *Knowing and Remembering*.

p. 134. Emily is quoted from Nelson, *The ontogeny*.

p. 135. The interview of the girl of three years and eight months is quoted from McCabe, A., E. Capron, and C. Peterson. 1991. The voice of experience: The recall of early childhood and adolescent memories by young adults. In A. McCabe and C. Peterson (eds.), *Developing Narrative Structure*. Hillsdale, N.J.: Erlbaum.

p. 135. The privacy of children's thoughts: Flavell, J., S. Shipstead, and K. Croft. 1978. *What Young Children Think You See When Their Eyes Are Closed.* Unpublished manuscript, Stanford University.

p. 136. Peterson, C., and A. McCabe. 1983. *Developmental Psycholinguistics.* New York: Plenum Press.

p. 136. Michaels, S. 1991. The dismantling of narrative. In McCabe and Peterson, *Developing Narrative Structure.*

p. 137. Children and adults remembering trauma: Spiegel, D., and E. Cardena. 1991. Disintegrated experience: The dissociative disorders revisited. *Journal of Abnormal Psychology, 100,* 366–378.

p. 138. Goodman, G., and A. Clarke-Stewart. 1991. Suggestibility in children's testimony: Implications for sexual abuse investigations. In J. Doris (ed.), *The Suggestibility of Children's Recollections.* Washington, D.C.: American Psychological Association.

p. 138. Errors of omission: Ceci, S. 1991. Some overarching issues in the children's suggestibility debate. In Doris, *The Suggestibility.*

p. 139. Errors of commission: Dent, H. 1991. Experimental studies of interviewing child witnesses. In Doris, *The Suggestibility.*

p. 142. Self-criticism in nine-year-olds: Harter, *Developmental perspectives.*

p. 145. Regarding the increased capacity for information processing, consult Flavell, J. 1985. *Cognitive Development.* Englewood Cliffs, N.J.: Prentice-Hall.

p. 146. Poker chip experiment: Osherson, D., and E. Markman. 1975. Language and the ability to evaluate contradictions and tautologies. *Cognition, 3,* 213–226.

p. 148. Elkind, D. 1981. *Children and Adolescents.* New York: Oxford University Press.

p. 148. Dan McAdams is quoted in J. Kotre and E. Hall. 1990. *Seasons of Life.* Boston: Little, Brown.

p. 149. Levinson, D. 1978. *The Seasons of a Man's Life.* New York: Knopf. Also: Roberts, P., and P. Newton. 1987. Levinsonian studies of women's adult development. *Psychology and Aging, 2,* 154–163.

p. 150. Modestin, J. 1992. Multiple personality disorder in Switzerland. *American Journal of Psychiatry, 149,* 1, 88–92.

p. 151. Concerning MPD outside of North America, the Netherlands may be an exception to the rule. Certain psychiatric facilities there report MPD with relative frequency. See Modestin, Multiple personality.

p. 151. MPD's irregular history is related by Hacking, I. 1991. Two souls in one body. *Critical Inquiry, 17,* 838–867.

p. 151. Hacking, Two souls, used the metaphor of the remote-control device.

p. 152. Watkins, J. 1984. The Bianchi (L. A. Hillside Strangler) case: Sociopath or multiple personality? *International Journal of Clinical and Experimental Hypnosis, 32,* 67–101.

p. 152. Arguing that Bianchi was consciously faking were Orne, M., D. Dinges, and E. Orne. 1984. On the differential diagnosis of multiple personality in the forensic context. *International Journal of Clinical and Experimental Hypnosis, 32,* 118–169. Arguing for unconscious creation was Allison, R. 1984. Difficulties diagnosing the multiple personality syndrome in a death penalty case. *International Journal of Clinical and Experimental Hypnosis, 32,* 102–117.

p. 152. This report of dissociation is quoted from Gelinas, D. 1983. The persisting negative effects of incest. *Psychiatry, 46,* 312–332.

p. 153. Concerning "Sybil" see Sileo, C. 1993. Multiple personalities: The experts are split. *Insight,* October 25, pp. 18–22.

p. 154. On recollections of past lives see Reveen, P. 1987–88. Fantasizing under hypnosis: Some experimental evidence. *The Skeptical Inquirer, 12,* 181–183. Also see Spanos, N. 1987–88. Past-life hypnotic regression: A critical view. *The Skeptical Inquirer, 12,* 174–180.

p. 155. Luria, A. 1968. *The Mind of a Mnemonist.* New York: Basic Books.

p. 156. Stern, *Diary of a Baby.*

p. 158. McCabe, Capron, and Peterson, The voice of experience.

Chapter Six: Memory in the Mature

p. 162. Levinson, D. 1978. *The Seasons of a Man's Life.* New York: Knopf.

p. 162. Helson, R., and P. Wink. 1992. Personality change in women from the early 40s to the early 50s. *Psychology and Aging, 7,* 46–55.

p. 162. Teltsch, K. 1989. "Midlife crisis" is investigated by one who doubts it's there. *New York Times,* December 12, p. C3. The psychologist referred to is Gilbert Brim.

p. 162. Recalling early emotional problems: Robins, L. 1985. Early home environment and retrospective recall: A test for concordance between siblings with and without psychiatric disorders. *American Journal of Orthopsychiatry, 55,* 27–41.

p. 163. Attitude change from 1973 to 1982: Markus, G. 1986. Stability and change in political attitudes: Observed, recalled and explained. *Political Behavior, 8,* 21–44.

p. 164. Changes in political attitudes, 1972–1976: Niemi, G., R. Katz, and D. Newman. 1980. Reconstructing past partisanship: The failure of party identification recall questions. *American Journal of Political Science, 24,* 633–651.

p. 164. Ross, M. 1989. Relation of implicit theories to the construction of personal histories. *Psychological Review, 96,* 341–357.

p. 164. Vaillant, G. 1977. *Adaptation to Life.* Boston: Little, Brown.

p. 165. Regarding a culture's origin stories see Mead, M. 1978. *Culture and Commitment.* New York: Columbia University Press.

p. 166. ". . . I was gathering in those years too . . ." Kotre, J. 1984. *Outliving the Self.* Baltimore: Johns Hopkins University Press.

p. 167. The study of Catholics and ex-Catholics: Kotre, J. 1971. *The View from the Border.* Chicago: Aldine-Atherton.

p. 167. Ross, Relation of implicit theories.

p. 168. Linton, S., and L. Melin. 1982. The accuracy of remembering chronic pain. *Pain, 13,* 281–285.

p. 168. Research on the study-skills program is presented in Ross, Relation of implicit theories.

p. 168. Remembering personal adjustment twenty-five years later: Woodruff, D., and J. Birren. 1972. Age changes and cohort differences in personality. *Developmental Psychology, 6,* 252–259.

p. 168. Sixty-seven-year-olds rate their memory at thirty-eight: McFarland, C., W. Turnbull, and M. Giltrow. 1988. Biased recollections in the elderly. Unpublished manuscript.

p. 169. Whitbourne, S., and D. Dannefer. 1985. The "life drawing" as a measure of time perspective in adulthood. *International Journal of Aging and Human Development, 22,* 77–85.

p. 170. Rubin, D., S. Wetzler, and R. Nebes. 1986. Autobiographical memory across the lifespan. In D. Rubin (ed.), *Autobiographical Memory.* Cambridge: Cambridge University Press.

p. 171. The study of college students remembering school terms was done by Robinson, J. 1986. Temporal reference systems and autobiographical memory. In Rubin, *Autobiographical Memory.*

p. 172. Mackavey, W., J. Malley, and A. Stewart. 1991. Remembering autobiographically consequential experiences: Content analysis of psychologists' accounts of their lives. *Psychology and Aging, 6,* 50–59.

p. 172. Remembering national and world events: Schuman, H., and J. Scott. 1989. Generations and collective memory. *American Sociological Review, 54,* 359–381.

p. 172. Studies on increased reflectiveness in the middle years are summarized by Cohler, B., and R. Galatzer-Levy. 1990. Self, meaning, and morale across the second half of life. In R. Nemiroff and C. Colarusso (eds.), *New Dimensions in Adult Development.* New York: Basic Books.

p. 174. The entire Chris Vitullo story can be found in Kotre, *Outliving the Self.*

p. 175. ". . . to live on my old-age pension . . ." Wong, P., and L. Watt. 1991. What types of reminiscence are associated with successful aging? *Psychology and Aging, 6,* 272–279.

p. 177. Butler, R. 1963. The life review: An interpretation of reminiscence in the aged. *Psychiatry, 26,* 65–76.

p. 178. Zuniga, M. 1989. Mexican-American elderly and reminiscence: Interventions. *Journal of Gerontological Social Work, 14,* 61–73.

p. 179. Keawkungwal, S. 1984. *Life Satisfaction of Thai and American Elderly as Related to Psychosocial Variables.* Dissertation submitted to the University of Maryland.

p. 179. The Washington oral history project is described in Manheimer, R. 1983. History on a human scale. *History News,* September, pp. 17–22.

p. 181. Noyes, R., and R. Kletti. Panoramic memory: A response to the threat of death. *Omega, 8,* 181–194. Also see Gallup, G. 1982. *Adventures in Immortality.* New York: McGraw-Hill.

p. 182. On the life review in extreme old age see Lieberman, M., and S. Tobin. 1983. *The Experience of Old Age.* New York: Basic Books.

p. 183. PET scans of twenty-year-olds and eighty-year-olds: Selkoe, D. 1992. Aging brain, aging mind. *Scientific American, 267, 3,* 134–142. PET stands for positron emission tomography.

p. 183. Regarding genetic origins of Alzheimer's disease see Murrell, J., M. Farlow, B. Ghetti, and M. Benson. 1991. A mutation in the amyloid precursor protein associated with hereditary Alzheimer's disease. *Science, 254,* 97–99. Also: Marx, J. 1991. Mutation identified as a possible cause of Alzheimer's disease. *Science, 251,* 867–877.

p. 184. The relation of age to senile dementia: Preston, G. 1986. Dementia in elderly adults: Prevalence and institutionalization. *Journal of Gerontology, 41,* 281–287.

p. 184. Bliven is quoted in Cowley, M. 1980. *The View from 80.* New York: Viking Press.

p. 184. Feeling young when working past sixty-five: Barak, B., and B. Stern. 1986. Subjective age correlates: A research note. *Gerontologist, 26,* 571–578.

p. 185. Tobin, S. 1991. *Personhood in Advanced Old Age.* New York: Springer.

p. 185. The story of the eighty-four-year-old widow is from Tobin, S. 1991. Preservation of the self in old age. *Social Casework: The Journal of Contemporary Social Work,* November, pp. 550–555.

p. 186. "We had a small jewelry store . . ." Tobin, *Personhood.*

p. 186. Lyman, A., and M. Edwards. 1989. Poetry: Life review for frail American Indian elderly. *Journal of Gerontological Social Work, 14,* 75–91.

p. 187. A discussion of the ageless self appears in Kaufman, S. 1986. *The Ageless Self.* Madison: University of Wisconsin Press.

p. 187. ". . . it has nothing to do with age . . ." Kotre, J., and E. Hall. 1990. *Seasons of Life.* Boston: Little, Brown.

Chapter Seven: "In the Beginning"

p. 190. Bronte, E. 1901. *Wuthering Heights.* New York: Knopf.

p. 193. On sex differences in the age of first memories see Pillemer, D., and S. White. 1989. Childhood events recalled by children and adults. In H. Reese (ed.), *Advances in Child Development and Behavior.* Vol. 21. New York: Academic Press.

p. 193. Rule, W., and G. Jarrell. 1983. Intelligence and earliest memories. *Perceptual and Motor Skills, 56,* 795. On the same subject see Rabbitt, P., and L. McInnis. 1988. Do clever old people have earlier and richer first memories? *Psychology and Aging, 3,* 338–341.

p. 194. Age of recall and the content of early memories: Usher, J., and U. Neisser. 1993. Childhood amnesia and the beginnings of memory for four early life events. *Journal of Experimental Psychology: General, 122,* 155–165. For a critique of this article see Loftus, E. 1993. Desperately seeking memories of the first few years of childhood: The reality of early memories. *Journal of Experimental Psychology: General, 122,* 274–277.

p. 194. Trauma, transition, and trivia in early memories: Kihlstrom, J., and J. Harackiewicz. 1982. The earliest recollection: A new survey. *Journal of Personality, 50,* 134–148. Also see Rabbitt and McInnis, Do clever old people?

p. 194. Sources referring to the visual content of early memories: Kihlstrom and Harackiewicz, The earliest recollection. Also: Cohen, G., and D. Faulkner. 1988. Lifespan changes in autobiographical memory. In M. Gruneberg, P. Morris, and R. Sykes (eds.), *Practical Aspects of Memory.* Vol. I. Chichester: Wiley. And: Bruhn, A. 1990. *Earliest Childhood Memories.* Vol. I. New York: Praeger.

p. 194. On the out-of-body perspective in memory see Kotre, K. 1990. The external observer in autobiographical memories. Unpublished master's thesis,

University of Michigan. And: Nigro, G., and U. Neisser. 1983. Point of view in personal memories. *Cognitive Psychology, 15,* 467–482.

p. 195. The Goethe story appears in Freud, S. 1917. A childhood recollection from *Dichtung und wahrheit.* In J. Strachey (ed.), *The Standard Edition of the Complete Psychological Works of Sigmund Freud.* Vol. 17. In a 1910 analysis of Leonardo da Vinci's earliest memory, Freud said that memories could be altered and even falsified to serve needs in the present. He concluded that Leonardo's memory of a vulture perching on his bed was really an adult fantasy transposed to childhood. Despite this awareness of the present tense, Freud's basic assumption was usually that the significance of memories lay in the past.

p. 198. Eisenhower, D. 1967. *Stories I Tell to Friends.* New York: Doubleday.

p. 198. Meir, G. 1975. *My Life.* New York: G. P. Putnam's Sons.

p. 199. The Papert and Einstein examples are from Huyghe, P. 1985. Voices, glances, flashbacks: Our first memories. *Psychology Today,* September, pp. 48–52.

p. 199. Plomin, R., G. McClearn, N. Pedersen, J. Nesselroade, and C. Bergman. 1988. Genetic influence on childhood family environment perceived retrospectively from the last half of the life span. *Developmental Psychology, 24,* 738–745.

p. 200. Numerous studies relating the content of early memories to the present condition of one's life are cited in Kotre, K. 1994. Autobiographical memory and the self. Unpublished paper, University of Michigan.

p. 200. Davidow, S., and A. Bruhn. 1990. Earliest memories and the dynamics of delinquency: A replication study. *Journal of Personality Assessment, 54,* 601–616.

p. 201. A change in the earliest memory following institutionalization: Tobin, S., and E. Etigson. 1968. Effect of stress on earliest memory. *Archives of General Psychiatry, 19,* 435–444.

p. 201. The story of "Jane" appears in Eckstein, D. 1976. Early recollection changes after counseling: A case study. *Journal of Individual Psychology, 32,* 212–223.

p. 203. Adler, A. 1931. *What Life Should Mean to You.* Boston: Little, Brown.

p. 203. Changing early memories among high-schoolers: Kihlstrom and Harackiewicz, The earliest recollection.

p. 204. On contrast and continuity in the life story see Hankiss, A. 1981. Ontologies of the self: On the mythological rearranging of one's life history. In D. Bertaux (ed.), *Biography and Society*. Beverly Hills, Calif.: Sage.

p. 205. A man's first memory of a trip to the hospital: Kotre, J. 1984. *Outliving the Self*. Baltimore: Johns Hopkins University Press.

p. 205. A woman's first memory of her mother leaving: Kotre, J., and E. Hall. 1990. *Seasons of Life*. Boston: Little, Brown.

p. 211. Adams, V. 1983. Remembering the first drink. *Psychology Today*, May, p. 82.

p. 211. A woman's memory of a new church: Kotre, *Outliving the Self*.

p. 213. First times outnumber last times: Cohen and Faulkner, Lifespan changes.

p. 214. On the Arunta and the Na-khi see Eliade, M. 1959. *The Sacred and the Profane*. New York: Harcourt, Brace.

Chapter Eight: Memory Inspirited

p. 218. ". . . they put it in my mouth . . ." Kotre, J. 1984. *Outliving the Self*. Baltimore: Johns Hopkins University Press.

p. 218. ". . . all the freedom we wanted . . ." Kotre, *Outliving the Self*.

p. 218. ". . . any more wonderful for me . . ." Kotre, J., and E. Hall. 1990. *Seasons of Life*. Boston: Little, Brown.

p. 218. ". . . and that was it . . ." Kotre, *Outliving the Self*.

p. 219. Revere, V., and S. Tobin. 1980. Myth and reality: The older person's relationship to his past. *International Journal of Aging and Human Development*, *12*, 15–26. Also see Lieberman, M., and S. Tobin. 1983. *The Experience of Old Age*. New York: Basic Books.

p. 220. ". . . by God . . ." Wacker, R. 1985. The good die younger. *Science*, *6*, 67.

p. 220. On establishing how we wish to be remembered see Unruh, D. 1983.

Death and personal history: Strategies of identity preservation. *Social Problems, 30,* 340–351.

p. 221. Tobin, S. 1991. Mythicizing parents when old. Paper presented at the ninety-ninth annual convention of the American Psychological Association, San Francisco, August 18.

p. 223. Haley, A. 1976. *Roots.* Garden City, New York: Doubleday.

p. 228. Stone, E. 1988. *Black Sheep and Kissing Cousins.* New York: Penguin.

p. 233. The life story of the nun appears in Kotre, *Outliving the Self.*

p. 234. The story of the twenty-one-year-old woman and her deceased father appears in Kotre, J. 1979. *Simple Gifts.* Kansas City: Andrews and McMeel.

p. 234. The story involving a grandfather's sculpture is from Kotre, *Outliving the Self.*

p. 235. The Moscone incident is described in Unruh, Death and personal history.

p. 236. The Hashoian memories are from Kotre, J., and K. Kotre. 1990. Of seasons and survivors. *Seasons of Life Audiotapes,* Program 26. Ann Arbor, Mich., and Washington, D.C.: The University of Michigan and the Corporation for Public Broadcasting.

p. 237. Schwartz, B. 1990. The reconstruction of Abraham Lincoln. In D. Middleton and D. Edwards, *Collective Remembering.* London: Sage.

p. 240. Kingston, M. 1976. *The Woman Warrior.* New York: Knopf.

INDEX